Beyond Bureaucracy?

The professions in the contemporary public sector

Edited by
MARTIN LAFFIN
University of Glamorgan

Routledge
Taylor & Francis Group

LONDON AND NEW YORK

Contents

List of contributors   vii

Foreword   ix
Martin Laffin

1   The professions in the contemporary public sector   1
    Martin Laffin

2   Medicine   18
    David J. Hunter

3   Nursing   38
    Stephen Ackroyd

4   The accounting profession in local government   56
    Linda A. Keen and Michael P. Murphy

5   Planning   76
    Huw Thomas

6   Social services   91
    Roger Clough

7   Social housing management   108
    Richard Walker

8   Environmental health   129
    Paul Thomas

9 School teaching   146
   Eric Hoyle and Peter D. John

10 Higher education   162
   Mary Henkel

11 The police service   183
   Barry Loveday

12 Justice in the lower courts   201
   John W. Raine

13 Conclusion   218
   Martin Laffin

Index   227

List of contributors

Stephen Ackroyd is Professor of Organisational Behaviour, the Business School, University of Lancaster.

Roger Clough is Professor of Social Care, University of Lancaster.

Mary Henkel is Senior Lecturer, Centre for the Evaluation of Public Policy and Practice, Brunel University.

Eric Hoyle is Emeritus Professor of Education, University of Bristol.

David J. Hunter is Professor of Health Policy and Management, Nuffield Institute for Health, University of Leeds.

Peter D. John is Lecturer in Education, University of Bristol.

Linda A. Keen is Lecturer in Human Resource Management, Canterbury Business School, University of Kent.

Martin Laffin is Professor of Public Policy and Management, Business School, University of Glamorgan, Wales.

Barry Loveday is Principal Lecturer, Institute of Police and Criminological Studies, University of Portsmouth.

Michael P. Murphy is Senior Lecturer in Accounting, Canterbury Business School, University of Kent.

John W. Raine is Director, Institute of Local Government Studies, School of Public Policy, University of Birmingham.

Huw Thomas is Senior Lecturer, Department of City and Regional Planning, Cardiff University of Wales.

Paul Thomas is Principal Lecturer in Public Policy, Business School, University of Glamorgan, Wales.

Richard Walker is Lecturer, Centre for Housing Management and Development, Department of City and Regional Planning, Cardiff University of Wales.

Foreword

Martin Laffin

This book is intended as a contribution to the debate over the future of the public services in Britain. Professionalism has been and still is a major feature of the welfare state in Britain. Yet the political, social and economic context in which the professions emerged and flourished is changing rapidly. The professional ideal of disinterested expertise serving the public interest has lost much of its original gloss. Professional status and careers are threatened by major shifts in the structure of the welfare state which can be summed up as the decline of the 'big government' bureaucratic model. More specifically individual professions themselves face challenges to their special claims to expertise and public service from: politicians on both the right and left of politics, senior managers, new social movements and pressure groups, technological changes, and not least from those citizens whom they aspire to serve.

Beyond Bureaucracy? tackles the questions of how are these new challenges changing the professions? and how are the professionals themselves adapting? The book opens with a wide ranging essay detailing these challenges and providing a framework within which their implications for the professions can be understood. The following chapters then examine the changes taking place in eleven selected professions, ranging from medicine to the police. The final chapter then draws on those chapters to portray the condition of the public sector professions in Britain at the end of the twentieth century.

The chapters in this book were originally presented at a seminar in June 1997 at the University of Glamorgan. I would like to thank Professor Michael Connolly, Director of the Business School, University of Glamorgan, for kindly supporting the seminar. Professor Ken Young also gave valuable advice on the original conception of the book and in commenting on an earlier draft of chapter 1. I would also like to thank the following practitioners for their contributions as discussants to the June seminar, contributions which considerably improved the final book: Dr Rosie Tope, Dr Norman Mills, Mr Chris Lawrence, Mr Phil Roberts, Mr Keith Turner, Mr Ian Crawley, Mr Graham Jukes and Professor Adrian Webb. I would also like to thank Mr Christopher Cramphorn for his invaluable help in editing and preparing the final version of the book.

1 The professions in the contemporary public sector

Martin Laffin

To say that the contemporary public sector is undergoing a period of great change and turbulence has become a commonplace. The present challenge for both academics and practitioners is how to articulate the nature of that change. This book starts from the view that while our old categories of bureaucracy and professionalism should not be discarded, on their own they are no longer adequate to the task of conceptualising current public sector changes. Political, economic, social and technological changes are eroding the twin pillars of bureaucracy and professionalism that supported the modern welfare state. Bureaucracy provided the means whereby welfare could be extended to all, enabling universal coverage and equal treatment. It gave us the traditional notions of political control and organisational structure - hierarchy, functional specialisation and service uniformity - which until recently set the terms for debates over how government can best be organised and how accountability ensured. Similarly professionalism, which came to pervade government as the welfare state expanded, contributed a further framework of accountability within which expertise and knowledge could be harnessed to welfare ends and so be reconciled to a wider public interest.

The challenges now confronting government have stretched these two categories to or even beyond their limits. The certainties of bureaucratic government - expert officials carrying out defined functions, working with a clear chain of command and following clear rules and procedures - never an exact mirror of the messy realities of governing, now seem actually to distort rather than reflect present realities. The professions, once the great hope of the welfare state, are very obviously struggling to adapt their accounts and practices to retain their position within the public sector. The decline of traditional bureaucratic structures, which provided the basic conditions for their expansion, threatens a loss of organisational habitats for the professions. National and local policy makers are looking to sources other than the professions for ideas for change and advice. To many the professions even seem to complicate heedlessly the struggle to understand and act on pressing public problems: for them the ways in which the professions have divided up knowledge have become stumbling blocks rather than aids to understanding and action.

The aim of this book is to examine the state of the professions in the public sector during a period of unprecedented change. It asks what impact are these changes having on the professions? How are they seeking to adapt themselves both to changes in the organisational structure of the public services and to new ideas, particularly those stressing market mechanisms and generic management, on how those services should be delivered? The book sets out to answer these questions through comparative studies of ten professions within the public sector.

The title of the book - *Beyond Bureaucracy*? - has been selected to echo recent claims about where the public sector is going and where it is should go. This line of argument assumes that the traditional 'big government' bureaucratic model is in decline. The traditional model is of government as a set of bureaucratised organisations, with policy and service delivery functions vertically integrated, and largely driven by professionalism and due process. This model is losing relevance as a 'post-bureaucratic' shift is taking place in the structure and working of public sector agencies and, as importantly, a shift in the dominant assumptions about how public sector organisations work and should work.

This chapter is about the powerful challenges that this shift poses both to the bureaucratic position of the professions within the public sector and ideologically to traditional professional values and practices. One aim of this chapter is to introduce these challenges and explore their sources. The other aim is to set out an analytical framework for the following chapters: a framework which outlines the three different levels at which professionals work and exercise influence, and four different future scenarios for the professions.

Bureaucracy and professionalism in the expansion of the welfare state

Any discussion of bureaucracy is bound to hark back to Weber's classic bureaucratic ideal type based on functional specialisation, formal hierarchy, rules and clearly defined official roles. Classical management theory, much of it still a potent influence on how we think about organisations, was essentially an elaboration of the Weberian model. An elaboration that emphasised notions such as unity of command, span of control, separation of line and management functions and organisational careers.[1] These notions stressed the internal functioning of organisations, the classical theorists largely overlooking the environment and external relations of organisations, the unstated assumption was a certain and largely unchanging environment. Indeed Weber himself saw inward looking tendencies as inherent in bureaucracy: 'Every bureaucracy seeks to increase the superiority of the professionally informed by keeping their knowledge and intentions secret. ... in so far as it can, it hides its knowledge and action from criticism' (1948, p. 233).

Weber was acutely aware of the power of knowledge. He formulated his bureaucratic ideal type precisely to understand how the political will is translated into action, a translation that depends crucially on the bureaucratic deployment of expertise. For him the problems of democratic control posed by the modern state arose from bureaucrats' ability to control expertise and information. Recent public choice theorists have made the same point, although they have drawn rather different policy conclusions. Using economic analogies they have pointed to the monopoly or near monopoly position enjoyed by governmental bureaucrats that gives bureaucrats the opportunity to over-supply their services and manipulate their political masters (Downs 1966, Niskanen 1971). Their influential case has been that government monopolies should be broken up through the creation of competition either by selling off services or compelling government service providers to compete with each other.

A similar case can and has been made against the professions as monopolies. The essence of professionalism lies in the efforts of members of an occupation to maximise their freedom from control by others in the immediate work setting, in the management of professional work and in the regulation of the profession (Laffin 1986, p. 21). Other characteristics of professions - such as the possession of ethical codes, long periods of training and the existence of an occupational association - are less defining characteristics than the strategies used by members of an occupational group to win and maintain professional status. Their efforts to achieve such status are based on a monopoly of expertise which necessarily has to be sanctioned and enforced by government (Johnson 1972, Freidson 1994 and Larson 1977). The professions enjoy relative freedom from control and a licence to practise, but accept certain requirements or mandates that reassure policy makers and the lay public that they will not abuse their exclusive expertise and knowledge (Hughes 1958). Thus professionalism provides a framework of accountability in which the possession of expertise and knowledge can be harnessed to public policy ends yet be reconciled to a wider public interest. Such has been the public and political acceptance of the idea of professionalism that government until recent years has sponsored numerous professionalisation projects within the public sector. Particularly in the immediate post war period policy makers supported the creation and expansion of self-regulating professions as the major public policy response to social problems. Thus professionals have came to enjoy considerable discretion at work and considerable policy influence within the public sector.

The professions became pre-eminent influences on the evolution of the modern welfare state. They played a key role in forming the modern idea of a social problem, a role which I will argue later is now in decline. Professional claims became inseparable from the identification of social problems, the urgency and extent of such problems formed the essential rationale for professional expansionism:

> What was new in the twentieth century was the belief that most social problems, not just the obvious ones like sanitation and water supply, were the products of social organisation rather than individual inadequacy. ... Problems thus defined as institutional and societal rather than moral and individual cried out for collective, professional solutions rather than moral

discipline and exhortation. And once the legislative and administrative treatment began, the process of professionalization and feedback set in, by which the welfare professionals uncovered new problems which demanded further legislative and administrative solutions and the recruitment of still more welfare professionals. (Perkin 1989, pp. 356-57)

Such expansionism was based on the discovery of new or the capture of old social problems from others, and the definition of the professional services as an essential part of the 'solution'. The professions became autonomous sources of influence on public policy, autonomous in the sense of separate from yet using the routine channels linking central and local government (Laffin 1986, p. 121), and central government and other decentralised agencies. Moreover any recognition of professional claims within the national arenas typically produced knock-on effects at the local levels: the more prominent the profession at national level, the more likely its practitioners would be to enjoy control of the top jobs in the local organisation and influence over local policy.

The parallel expansions of the professions and bureaucracy in the post-war welfare state were complementary rather than competing processes (Larson 1977, p. 199). The professions colonised the new bureaucracies and extended the principle of professional exclusivity up the organisational hierarchy to include the top jobs. Tensions did arise between professional discretion and bureaucratic rules and authority, and between collegiality and hierarchy. These tensions were eased by the symbiotic aspects of the relationship - hierarchy provided careers for professionals, while the professions delivered the trained and committed specialists required to make bureaucracy work. As these bureaucracies mushroomed, new 'staff' professions (such as accountancy and personnel) as opposed to the public service, 'line' professions developed. Significantly these professions early on absorbed and advocated ideas of corporate and strategic management, often in the face of resistance from the public service professions (Laffin and Young 1989, p. 23).

The waning of bureaucracy and professionalism

The conditions under which the professions flourished have changed. The professions both in the private and the public sectors have lost prestige and influence. That loss is particularly evident in the case of the public sector professions. This loss reflects a fall in public confidence in 'big government' bureaucracy and the professions which are seen, rightly or wrongly, not to have delivered on their early, post-war promises of social transformation. The welfare state would not have happened in the absence of a widely shared confidence not simply in the capacity of governmental action to solve problems but also in the competence of the professions and bureaucracies to diagnose and act on those problems. Now that confidence has come to be seen as over-blown. The evidence of professional under-achievement has become the common currency of recent

4

political debate. To take one among many possible illustrations: what had been the educationalists' 'secret garden' of the school curriculum has been trampled on by politicians in the name of improving educational standards.

Professionals no longer enjoy a monopoly over the policy advice. The post-war welfare state was characterised by depoliticised (or, more accurately, non-party political) profession dominated policy making within well-established 'professional-bureaucratic complexes' or 'policy communities' (Rhodes 1986, Laffin 1986). The more established professions came to play a major role in these communities. These complexes and policy communities have been dispersed or have lost influence during the 1980s. Heclo notes a similar change in the US where what he calls the old world of establishments has disappeared into very fluid policy making networks (Heclo 1989). Even the UK civil service, the model profession, has become less trusted by ministers as a source of policy advice (Campbell and Wilson 1995).

Not only have the professions lost policy influence, they have also been subject to deep inroads into areas of professional practice formerly regarded as belonging to the self-regulating, professional domain. One obvious set of inroads has been how Conservative and Labour ministers have placed new and more detailed requirements on the world of professional practice, many of which are detailed in this book. Another, and related, set of inroads is the new accountability which has taken the form of a proliferation of bodies with inspectorial functions such as the Audit Commission and the Office for Standards in Education (OFSTED). The creation of these bodies indicates how far contemporary policy makers have turned away from their predecessors' reliance on self-regulating professions as instruments of public policy.

During the last Conservative government (1979-97) Conservative ministers, heavily influenced by new right thinking, identified the public sector professions, and the policy communities of which they were part as 'vested interests' hostile to Conservative policy. Accordingly they were marginalised in policy making. The Conservatives also sought to rein in public expenditure, taking further the previous Labour government's budget tightening. Thus while the period from 1945 to the late 1970s was characterised by steady growth in the public sector, from the late 1970s the rate of growth slowed considerably (though the Conservatives significantly failed to throw that growth into reverse) and spending levels began to fluctuate from year to year. They sought not only to cut expenditure but also to extract better 'value-for-money' which has inevitably meant that all in the public sector, including professionals, have become subject to a new and intense money-driven scrutiny of their work practices.

The most radical changes in the public services followed the 1987 Conservative electoral win. Change then happened with a vengeance as ministers released an avalanche of legislation which set in motion major shifts in the structure of the welfare state.[2] They were on a policy high: they had discovered that privatisation within the industrial public sector was 'workable'. Even more importantly not only had they just won a five year period of office but also the risks of losing the next election seemed remote given the disarray of the Labour opposition. Consequently ministers now felt confident about taking major political risks, even with that most sacred of cows - the national health service.

What was new after 1987, then, was the government's policy shift to apply market principles to the delivery of public services which has moved public service structures in a post-bureaucratic direction - at least partly driven by the search for tighter control over public expenditure. Of course the government had by then already become only too aware of the limitations of a simple rationalisation or retrenchment agenda (Pierson 1994). The internal marketisation of public services promised to attract much less resistance, certainly in electoral terms, and so achieve those elusive savings. Marketisation offered the chance to build cost containing mechanisms into public service delivery and extract more value for money from means such as cheaper labour on open rather than closed public sector labour markets. The new organisational structures, organised around the provider-producer split, also promised future opportunities for privatisation. Further these policies cast money saving policies in a positive form. Rationalisation or retrenchment policies on their own present problems of blame avoidance, whereas post-bureaucratic initiatives promise opportunities for what Weaver terms 'credit claiming' (1986). Such initiatives are also more likely to gain support among elite bureaucrats as they promise them a positive role (as change agents) rather than a negative role as cutters. Ministers were also attracted by the chance, limited by the big bureaucracy model of government, to distance themselves from the political fall-out arising from specific service cuts. Such reasoning appears to have been an important consideration behind the introduction of the internal market reforms in the NHS (Jenkins 1996, p. 72), though whether these reforms deflected political blame away from the government in practice is doubtful.

Competition, then, although often a long way from the economists' pure ideal, has become central to service delivery, as well as in the selection of policy ideas and advice. The post 1987 changes mean that government organisations now buy in a broad range of services from outside the public sector and even those still sourced from within are often 'market-tested' against alternative suppliers. In 1990 the government introduced internal markets into the National Health Service, requiring health authorities to purchase services from providers - NHS trusts and the independent sector - an innovation which curtailed clinical autonomy in favour of resource management (Wistow 1992, p. 114). Compulsory competitive tendering (CCT) for white collar staff, introduced by the Conservatives in 1992, entrenched a similar contractor-client relationship in local government. Although Labour has softened these requirements under its 'best value' requirements and committed itself to revoke the NHS internal market, the requirements for business like accountability remain.

Management through and by contract challenges both the continuing relevance of traditional professional skills and traditional claims to expertise by requiring them to be codified for contractual purposes - challenges which are illustrated in the following chapters. For the new contractor-client division cuts across the old functional divisions between professions and requires officers to exercise new skills of contract management and negotiation alien to the public service professions.

6

Events after the 1997 election indicate that Labour will modify rather than reverse this direction of public sector change. The Labour government is, of course, to some extent locked into this policy direction given the cost (financial, parliamentary time and other political costs) of reversing Conservative policy changes. New Labour also shares much of the Conservatives' antipathy towards 'big government' bureaucracy.

However the decline in confidence in big government and professionalism has its sources beyond just particular party platforms and expenditure restraints. One deeper source is the increasingly contested nature of policy knowledge. The division of knowledge and expertise among the professions, and between a profession and the laity, remained stable and certain during the professions' heyday. This stability was itself largely sustained by the professions' self-policing. But the traditional form of professionalism has been steadily undermined since the 1970s or even 1960s. Mass education has meant the proliferation of professionalisation strategies across occupational groups. Compared with the immediate post-war period, many more professions and would-be professions are now competing to lay claim to cognitive and moral territory for themselves - that is those social problems for which their competences and commitment are indispensable. In asserting these claims and counter-claims they must challenge the claims of other, competing professions, a process which itself generates uncertainty over what 'knowledge' is.

Professionals as well as professions are proliferating. We have indeed moved towards the professionalisation of everyone to answer Wilensky's (1967) question in the affirmative. Yet while professionals may expect their claims to be accepted on trust, their own educational achievements increase their scepticism of others' claims. Thus ironically the more of us that become professionals, the more professional claims will be challenged.

This markedly greater pluralism of knowledge is reshaping the political process. Policy makers, nationally and locally, are rethinking public policy in terms of new ideological frameworks. Ironically right and left have converged in their criticisms of the welfare state as too bureaucratically and professionally dominated and, therefore, unresponsive to the citizenry. The right has rediscovered individualism, using it to challenge the ideas of collective provision underpinning the welfare state professions: for as Perkin points out the welfare professions are based on a principle of social justice that involved the 'marriage of a comprehensive acceptance of the claims of social citizenship with the self-interest of the professionals who existed to meet them' (1989, p. 353).

New social movements, most notably feminism and environmentalism have also challenged the professional construction of knowledge and professional domination of how public policies are defined. Again mass education laid the basis for these new movements and the associated proliferation of policy ideas. These movements, on the right and the left, have disrupted the formerly orderly social construction of public policy knowledge which the professions created and sustained. New sources of policy knowledge and advice, particularly in the form of new or reinvigorated thinktanks are also displacing the policy role of the professions as 'change drivers'.

7

Technological change - as well as social, economic and political change - has challenged traditional assumptions about knowledge. In the past the professions have benefited from technological change. However recent developments, particularly in information technology, are making the professions more vulnerable to external control through codifying their practice as the 'availability of more robust and user-friendly procedures for constructing expert systems leads to more frequent development and use of in-house expert systems as components of organisational memories' (Huber 1990, p. 61). Any such future incorporation of expertise into software would have vital implications for the professions.

But technological change creates possibilities rather than drives change. Certainly many recent organisational innovations would not have occurred without the necessary technological capabilities. For example the idea of internal markets would probably not have diffused as rapidly if computerisation had not made their management feasible. Another example is how email and other forms of electronic communication are reducing the levels of hierarchy (but not necessarily the power of top management) within organisations and eroding conventional inter and intra-organisational boundaries. Generally technological changes contribute to the tendency for organisations to lose *some* traditional bureaucratic characteristics and become more diffuse; though most commentators note that the major organisational implications of new technology lay in the future. Whether these changes increase rather than decrease control by those at the top or in other organisations remains a matter of debate. Bellamy and Taylor (1994) point to how information technology applications reflect the interplay of political and bureaucratic agendas rather than any technological imperative. Similarly Huber argues that new electronic communications will simply exacerbate pre-existing trends towards centralisation or decentralisation in organisations rather than reverse them (1990, p. 57).

To sum up: there has been a marked shift in the political conventional wisdom that cuts across party lines and emphasises 'small government', market driven policy responses rather than 'big government' and profession dominated policy responses to problems. At the same time policy making arenas have become very competitive with many other policy actors, often hostile to professional claims to expertise and altruism, pushing the professions aside in the search for access and influence.

Post-bureaucracy or neo-bureaucracy?

The assumption behind this book is that the organisation of the contemporary welfare state is changing radically. How can this change be understood and explained?

Two broad schools of interpretation have emerged - that could roughly be termed the 'neo-bureaucratic' and the 'post-bureaucratic'. In the first school Pollitt (1990), Hood (1991) and Ferlie at al. (1996) build their analyses on the assumption that political and official policy makers are imposing a 'new public management' or 'managerialist' model on the public sector. Pollitt (1990), in particular, argues that this model is profoundly alien to the public sector which he sees as being driven in a neo-Taylorist direction (see Ackroyd, ch. 4, for a critique of this view). In a slightly different vein Hoyle and John in this volume describe a 'neo-bureaucratic' pattern of change evident in many schools. They point to how 'the structural looseness' of schools has been replaced by 'a neo-bureaucracy' characterised by 'sub-committees, working parties, problem solving teams, task-forces and the like' which develop 'mission statements, policy documents, appraisal schemes and so forth' (ch. 9).

In contrast the 'post-bureaucratic' view stresses how service delivery increasingly involves inter-organisational relationships rather than bureaucratic, intra-organisational relationships. The proponents of this view point to how the disaggregation of large government organisations is giving a key role to networks and markets in service delivery and policy formulation. Of course government services have always involved networks and markets, arguably in government until the end of the nineteenth century these modes of organisation were more important coordinating mechanisms than bureaucratic hierarchies. But now towards the end of the twentieth century, the argument goes, the high tide of bureaucracy is receding and government is increasingly characterised by a complex mix of bureaucracy, networks and markets (for early and stimulating statements of this view see Stoker 1989 and Hoggett 1991).

Rhodes (1997) has introduced the term 'differentiated polity' to refer to the ways in which politics and policies have become more fragmented and dominated by 'self-organizing, interorganizational networks'. He sees this process as reflecting increased functional and institutional specialisation which means that services are delivered by inter-governmental networks over which the centres (policy making cores) have only limited control. Kooiman similarly detects a shift in governing systems towards less centralised, more diffuse patterns of policy making and implementation involving a wider range of actors than those conventionally seen as 'political' actors:

> There seems to be a shift away from the more traditional patterns in which governing was basically seen as 'one-way' traffic from those governing to those governed, towards a 'two-way' traffic model ... . This means that the place of boundaries between state and society changes, but also that the boundaries themselves change in character. One could say they are becoming more permeable ... . No single actor, public or private, has all the knowledge and information required to solve complex, dynamic, and diversified problems; no actor has sufficient overview to make applications of needed instruments effective; no single actor has sufficient action potential to dominate unilaterally in a particular governing model. (1993, p. 4)

The argument in this book is similar to that of both Kooiman and Rhodes. However in this book these changes are referred to as 'post-bureaucratic'. This term is more self-explanatory than Kooiman's and Rhodes' terms and is more appropriate in this context as it focusses attention on the organisational locations of the professions

(Hoggett 1991 first used 'post-bureaucratic' in the context of change in British government, but the term is defined here rather differently).

The post-bureaucratic agenda has to be understood in historical context as the most significant change in the structure of the public services since at least 1945. The telling contrast is that with the 1970s corporate management movement which advocated a strengthened strategic role for local authorities and health authorities. Its advocates attacked traditional professionalism-as-departmentalism, which they argued impeded coordination and the evolution of a corporate view. The movement assisted in strengthening the roles of chief executive and treasurer but had a limited impact on the public service professions. Nevertheless that movement remained largely a set of ideas waiting for their historical moment. In contrast the post-bureaucratic agenda, which of course has incorporated some of the ideas of the earlier movement, is more radical, in that it seeks ways of replacing conventional bureaucratic relationships, as well as more closely matching the historical moment.

The direction of post-bureaucratic change can be summed up under three headings.

1. Organisational forms. The welfare state is becoming organisationally more diverse and pluralistic. New distinctions are emerging that cut across and challenge the older, hierarchical and functional or professional divisions characteristic of the post-war welfare state. One such new set of distinctions is based on the separation of policy and service delivery functions. Services are increasingly delivered through devolved organisations, many of which are in the non-profit and private sectors. Local authorities, in particular, are acquiring new business-like organisational cultures (Young 1996).

Meanwhile those government agencies that retain policy or purchaser roles are having to learn to work within a new and demanding 'local governance' context comprising a complex of public, private and non-profit organisations. The last government articulated this role as the 'enabling authority' meaning that the role of local government was not to provide services directly through their own employed staff but rather to create a political structure through which political demands could be expressed and the market used to respond with the appropriate services (Ridley 1988). More recently Osbourne and Gaebler (1992) have formulated a similar distinction as one between steering and rowing, a potent metaphor that has entered the language of many public sector policy makers.

2. Control and coordination relationships. Relationships of control and coordination are more complex and bear less and less relationship to the relative simplicities of hierarchical, employment relationships. The norm is moving away from that of superior and monopolistic bureaucrats implementing decisions towards a norm of negotiation between roughly equal parties - for example where health authorities (purchasers) negotiate to buy patient services from hospitals and other health organisations (providers). Inevitably the practice is messier than the theory given the inherent limitations of the contractual relationship in the provision of complex services. So relationships under quasi-markets differ significantly from those under pure markets - the competitors are often public or non-profit organisations, the medium of exchange is seldom cash but some transfer payment (cash following patient/student) and the consumer's wants are usually mediated by a proxy such as a GP or care manager (Rao 1996, p. 174). In fact it seems that the emerging relationships are a mixture of network and contractual elements, close to what are called strategic alliances in the private sector, in which trust as much as competition plays a key role.

The greater plurality of service delivery organisations and the consequent proliferation of relationships means that the problems of control and accountability have increased in complexity. Such problems require more focussed strategic policy advice or a corporate response, a response not always forthcoming from organisations retaining entrenched professional-functional divisions. For instance recent studies indicate that local authorities face very real difficulties in defining and creating such a strategic role for themselves (Rao 1996 and Lowndes forthcoming). Further problems arise as core agencies are only just beginning to acquire the staff competencies to manage contracts and complex service delivery networks. These problems have led to the importation of yet another powerful metaphor, again from the US, that of 'hollow government' (Goldstein 1992). 'Hollow government' refers to situations in which the policy core becomes so slimmed down that the policy makers can no longer retain effective control over the service providers.

The spread of non-bureaucratic relationships is associated with the advent of a new language of performance management as policy makers and managers struggle to cope with the problems of accountability in devolved systems. At least in theory managers are given greater freedom 'to get the job done' and are held accountable in terms of outcomes rather than adherence to due process. Thus performance management is post-bureaucratic to the extent that it stresses outcome rather than process or procedural, that is bureaucratic, measures.

3. Organisational boundaries. The traditional bureaucratic model implied clearly defined boundaries between elected politicians and appointed officers, between the public and private sectors and, within agencies, among functional specialisms and bureaucratic jobs. These boundaries are increasingly blurred. For instance in local government from the early 1980s the divide between the leading members and chief officers has become less distinct particularly with the rise of a new generation of better educated and assertive politicians (Laffin and Young 1989).

Significant changes are taking place in lateral, cross-functional as well as in vertical control relationships. Policy makers recognise increasingly that social problems cut across functional, professional boundaries and this recognition is a significant source of dissatisfaction with professional advice.

Relationships have changed significantly between the private and public sectors. The traditional bureaucratic model embodies an assumption that private interests should be kept quite separate from government, even though in practice relations were often close. Now the post-bureaucratic assumption is that the two should be arm in arm rather than at arms length: for example Young's survey reveals

11

considerable willingness within local government to work with the voluntary and, to a lesser extent, with the private sector among councils (1996, p. 37-8). This blurring is partly a direct consequence of central government policy - the rhetoric urges agencies to create private-public partnerships, though neglecting the original, anti-corruption reasons which preoccupied nineteenth century reformers. Contractual relationships, too, frequently resolve themselves into partnerships as both client and contractor discover the limitations of contractual relationships in the provision of complex public services.

To sum up: the argument is not that bureaucracy is disappearing but rather that it is in decline as other means of control and coordination gain in importance. Neither is the argument that a post-bureaucratic ideal type comparable to Weber's bureaucratic type is emerging, such an argument is at best premature - a point recognised even by the stronger (and in my view utopian) exponents of a 'post-bureaucratic' organisational type (Heckscher and Donnellon 1994). Neither is it to suggest that there is a trend towards those in jobs lower down organisations being empowered. As Hoggett (1996) points out the evidence for such a change is very limited. In fact the evidence in this book indicates that recent change has redistributed power among different jobs, such as from teachers to headteachers and from directors of education to headteachers, rather than bringing about a new Eden in which everyone enjoys greater freedom at work. Furthermore some professions, like nursing, appear to be experiencing a loss of influence over their work at both practice and management levels.

Three levels of professionalism

The classic studies of professionalism have tended to treat a profession as homogeneous, assuming considerable coincidence of interest among practitioners. Even during the heyday of professionalism this assumption was questionable, but recent change has made it even more so. Far from being homogeneous, the professions are hierarchically layered within the welfare state. Those professionals at each layer have different interests than those at other layers. Three layers are distinguished in this book as the basis for analysis in the later chapters - the national or macro, institutional or meso and practice or micro.

1. National or macro level. A major characteristic of the professions is that they have national associations to represent and advance the interests of their members. A key function of these associations is the promotion of accounts of professional practice and as a pressure group in relation to central government. In so doing they have acted, in the past at least, as autonomous sources of policy.

As noted earlier the once stable, cosy relationships with central government policy makers have been replaced by a more uncertain and politicised world. The challenge for the professions is daunting. A few, like the police, have been able to retain and even expand their policy role. But most professions have inevitably lost ground. The new, more competitive policy marketplace demands new strategies -

new alliances and less technical policy analysis - if they are to continue to be significant policy players. They may even go beyond these strategies and seek to redefine their professional accounts (the skills and knowledge and ideals of professional practice) to respond to the new realities. Some may well try defensively to absorb at least some of the new post-bureaucratic ideas and language into their own professional accounts, though such changes to the professional accounts can often meet resistance from rank and file members who still remain attached to the old professional values.

2. *The institutional or meso level.* This level is that at which the elite professionals operate, heading up the major institutions (individual local authorities, health authorities, universities, police services). They collaborate with the locally elected or appointed policy makers to interpret, modify, apply and sometimes evade central government policy. Traditionally they have justified their managerial role in professional terms - the need for professional (expert and disinterested) advice and for professionals to be managed by their own kind. They have also formed the pool from which the national level professional leaders have been drawn.

3. *The practice or micro level.* Those practitioners actually delivering services face new and intensified top-down demands for accountability which are seldom easily reconciled with both their own professional ideals and discretion as well as the pressing realities of everyday practice (the classic analysis is Lipsky 1979 on street-level bureaucrats). The work of the frontline practitioner has been further complicated by the increased political demands to prescribe professional practice.

The future of the professions: four scenarios

The organisational and social conditions of the professions have and are changing significantly and in many cases do threaten traditional professional assumptions. As will be seen in the course of this book, the professions are facing broadly similar pressures though they display different capacities in how they are adapting to these pressures. For the purposes of analysis in this book four broad possible scenarios are outlined as follows.

1. *Limited change.* Under this scenario the professions or certain professions would continue to enjoy positions of job exclusivity and policy influence. But to maintain this position would require some change by the profession - accounts of professional practice would be likely to have to absorb new demands for generic (that is non-service specific) management competencies necessary for contract management and for strategic planning (especially service coordination). Debate would be likely to rage within the profession over the extent to which these bundles of new competencies could be integrated with the existing professional set of competences, and the balance between the new and the old competences in making selection, promotion, training decisions. Medicine is likely to fit this scenario.

2. *Professional elitism*. According to this scenario 'policy' and service delivery functions are organisationally separated. Core policy government agencies (local authorities, health authorities, central departments) are reformed around small, elite professional groups who advise the formal policy makers and monitor the service deliverers. Those within the core continue to cherish and deploy distinctively professional claims, while the rank and file practitioners experience increasing difficulty in sustaining professional claims and professional exclusivity, becoming 'deskilled' or 'proletarianised'. The career link between practice and management, which had become characteristic of the public service professions, would become attenuated. Freidson (1994, p. 9) argues that such elite or leading professionals would still be able to use their claims to expertise to resist pressures to rationalise their work and even to enhance their status and autonomy at work. This scenario is close to his argument that the essential elements of professionalism are not disappearing but are taking a new form: 'Professionalism is being reborn in a hierarchical form in which everyday practitioners become subject to the control of professional elites who continue to exercise the considerable technical, administrative, and cultural authority that professions have had in the past' (1994, p. 9). Under this scenario the elite professionals would see their role as strategic and divorced from service provision.

3. *Deprofessionalisation*. In this scenario certain professions would disappear or at least lose considerable professional standing. Some commentators have argued that the professions are becoming 'deprofessionalised' or 'proletarianised' as professional work becomes more and more rationalised or codified (Murphy 1990, see Reed 1996 for a useful overview of these arguments). A cull of professions may take place whereby some professions are disbanded or absorbed into others. In local government such a process could conceivably go further, amounting to an 'implosion scenario' as the remaining professions (at least at the elite levels) fold into a general managerial profession roughly comparable to the US city management profession.

4. *Professional flight*. Large numbers of professional practitioners may move to the service providing organisations, in the private and voluntary sectors, and build their career structure within these organisations. In other words many professionals are likely to elect to go with the contractor side rather than the client side. Housing management could take this path, returning to its roots within the housing association movement. Social work too could follow its American colleagues and recolonise the voluntary sector.

Conclusion

The professions in the public sector are having to adjust to new social, technological, political and economic realities quite different from those that drove their rise to political and bureaucratic prominence. The following chapters seek to detect and analyse the common patterns across the eleven professions in the light of the framework outlined in latter half of this chapter. The concluding chapter will then return to the questions raised in this chapter through an overview of change within those professions

Notes

1   As Stewart points out the modern welfare state was based on the assumptions of the administrative efficiency movement of the early twentieth century (such as Gulick and Urwick 1937) which stressed functionalism (organisational forms based on professional divisions), uniformity of service delivery and hierarchy (Stewart 1985). As Stewart emphasises these principles matched the time and made the large scale welfare state organisationally possible.

2   '... the basic structure of the welfare state in 1987 was much the same as in 1979. The vast majority of the population was still served by state-funded and state-provided systems of education, health care, social services and social security. Even the proportion of national resources going into public welfare did not change significantly; in 1987/88 it was exactly the same proportion of the Gross Domestic Product (23 per cent) as it had been in 1978/79.' (Le Grand and Bartlett, 1993, p. 2)

References

Ackroyd, S. (1996), 'Professions and Organisational Change in the UK', *Organisation Studies* Vol. 17, No. 4, pp. 599-621.
Bellamy, C. and Taylor, J. (1994), 'Introduction: Exploiting IT in Public Administration - Towards the Information Polity?' *Public Administration*, Vol. 72, No. 1 (Spring), pp. 1-12.
Campbell, C. and Wilson, G. (1995), *The End of Whitehall: Death of a Paradigm?* Oxford: Blackwells.
Downs, A. (1966), *Inside Bureaucracy*, Little, Brown and Co.: Boston.
Ferlie, I., Ashburner, L., Fitzgerald, L. and Pettigrew, A. (1996), *The New Public Management in Action*, Oxford University Press: Oxford.
Freidson, E. (1994), *Professionalism Reborn: Theory, Prophecy and Policy*, Polity: Cambridge.
Goldstein, M. (1992), *America's Hollow Government*, Business One Irwin: Homewood, Ill.
Gulick, L. and Urwick, L. (1937), *Papers on the Science of Administration*, Columbia University Press: New York.

Heckscher, C. and Donnellon, A. (1994), *The Post-Bureaucratic Organization: New Perspectives on Oganizational Change*, Sage: Thousand Oaks.

Heclo, H. (1989), 'The Emerging Regime' in Harris, R. and Milkis, S. (ed.), *Remaking American Politics*, Westview: Boulder.

Hoggett, P. (1991), 'A New Public Management in the Public Sector?' *Policy and Politics*, Vol. 19, No. 4, pp. 243-256.

Hoggett, P. (1996), 'New Modes of Control in the Public Service', *Public Administration*, Vol. 74, No. 1 (Spring), pp. 9-32.

Hood, C. (1991), 'A Public Management for All Seasons? *Public Administration*, Vol. 69, No. 1, pp. 3-19.

Huber, G. (1990), 'A Theory of the Effects of Advanced Information Technologies on Organisational Design, Intelligence, and Decision Making', *Academy of Management Review*, Vol. 15, No. 1. pp. 47-71.

Hughes, E. (1958), *Men and Their Work*, Free Press: Glencoe, Ill.

Johnson, T. (1972), *Professions and Power*, Macmillan: London.

Jenkins, S. (1996), *Accountable to None: The Tory Nationalization of Britain*, Penquin: Harmondsworth.

Kooiman, J. (1993), 'Governance and Governability: Using Complexity, Dynamics and Diversity' in Kooiman, J. (ed), *Modern Governance*, Sage: London.

Laffin, M. (1986), *The Professions and Policy: The Role of the Professions in the Central-Local Government Relationship*, Gower: Aldershot.

Laffin, M. and Young, K. (1990), *Professionalism in Local Government*, Longmans: London.

Larson, M. S. (1977), *The Rise of Professionalism: A Sociological Analysis*, University of California Press: Berkeley.

Legrand, J. and Bartlett, W. (1993), *Quasi-Markets and Social Policy*, London: Macmillan.

Lipsky, M. (1979), *Street-level Bureaucracy*, Sage: New York.

Lowndes, V. (forthcoming), 'Management Change in Local Government' in Stokes, G. (Ed), *The New Management of Local Government: Markets, Hierarchies and Networks*, Macmillan: Basingstoke.

Murphy, R. (1990), 'Proletarianization or Bureaucratization: the Fall of the Professional' in Tordenstahl, R. And Burrage, M (ed.), *The Formation of Professions*, Sage: London.

Niskanen, W. (1971), *Bureaucracy and Representative Government*, Hawthorne, N.Y.: Aldine.

Oppenheimer, M. (1973), 'The Proletarianization of the Professional', *Sociological Review Monograph* No. 20, pp. 213-27.

Perkin, H. (1989), *The Rise of Professional Society England Since 1880*, Routledge: London.

Pierson, P. (1994), *Dismantling the Welfare State? Reagan, Thatcher and the Politics of Retrenchment*, Cambridge University Press: Cambridge.

Pollitt, C. (1990), *Managerialism and the Public Services: The Anglo-American Experience*, Blackwell, Oxford.

Rao, N. (1996), *Towards Welfare Pluralism: Public Services in a Time of Change*, Dartmouth: Aldershot.

Rao, N. and Young, K. (1995), *Competition, Contracts and Change: The Local Authority Experience of CCT*, Joseph Rowntree/LGC Communications, London.

Reed, M. (1996), 'Expert Power and Control in Late Modernity: An Empirical View and Theoretical Synthesis,' *Organisation Studies*, Vol. 17, pp. 573-597.

Rhodes, R. (1986), *The National World of Local Government*, Allen and Unwin: London.

Rhodes, R. (1996), *Understanding Governance: Policy Networks, Governance, Reflexivity and Accountability*, Open University Press: Buckingham.

Ridley, N. (1988), *The Local Right: Enabling not Providing*, Centre for Policy Studies: London.

Stewart, J. (1985), 'The Functioning and Management of Local Authorities', in Loughlin, M., Gelfand. M. and Young, K. (ed.), *Half a Century of Municipal Decline 1935-1985*, Allen and Unwin: London, pp. 98-120.

Stoker, G. (1989), 'Creating a Local Government for a Post-Fordist Society' in Stewart, J. and Stoker, G. (ed.), *The Future of Local Government*, Macmillan: Basingstoke.

Weaver, R. (1986), 'The Politics of Blame Avoidance', *Journal of Public Policy*, Vol. 6, No. 4: 371-98.

Weber, M. (1948), 'Bureaucracy' in Gerth, H. and Mills, C. (ed.), *From Max Weber: Essays in Sociology*, Oxford University Press: New York.

Wilensky, H. (1964), 'The Professionalization of Everyone?', *American Journal of Sociology*, Vol. 70, pp. 148-9.

Wistow, G. (1992), 'The National Health Service' in Marsh, D and Rhodes, R (ed.), *Implementing Thatcherite Policies: Audit of an Era*, Buckingham, OU Press, pp. 100-16.

Young, K. (1996), 'Reinventing Local Government? Some Evidence Assessed', *Public Administration*, Vol. 74, No. 3 (Autumn), pp. 347-67.

Acknowledgements

The author would like to thank the other contributors to the book for their comments on an earlier draft of this chapter.

2 Medicine

David J. Hunter

A feature of health care reform in the UK over the past six years or so has been the progressive erosion of professional autonomy in favour of ever-growing management dominance (Harrison and Pollitt 1994). The changes in the NHS which began to be introduced in 1991 have sought to replace a producer-led culture, that is one dominated by professional priorities and practices, with a consumer-driven one in keeping with the former Conservative government's commitment to marketising much of the public sector, including health care. Moving from hierarchies and outmoded command and control structures to markets and looser, decentralised structures became the hallmark of the former government's public sector reform strategy. The new Labour government is not unsympathetic to many of the changes introduced by its predecessors but, in the case of the NHS, is committed to ending the internal market introduced by the Conservatives. A white paper was published in December 1997 which set out the government's policy for a NHS free from market principles and competitive practices.

To portray the 1991 changes in the rather stark terms used above does violence to the complexities of what has actually occurred in practice. In particular the power shift has not all been in one direction, that is from the professions to management. The 'new managerialism' may have exerted a potent influence on the development, shape and morale of the professions in health care, especially the medical profession, but countervailing pressures have also been at work. Not all doctors were opposed to the reforms, even if at a collective level their professional associations were hostile, and many, notably general practitioner fundholders, have done very well out of them. Conversely not all managers favoured the changes despite the opportunity they afforded collectively for raising their status and securing their position as leaders and change agents within the NHS.

This chapter builds on an earlier review of health care personnel in health and health care management (Hunter 1996). The review examined the state's increased influence over how professionals practise and use resources. One conclusion was that a mismatch existed between the management style favoured by policy makers and reformers, and the necessary flexibility required in the skill mix and organisation of clinical work. That conclusion remains valid.

The chapter is in three sections. Firstly the rise of managerialism within the health care sector is described and placed in its historical context, including a resume of the argument referred to above. Secondly the role of doctors in management is assessed in the light of two contrasting models of management. Thirdly likely future developments are assessed especially given the Labour government's intended abolition of the internal market in health care. Will a new ethic and value base, seeking to restore the notion of public service, mark the end of the revolution known as the 'new public management'? Will this mean a move towards collaborative rather than competitive behaviour? Or is the abolition merely a presentational shift which will do little more than slightly modify the direction of change under the former Conservative government? The implications of the trend to encourage doctors in management will also be reviewed. Will doctors simply be sold the prevailing model of management which draws heavily on economic rationalism? Or will they begin to evolve their own particular brand of management which draws on professional values and concepts of organisation? Are these emerging organisational and managerial forms coming to constitute something 'beyond bureaucracy' or are they closer to traditional hierarchical forms regardless of the rhetoric or packaging surrounding them?

The new managerialism and the medical profession

The management problem in the NHS has been a persistent feature in its evolution. The quest for improved management has generated a succession of reforms of the Service, beginning with its first major reorganisation in 1974, and has resulted in the importation into the NHS of managerial concepts and principles borrowed from the commercial sector. As the NHS celebrates its fiftieth birthday the search for better management continues.

The NHS is like no other organisation in the public or private sectors. It is a distinctive type of formal organisation which deviates significantly from the Weberian model of bureaucracy. Its uniqueness lies in the fact that it is a split organisation with a bureaucratic component and a professional component (Susser and Watson 1971). This split organisational form underlies many of the management problems and tensions in the NHS. The organisational form of the NHS and the distribution of power and authority within it are deeply affected by the doctors' special relationship to their patients. Other professional or semi-professional groups, notably nurses, are present in the NHS, but the medical profession has had and continues to have a unique authority. Rowbottom has expressed the point well:

> the position of doctors... presents a fascinating, and possibly unique, situation to any student of organisation. Never have so many highly influential figures been found in such an equivocal position - neither wholly of, nor wholly

divorced from, the organisation which they effectively dominate. (1973, p. 73)

An abiding feature of the NHS throughout its successive reorganisations has been the interactions among the deliverers of health care (primarily the medical profession), the administrators (now known as managers) who control the overall budgets and who are accountable for the day-to-day running of the NHS, and the boards or authorities which act as the governing bodies.

The relationship between the medical profession and managers is characterised by two different sets of aims and objectives as well as different values. Doctors insist upon treating individual patients in the manner they see to be in the patients' best interests and see themselves as being accountable to the patients they serve and to their own conscience. In contrast managers are concerned with the operation of the NHS as a whole and with ensuring that resources benefit the needs of a particular population or community rather than simply those of any single individual. This tension lies at the heart of the management challenge within the NHS and accounts for the ambivalence many doctors feel over the management function. It is an ambivalence which has been compounded by the particular models and styles of management which have been introduced at various stages over the past twenty five years or so.

The concept of clinical autonomy may be a rather nebulous and increasingly discredited one but it retains some validity. Managers have no right to direct in the area of care and treatment, they can only discuss and persuade. As a result peer pressure through instruments like clinical audit, guidelines and protocols offers the more effective means for challenging doctors' decisions and modifying them in line with best clinical practice.

While the medical profession may possess the potential to exercise considerable influence over how resources are used at a micro level, constraints restrict their autonomy. Medical dominance is no longer unfettered, if it ever was which is doubtful. In keeping with changing techniques and disease patterns, the medical profession is now dependent on many other skills and services. These serve as constraints on the medical profession's hegemony because doctors cannot ignore others' views and are required to work within teams. This increasing division of labour within medicine, which has yet to run its full course, represents a major challenge to medical dominance (Armstrong 1976).

Although the traditional specialities within medicine or clinical care have managed to resist the growing influence of the nursing profession and of general practice, and more recent developments in community pharmacy, it seems likely that their ability to continue such restrictive practices cannot survive for much longer. Indeed the 1991 NHS market-style reforms, with their separation of purchasers and providers, have shifted the balance of power from hospital consultants to fundholding general practitioners. By virtue of holding budgets with which to purchase services, GPs have been able to secure changes in hospital practices and quality of service which, it is claimed, would not otherwise have occurred or been possible. The problem with assessing these claims is that the

20

reforms have not been thoroughly or independently evaluated. A particular problem lies in attributing causation to a change in management or organisation as opposed to some other factor.

Partly to challenge the medical profession's monopoly and to inject greater management rigour into the efficient use of resources, the NHS has since the early 1970s been subjected to almost continuous structural change. While the details and precise forms of these restructuring exercises need not detain us, they all share some common themes and purposes which are important for an assessment of the shifting frontier between medicine and management.

The first major reorganisation of the NHS in 1974 provided policy makers with an opportunity to challenge the exclusiveness of the medical profession in deciding what, and how, services should be provided and to whom. The encroachment of managerialism into medical territory began innocently enough. The management of local services was vested in medical, nursing, lay and financial officers. These corporate bodies operated as consensus management teams which meant that decisions could only be agreed if all team members were unanimous. If the team failed to reach agreement, the matter was passed to the level above for resolution. Consensus management enhanced the status of the nurse and finance director as equal members of the management group alongside the doctor and lay manager. Nurses in particular welcomed the seat at the top table as recognition of the significant contribution they made to policy and their place as the largest single group of NHS employees.

The 1974 reorganisation did not end the search for improved management. Paradoxically it fuelled yet more intensive attempts to tackle what were perceived to be continuing problems in health services management (Harrison, Hunter and Pollitt 1990). By the late 1980s consensus management became discredited and was accused of giving rise to lowest common denominator decisions.

There was also criticism of the lack of a unified authority in the NHS and the length of time taken to reach decisions (Harrison 1982). The absence of clear responsibility was perceived to be the fundamental flaw in the 1974 model (Maynard 1983). Apart from those who believed that consensus management had led to weak management sapping individual responsibility, others argued that the 1974 reorganisation imported too many inappropriate management concepts into a public service. It was a criticism which would surface in later NHS management changes. Burns (1994, p. xx) for instance was critical of the 'recrudescence of hard line managerialism' and a primitive, already outdated managerialism at that. He contrasted the supporting, enabling role of management with the controlling, hierarchical one and feared that the latter had been in the ascendant since 1974. Finally NHS practitioners themselves were critical of what they regarded as an unnecessarily complex, cumbersome and overbearing structure. There was some talk of replacing consensus management teams with a system of chief executives although the medical profession saw this as unacceptable.

A chief executive would be in charge of all professional personnel - a position of command which had no parallel then in the NHS as far as medical staff were concerned since each consultant enjoyed virtual autonomy. There was no constituency at the time anywhere in the UK for such heretical thoughts. As Klein (1974) has argued, the creation of consensus management teams was the only way out of the impasse resulting from professional intransigence over the desirability of a chief executive figure who would run the Service within each authority.

Criticism of the 1974 reorganisation finally persuaded the government to set up a Royal Commission on the NHS in 1976. The Commission advocated modifications rather than a wholesale restructuring to improve the operation of consensus management (Royal Commission on the NHS 1979). The incoming Conservative government endorsed this view, having no wish to antagonise the medical profession.

Further change in the management of the NHS had to await the Griffiths inquiry into the management of the Service in 1983. Roy Griffiths was then Deputy Chairman and Managing Director of the Sainsbury's group and represented the perfect businessman type that the Conservatives saw as resolving public sector management problems.

The Griffiths report, a brief 23 page letter for action, resulted in the introduction of general managers in place of team management (NHS Management Inquiry 1983). General managers were a response to what Griffiths saw to be the state of 'institutionalised stagnation' in the NHS, the result of labyrinthine consultation processes and consensus management teams. Griffiths' charge that the NHS lacked a clearly defined general management function caught the spirit of the times. Even so, and often overlooked, Griffiths did not seek to diminish the value of consensus among managers as distinct from formalised consensus decision-making. In his view a general manager was to 'harness the best of the consensus management approach and avoid the worst of the problems it can present' (NHS Management Inquiry 1983). However in the rush to implement Griffiths' proposals consensus was little in evidence. Certainly there was much opposition to the proposal for general managers at all levels of the NHS from among the professions, particularly nurses who believed, correctly, that they would lose the hard won gains which consensus management had provided. A belief reinforced by Griffiths' comment about doctors being the 'natural managers'. No longer would nurses have a seat at the top table within a team of equals.

The government was keen to implement Griffiths' proposals with all possible speed. What was puzzling is that only a few years earlier the same government, albeit under a different Secretary of State, had rejected the idea of chief executives and any shift away from consensus management. What had changed so dramatically? There is probably no single answer. A key factor was growing anxiety in Treasury circles that the Service had an insufficient managerial grip on expenditure. If the NHS was to receive further injections of funds then it had to demonstrate its ability to manage its resources effectively. Improved management was the Secretary of State's weapon to demonstrate to the Treasury that the NHS meant business.

In all this manoeuvring the professions were effectively overlooked at a national consultative level. From a position adopted in 1948 where their sensibilities and freedoms were not to be disturbed, the government no longer regarded this implicit understanding with the professions as sacrosanct particularly given Treasury pressures. Griffiths offered a government anxious for a management fix the perfect solution. His prescription for crisper management was just what was needed even if it did mean confronting, and subsequently modifying, even if only modestly, the interests and influence of the various stakeholder groups.

Whether the introduction of general management has fundamentally altered the prevailing culture in the NHS is debatable. In some ways events moved too fast to allow the Griffiths changes to settle down properly. Scarcely had the new breed of general managers been appointed, when talk of further reform began. In the wake of a funding crisis in the late 1980s, a 1989 white paper proposed an internal market for the NHS and a clear separation between the funders and purchasers and the providers of health care. Although the 1989 proposals built upon Griffiths, many criticised them as unnecessary and premature given the 1983 general management changes had not matured.

Moreover talk of markets and competition had an alienating effect on public service professionals attached to a different set of values. Other criticisms levelled at the 1991 changes included that they made hospitals and practitioners compete with one another instead of collaborating; that professionals lost influence over strategic issues at a purchasing level; and that management had been taken over by an accounting mentality obsessed with the financial bottom line and little else, as evidenced by the efficiency index with its narrow focus on means (activity levels) rather than ends (health outcomes).

Harrison (1988) concluded that post-Griffiths management changes had resulted in NHS managers becoming more clearly agents of government, as a result of the chain of command in place from centre to periphery; and that while the frontier of control between government and doctors had shifted a little in favour of the former, as yet only limited evidence suggested that managers had secured greater control over doctors. Indeed much of the impetus behind the 1991 NHS changes can be seen as an attempt to secure such a shift. Not surprisingly the health care professions led by the British Medical Association were virtually unanimous in opposing the changes. The reasons are explored below. Before turning to these, let us return briefly to the notion of management and what the cult of managerialism meant in the context of the NHS.

If as Drucker claims, 'management world-wide has become the new social function' (1990, p. 218), this has profound implications for all organisations including health services. Within the health care sector, the global revolution in the organisation of health services in the past decade or so has centred on improved management. Management has been held up as the principal instrument through which many of the objectives of health care reform can be achieved. However, as was noted earlier, serious questions have been raised over the appropriateness of the particular management concepts within a health service context.

In seeking to shift from hierarchies to markets when it introduced its NHS changes in 1991, the Conservative government was never as unequivocal in undertaking the shift as it tried to make out (Hunter 1997). Certain features of the changes in management style and content represented a rather odd and uneasy mix of the old (hierarchies, command and control systems) and the new (markets and competition) which did not sit easily together - as indeed subsequently proved to be the case. For instance the 1989 white paper, *Working for Patients*, stressed the chain of management command which, as a result of the introduction of general management, ran from districts through regions (the 14 former Regional Health Authorities which disappeared in April 1996 to be replaced by eight Regional Offices) to the NHS Chief Executive and through him to the Secretary of State for Health and then Parliament. But as Harrison et al point out: 'this was rather a curious cuckoo in the nest of the provider market. Markets, of any kind, are not run by a single clear chain of command. On the contrary "a market system is a 'spontaneous order' monitored by its feedback, it conflicts with a 'rational order' shaped by targets" (Sartori 1987, p. 400)' (1992, p.119).

Curiously this ambivalence about encouraging markets on the one hand while being reluctant to let central control go on the other has resulted in an even tighter central grip on the NHS than anything which preceded it. It may be a peculiarly British phenomenon. As Hoggett (1996, p. 27) observes more generally in the restructuring of the public sector in Britain, elements of decentralised, hands-off market based approaches to delivering public services have been 'dwarfed by visible elements of centralisation... and the extended use of hands-on systems of performance management creating a form of "evaluative state" .' For Hoggett the public sector in Britain in the 1990s exemplified an 'uneasy combination of the new and the old, the hands-off and the hands-on, the sophisticated and the crude, freedom and surveillance, quality and quantity' (1996, p. 28). In Handy's words we should not be dismayed by the 'contradictions and surprises of paradox. [It] has to be accepted, coped with and made sense of' (1994, pp. 17-8).

The excessive degree of centralisation and formalisation had unforeseen consequences on the dynamics of the NHS. As Jenkins observes: 'the centralisation of the Service left an uneasy feeling that a professional relationship of trust between patient and doctor and hospital and community had been broken'(1995, p. 88). Jenkins contrasted the monster created principally by Margaret Thatcher and Kenneth Clarke with Bevan's original model for the NHS: 'His health service was concerned simply with offering doctors and nurses an administrative apparatus "for them freely to use in accordance with their training for the benefit of the people of the country".' (1995, p. 86).

Bevan's model was the profession dominated NHS which had survived largely intact until the first half of the 1980s. Griffiths questioned this model and sought to strengthen management to shift the emphasis, and eventually the balance of power, from producers to consumers in line with commercial practice - the world with which he was most familiar. The market rhetoric of *Working for Patients* endorsed this approach and sought to take it further by talk of 'money following the patient', and through GP fundholding which would allow GPs to hold budgets to be able to respond more flexibly and appropriately to patients' wishes.

But the government was never prepared to see the NHS in pure market terms. Rather the terms 'managed market' and 'managed competition' were employed to make a distinction between the theory of pure markets on the one hand and the government's commitment to a public service on the other. As a former Secretary of State for Health, Virginia Bottomley, told the House of Commons in 1991 at the time the reforms were being implemented, the NHS 'is not a market where the outcome is allowed to fall where it will, because it is a managed public service'. Much of the thinking underpinning the 1991 NHS changes was informed by notions and concepts which have come to be referred to as 'new public management' (Hood 1991).

The 'new public management' (NPM) was not confined to the NHS nor even to the UK. It can best be described as an international movement which overtook public administration globally across a range of public policy spheres. Of particular importance was the emphasis in NPM on standard-setting, performance management, and target setting in the sphere of professional influence. Also important was the stress on private sector management and the move away from the traditional public service ethic which owed more to sound administration than management.

In the NHS the application of NPM principles involved the introduction of an internal market in the form of a purchaser-provider separation of responsibilities and the emergence of a 'contract culture'. Health authorities, and increasingly GPs who are taking over the purchasing function, are required to assess the health needs of their communities and meet these in the most cost effective way. Provider units bid for contracts to provide services. They are essentially small businesses (although denied the freedoms open to these) which have two aims: to maximise income and expand their services in order to survive.

The upshot of all these developments on the medical profession has been closer bureaucratic control of its activities - a clear example of a policy paradox. But whether its former dominance is now subject to erosion through deprofessionalisation or proletarianisation is unclear (Larkin 1993). Its autonomy is certainly under threat from management as well as from health services researchers intent upon challenging medical practice variations and from active consumers.

The impact of marketisation on the NHS has had, it has been argued, a corrosive effect on the former 'high-trust' relationships between doctors and managers and between doctors and patients (Harrison and Lachmann 1996). Trust implies mutual understanding and respect. Whatever its shortcomings, and there were many, the pre-1984 NHS was based on 'high-trust' relationships in which the parties involved observed mutual obligations which were not precisely defined. That these relationships may not always have been evident in practice does not negate the assumptions underpinning the management style then operating. In contrast the post 1984 and 1991 changes replaced a consensus model with a model based on the management of conflict (Day and Klein 1983). The new model implies low trust relationships: everything must be defined, documented, formalised and transformed into a quasi-contractual relationship. In his seminal study of labour management issues Fox (1974) defined 'high-trust' relationships as ones in which the participants: share (or have similar) ends and values, have a diffuse sense of long term obligation, offer support without calculating the cost or expecting an immediate return, communicate freely and openly with one another, are prepared to trust the other and risk their own fortunes in the other party, give the benefit of the doubt in relation to motives and good will if there are problems. In contrast 'low-trust' relationships are ones in which the participants: have divergent goals, have explicit expectations which must be reciprocated through balanced exchanges, carefully calculate the costs and benefits of any concession made, restrict and screen communications in their own separate interests, attempt to minimise their dependence on the other's discretion, are suspicious about mistakes or failures, attributing them to ill-will or default and invoke sanctions.

Fox argued that purely economic exchanges, and those relying on formal contracts, institutionalised the dynamics of low trust and low discretion. Conversely social exchange entails judgement in task performance and loyalty and sustains 'high-trust' relationships and high levels of work discretion. Fox claimed that with markets and contractual relations permeating every sector of social and public life, the reciprocity and diffuse obligations essential for 'high-trust' relationships were being progressively undermined. Flynn, Williams and Pickard (1996) demonstrate in their study of contracting in community health services that high discretion work (e.g. complex professional services) necessitates high levels of trust: 'Dogmatic attempts to codify, formalise and prescribe such high-discretion work will not only be unfeasible but also counterproductive, because prescriptive contracts are inappropriate for tasks characterised by indeterminacy and uncertainty, and the use of sanctions (resting upon distrust) will undermine the contractual relationship' (1996, p.143).

The arrival of markets, even at a rhetorical level, and aggressive consumerism have seriously eroded 'high-trust' relationships. The cult, or celebration, of the type of managerialism known as NPM and its impact on the medical profession is of particular interest in this respect. A link can be traced to the increasing subjugation of doctors to the edicts of the new managerialism, with their stress on control and accountability, and doctors' growing frustration at seeing their power base challenged if not eroded.

The concerns of the medical profession can, with some justification, be dismissed as naked protectionism but they are understandable and not entirely without foundation. They cannot summarily be dismissed as being of no consequence or substance. As Pollitt (1993) argues, the new orthodoxy of managerialism amounted to 'a set of beliefs and practices, at the core of which burns the seldom-tested assumption that better management will prove an effective solvent for a wide range of economic and social ills.'

Compounding the hostility to management in the NHS and contributing to the erosion of trust between doctors and managers was doctors' perception of managers as the agents of ministers rather than as a group of enablers and facilitators who existed primarily to support doctors. Ironically given their opposition to the NHS concept in the first place, doctors saw themselves as the sole remaining guardians of the founding principles of the NHS with managers cast as the NHS's greatest enemy (Wall 1996). Thirty years ago managers were not expected to be assertive. Their task was to create an environment for doctors to practice medicine. Now doctors see managers ruling the roost with clinical work subordinated to the ever growing demands of financial management. Doctors are victims of managers who use their power to coerce doctors into compliance. Developments such as managed care and integrated care pathways, imports into Europe from the US, are the latest examples of this type of aggressive management.

As the power balance between doctors and managers has shifted seemingly inevitably and inexorably towards managers, doctors, albeit with some exceptions, have become increasingly vociferous and strident in their condemnation of the NHS in general and cult of managerialism in particular. Even if, as Gray and Jenkins (1995) conclude, the changes may have been more about form than substance, undoubted signs of major substantive change do exist. The nature of power and politics in the health service has been altered which 'has been at the expense of the professionals and to the advantage of the managers' (Gray and Jenkins 1995, p.29). The position of managers is now pivotal even if politicians feel ambivalent about them and are intent upon reducing their numbers. They are also dependent on these very same managers when it comes to implementing any change.

Management and the medical profession

The national associations representing the principal health care professions have generally been opposed to the 1991 NHS changes. They see the introduction of markets into medicine as conflicting with a caring ethos and management systems as absorbing significant sums of money better spent elsewhere. Yet while the Royal Colleges and particularly the BMA have been vociferous and persistent critics of the so-called 'infernal market', the medical profession has accepted that practitioners must adopt a more corporate position on policy and management issues given limited resources, and that the needs of the individual must be balanced against collective needs.

The BMA's attempt to define core values for the medical profession is a significant recognition of the shift that has occurred. Another development has been the production of clinical guidelines and protocols which codify best practice and are intended to be used by clinicians when they make decisions about treatment options. It would be wrong to assume that because the medical profession has produced such tools nationally they are then adopted locally. Klein (1995), for instance, maintains that a distinction can be made between individual and collective professional autonomy. He suggests that the individual autonomy of clinicians is shrinking as a consequence in part of the 1991 NHS reforms which, in the case of trust hospitals, gave the same incentives to managers and professionals who had a shared interest in ensuring the viability and survival of the hospital in which both groups worked. In contrast Klein argues that collectively the medical profession has accepted greater responsibility for 'putting its house in order' and for rooting out inefficient practices and bad doctors. He concludes that 'the medical profession appears to be ready to restrict the autonomy of individual clinicians in order to strengthen collective professional autonomy' (Klein 1995, pp. 243-44). Thus the medical profession is aiming to retain control over the regulation of the health care market as well over issues of quality of care and accreditation to avoid managerial intervention. The Royal Colleges, BMA and GMC in these respects are no less powerful now than they have always been even if their direct involvement in policy formulation virtually ceased under the last government.

Klein's argument may be a little too neat and tidy. The dictates of the new structures or claims of managers may not be reflected in practice. Allen's (1997) study of junior doctors' attitudes suggests that professional values are more potent features of medical life and work than employment by a particular hospital trust. A new logo, board of directors and corporate strategy do not mean that doctors suddenly become corporate players. Their professional beliefs are too strong for that and certainly transcend individual hospital boundaries.

Evidence for this can be found in the rash of trust mergers that is breaking out across the country as part of the Labour government's wish to end the internal market. One of the drivers behind the mergers has been pressure from clinicians to end what they regard as an absurd system which breeds competition and duplication in place of professional co-operation across hospital and organisational boundaries. As a former Chairman of the BMA Council, Jeremy Lee-Potter, observes the system of competing trusts and multiple small fundholding business 'has damaged [the NHS's] immensely valuable medical networking systems. No longer can doctors in different hospitals freely help each other out with information and second opinions...' (Lee-Potter 1997, p. 247).

The activities of the British Association of Medical Managers (BAMM) and other organisations suggest that more clinicians are entering senior management positions and this trend is likely to continue and grow. The numbers of clinical director and medical director posts have expanded but the job satisfaction of many of them is limited. May be this is why BAMM's growth has been steady though not spectacular with currently just 800 members. In a *British Medical Journal* editorial clearly intended to increase BAMM's appeal, the chief executive and the *BMJ* editor claim that the best health care management requires doctors to become more involved and increase their management skills. They argue that 'doctor managers put patient care and clinical outcome ahead of the financial imperative, and this ultimately is the only way to develop the business of healthcare systems - looking after patients' (Simpson and Smith 1997, p.1636). They continue: 'No matter how much a chief executive's values may coincide with those of clinicians, he or she is vulnerable if there is direct conflict between what is right for patient care and what is demanded from above' (p. 1637).

Despite any erosion of their power at a national level, doctors at a micro level have proved themselves resistant to change:

medical micro-power is essentially conservative - it is a power to resist change that comes from outside, to resist not necessarily by battles at meetings and other 'first face' campaigns (though they may also occur) but rather by silent, individualistic non-compliance - a 'second face' refusal to become engaged or involved. That is one reason why it is so hard to beat - medical micro power is not organised influence. (Harrison, Hunter, Marnoch and Pollitt 1992, p.140)

The new managerialism is undermining medical dominance in various ways. For instance in areas of quality and clinical audit, and more recently through the research and development strategy and related notions of clinical effectiveness and evidence-based medicine (EBM), the medical profession is being subjected to more systematic and rigorous managerial assessment and, in the jargon, performance management. It, along with other professions, is coming under closer scrutiny and is being held to account for its effectiveness and efficacy. Even if quality and audit are presented as educational devices which doctors can operate and apply themselves in the form (and safety) of self-review and peer review, the reality is that the boundary between medicine and management is being progressively breached.

Developments in quality, audit and monitoring together constitute 'a significant incursion into the medical domain. They represent a trimming of doctors' micro-power, because they open a management window...onto those core medical activities of diagnosis, admissions, prescribing therapies and deciding on discharges' (Harrison et al 1992, p.143). Because many of these developments are in part being driven by cost considerations, and not primarily by considerations of quality or service improvement, they are viewed by doctors with a degree of scepticism if not outright hostility. The concern, too, is that techniques derived from EBM will reduce medicine to cookbook principles and deprofessionalise the craft of medicine. Of course if doctors lead the developments in clinical effectiveness at both national and local levels then they should have little to fear but anxieties do nevertheless exist and need to be acknowledged regardless of how rational or irrational they may be.

Despite the encroachment by management into medicine, its impact on practice and behaviour should not be overstated. Clinical effectiveness has yet to make significant inroads into medical practice. The micro-management of medical work remains weak and will probably always remain so until clinicians manage themselves and their work (Burns 1996). The point is endorsed by Simpson and Smith (1997, p.1637) who argue that 'all clinicians must know something about management, even if it is to be able followers rather than leaders'. However not all doctors feel so inclined. Lee-Potter, a former Chairman of the BMA Council, maintains that 'relatively few' doctors actually want to be managers.

Yet as Lee-Potter, among others, has argued, some form of accommodation must be found between managers and doctors. Using the term 'sides' intentionally, Lee-Potter believes that to integrate the training of managers with that of doctors at some stage in their careers would bring them together: 'The intention would not be to turn doctors into managers or vice versa, but simply to familiarise each group with the other's priorities, skills and problems faced, and help to achieve better teamwork and thus a better health service' (Lee-Potter 1997, p. 250). Other ways of involving doctors in management at a higher level would be to allow clinical directors to become members of hospital management boards.

Do younger doctors have a more positive view than their elders of the management function? A recent BMA survey of young doctors' views of their core values indicates that they do not (Allen 1997). The survey found considerable hostility towards management whose apparently conflicting culture and different ethos doctors feel prevent them from practising medicine to the benefit of their patients. Doctors were particularly concerned about the increasing demands placed on them by 'managers with clipboards'. There were demands to maintain throughput and numbers and to account for their time in ways unheard of in the days of their predecessors.

These young doctors saw management as becoming increasingly intrusive and aggressive in questioning the commitment of doctors through their working practices. Many felt 'hassled' by management to speed up their consultations and to see more patients. The view was expressed that consultants were becoming less and less empowered because they are becoming more like 'technical monkeys'. A great cultural divide existed between doctors and managers particularly when it came to understanding the core values of the medical profession. Doctors presented a bleak picture of misunderstanding and territorial separation which illustrated the width of the gulf between them and managers. Managers were perceived as individuals who 'don't know what we do and they don't want to know either' (Allen 1997, p.8).

Linked to these negative views of management was a more pervasive set of concerns around growing pressure of work and loss of autonomy which contributed to mounting work-related stress. Early retirement was seen as the only goal worth aspiring to. Loss of autonomy pervaded many of the discussions. Yet the doctors surveyed did not feel they would increase their autonomy by taking a more managerial role. Managers were seen as a different species. As one subject put it: 'Managers don't share the same ethics as us, and so it's assumed that if you cross the road and become a manager, you've lost some of those values that are held dear to doctors' (Allen 1997, p.11).

Perceptions such as this had important implications for discussions of whether doctors should or could take on more managerial roles. Some referred to colleagues who had taken on more managerial responsibilities in the new culture as 'traitors' or as having 'copped out'. But there was a preference for dealing with managers who had been clinicians because their judgement could be trusted. Significantly this trust was mostly based on the perception that the manager with a medical background still shared the same core values as the doctors, while managers were perceived to have a different value system. Yet some respondents gave examples of the ways in which the core values of medical managers could be overruled by management, particularly on issues of quality compared with numbers.

Not all management incursions can be condemned outright or rejected as having no useful public purpose. As Allen notes, many of the demands for greater accountability, measurable outputs and more throughput are well founded and have sought to remove some restrictive practices. Not all professionals perform in ways which uphold the high ideals and standards set for them. The privileges they enjoy can be abused in ways which appear self-serving and protectionist. Other aspects of the management revolution, however: 'have succeeded only in demotivating and demoralising professionals who have sought to maintain core values in a world which has become increasingly wedded to efficiency and the management culture' (Allen 1997, p.14).

Could it even be that the type and style of management that has been developed within the NHS is inappropriate for the task? Significantly not all managers accept the framework within which they are expected to operate with its stress on means rather than ends. After all, the BMA survey emphasised the unanimity over the cultural divide between doctors and managers which was proving wholly counterproductive and stress inducing. The two groups occupied two quite separate and distinctive worlds. While younger doctors did acknowledge the need to modernise the profession, they remained wedded to a commitment to provide competence, care and compassion for those in need. But they were resistant to what many saw as a managerial take-over which, if successful, would threaten their values and practice. Whether or not this is a fair or accurate portrayal of reality as seen by others is not the point. It is the reality for these particular members of the medical profession.

Even so some countervailing pressures are constraining the advance of management and its assault on clinical autonomy (Hunter 1992, Harrison and Pollitt 1994). Doctors' specialist knowledge remains irreplaceable which itself places limits on managers' incursions into medical territory. Managers and politicians, on their own admission, remain heavily dependent on the medical profession.

Myths and models of management

A vital distinction must be drawn between managing the NHS and those responsible for providing health care on the one hand and the particular model of management selected for the task on the other. Few would disagree with the diagnosis of the NHS's weaknesses which was produced to justify the 1991 changes. The objections have more to do with a style of management and cult of managerialism reflecting accounting rather than clinical or quality of service criteria. Accommodating these two sets of values is unlikely to prove straightforward.

Equally to polarise crudely the respective managerial and professional domains is simplistic and unhelpful. Many doctors, as does the BMA's code on core values, accept the need to manage resources optimally and support the drive to base decisions on knowledge and evidence of effectiveness. On the other side of the management-medicine divide (and however much managers and others may protest at the use of such language, a divide remains) are many managers who are frustrated by the obsession with an efficiency index which has little to say about effectiveness and outcomes. So there is indeed a need, as Lee-Potter claims, for an honest dialogue between the two groups although whether this is likely to happen is probably doubtful. Lee-Potter gives the game away in the following passage:

> Doctors are unavoidably elitist. They have been used to being amongst the brightest in their schools, they have had to work longer and harder while at university... . The lot of a junior doctor is a hard one, and it does not get much

31

easier during the rest of a medical career, whether in hospital or general practice. From this point of view, the path to chief executive of a trust hospital, on a salary equal to or higher than that of a consultant with at least a 'B' merit award... looks much easier. If the truth were told it probably is. (1997, p. 249)

But whatever the cultural differences separating doctors from managers, unless managers are themselves doctors or nurses as is likely to happen to an increasing degree, the model and style of management adopted cannot be ignored. Not all management is the same. As has been noted, a principal criticism of the new managerialism which swept through the NHS in the 1980s and 1990s is the exaggerated faith shown in private sector values. This faith, insists Mintzberg (1996), is dangerous when applied to health care and other complex professional services.

He disposes of three popular myths concerning management and its application to public policy. Firstly activities can be isolated and treated as discrete entities rather than being regarded as interconnected. Secondly performance can be fully and properly evaluated by objective measures. Such a goal is rarely possible or even appropriate in an area like health care. Thirdly activities can be entrusted to autonomous professional managers held responsible for their performance. Faith is placed in managers trained to manage. But, as the BMA study of junior doctors' views demonstrated, it was precisely these features of the new managerialism which concerned the respondents and were the cause of so much personal and professional acrimony and stress. The medical profession's core values stress caring and compassion, multi-disciplinary team working and community responsibility (BMA 1995). However much we may wish that the activities of government were otherwise and were subject to clear and precise measurement, the reality is more akin to Handy's acceptance of paradox and ambiguity which are heavily to the fore in public policy. Many activities undertaken by government, like health care, require soft judgement.

Two of Mintzberg's five models for managing government are pertinent to the present discussion: the government-as-network model, and the normative-control model. The first model is the opposite of the new public management which has prevailed in the NHS over the past decade or so although it closely resembles how groups of doctors often operate and organise themselves. It is loose instead of tight, free-flowing instead of controlled, interactive instead of sharply segmented. Government organisations are viewed as single interconnected systems, complex networks of temporary relationships fashioned to work out problems as they arise. The second normative-control model is not about systems or structures but about soul. Attitudes count, not numbers, and control is rooted not in hierarchy but in values and beliefs. The model is quite close to those fashionable management theories which have informed NHS changes since the mid-1970s.

As Mintzberg makes clear, there is no one best model although some models are more appropriate than others depending on the task. He claims that the network model is applicable to many of the complex, unpredictable activities of today's governments. Mintzberg also favours a major shift of emphasis to the normative model. He believes it addresses the unique aspects of government with its vagaries, nuances and difficult trade-offs among conflicting interests. And for Mintzberg this is an especially important ingredient when it comes to client-oriented professional services such as health care 'which can never be better than the people who deliver them' (Mintzberg 1996, p.82). Professionals need to be freed from the stifling controls of government bureaucracy and the narrow pressures of market competition. For this to become a reality, it will be necessary to temper the influence that business values and the new managerialism exert on government and on particular policy sectors like health.

Moving towards one or other, or perhaps a mix, of these two models could be what the government intends by ending the internal market in the NHS. The next and final section considers the possibilities a little further. Not all the trends are favourable or point in the direction of these models. Other developments on the management front, also imports from the US, reinforce two further models mentioned but discarded, despite their popularity, by Mintzberg, namely, the government-as-machine model and the performance-control model.

The management developments to which Mintzberg refers in the health sector, and usually referred to as managed care and integrated care pathways, are aimed at controlling the activities of the medical profession even more closely and aggressively than hitherto (Fairfield, Hunter, Mechanic and Rosleff 1997). Managed care has many definitions but the principal components are essentially the same. It is a planned approach to the delivery of medical services which seeks to control costs and improve quality of health care by a variety of methods which might include controlling access to health care, case note review of treatment standards and the use of financial incentives to encourage efficiency (Burns and Ellis 1997).

As Burns and Ellis point out, managed care by its nature alters the decisions doctors make about their patients because 'it seeks to limit clinical freedom where that freedom might result in inefficient or ineffective treatment being prescribed' (p. 1). In the US managed care is experiencing something of a backlash from doctors resentful of the intrusion by managers and accountants who in effect determine the parameters within which doctors can operate. Patients are also increasingly opposed to managed care schemes since it is believed they actually disempower them and reduce the choices available to them. In particular, they restrict access to specialist care. Whether managed care in a European context can avoid the problems encountered in the US remains to be seen. Certainly the intention would be to adopt a consensus approach rather than a conflict one where possible. Also systems like the British NHS are already managed care organisations on a macro scale. Much of what is proposed is a natural extension of the performance management philosophy evident within the Service in recent years. The obstacle is likely to be the non-medical general managers within trusts and health authorities who fail to understand the business they are in and who are therefore, with honourable exceptions, reluctant to confront or challenge clinicians. This state of affairs constitutes another paradox because at a time when managerialism is riding high, many of its beneficiaries are unable to utilise it to effect lasting change or to modify the behaviour of those who are largely responsible for driving and shaping health care services.

Conclusion: future developments

Is the government likely to take the NHS and its managerial perspective in a dramatically new direction? Probably not. Labour supports, privately if not publicly, much in the management changes introduced by the last government and is also committed to the previous government's spending plans. In order to create the resources to develop services, the government will find it needs more effective management. It is likely to see a major developmental challenge here for doctors especially primary care physicians who will be spearheading new forms of locality commissioning. The framework for this agenda was put in place by the previous government but with Labour's full support. In this scenario it is conceivable that, as Harrison and Pollitt (1994, p.137) put it: 'the interests of management are themselves likely to become more fragmented, various and conflictual'. It may also be the case that as new organisational forms take root among groups of primary care doctors, these forms move away from managerial hierarchies towards independent groupings or partnerships.

Ham (1996) offers a glimpse of the future when he speculates over new forms of ownership and delivery being actively encouraged and old forms rediscovered. In particular he mentions self-governing community health agencies which would strengthen and rebuild community solidarity. While public funds would continue to be the source of funding health care and there would be public regulation of standards, the provision of services might be organised through diverse forms of organisation which owe more to the mutual societies and co-operative ventures than to pre-existing structures. Such organisational forms would certainly appeal to New Labour with its wish to see innovative public-private partnerships flourish.

Similarly Harrison and Pollitt (1994) foresee 'an escape from hierarchy' in the form of independent partnerships or firms which would hire their services back to the main purchasing or providing agencies - a model already reflected in the way general practitioners operate. While for-profit schemes might hold less appeal, not-for-profit ventures would be immensely attractive. They would also represent a means for encouraging local community ownership of health care services.

However while such thinking would clearly take the NHS beyond bureaucracy, countervailing pressures are at work and policy tensions and contradictions present. The Labour Party remains wedded, as does the public who voted for them, to a national health service which is committed to equitable levels of and access to services. A criticism of recent years, somewhat ironically in view of the massive re-centralisation that has occurred, has been how increased local discretion and variation has resulted in services being provided in some parts of the country but not in others. The issue for Labour is how to balance national uniformity, or at least the attempt to secure it, with local differences. If there are to be limits to diversity and its tolerance, then what are these and how far is a national approach contingent upon a return to hierarchy? While the government may seek a blend of hierarchies and markets, albeit not-for-profit ones, how far will this be possible in practice with a medical profession and public who appear to favour a more centrally planned approach to the allocation and use of resources?

How far medicine will be allowed, or wish, to move into the uncharted waters beyond bureaucracy remains unclear. But neither the government nor the medical profession may have the luxury of coming to a considered view. The imperatives of developments in medical technology may make the decision for them. Not only will advances in health technology change the organisation and structure of services, but they will also demand new modes of working and different skills (Hunter 1996). Skill mix issues will be to the fore and more flexible styles of working will be required even though such developments appear to run counter to the prevailing orthodox management solutions, resting on the Taylorist school of scientific management rather than more recent management theories.

Those preparing and positioning the NHS for the 21st century might be best advised to consider Mintzberg's two models: the network model and the normative model. Therein may lie the means of restoring the medical profession's faith in management that connects with their reality and beliefs as distinct from industrial models of management imported into the NHS but which are seen as alien and alienating. As part of this redefinition of management a renegotiation could take place over what is meant by clinical discretion and in the demarcation between professional and managerial responsibilities. The BMA core values initiative, itself an unprecedented venture, can be seen in this context. It represents a significant acknowledgement of the need for clinicians to think more broadly about their role and responsibilities. Managers, who lack an explicit ethical code but who support the need for one, might take note.

References

Allen, I. (1997), *Committed but Critical: An Examination of Young Doctors' Views of their Core Values*, British Medical Association: London.

Armstrong, D. (1976), 'The Decline of the Medical Hegemony: A Review of Government Reports during the NHS', *Social Science and Medicine*, 10.

British Medical Association (1995), *Core Values for the Medical Profession in the 21st Century*, Report of a Conference, 3-4 November 1994, BMA: London.

Burns, H. (1996), *Making Outcomes Matter*, Speaking Up No. 5, National Association of Health Authorities and Trusts: Birmingham.

Burns, H. and Ellis, B. (1997), 'Why a New Journal?' *Journal of Managed Care*, Vol. 1. No. 1, pp. 1-2.

Day, P. and Klein, R. (1983), 'The Mobilisation of Consent versus the Management of Conflict: Decoding the Griffiths Report', *British Medical Journal*, No. 287, pp. 1^13-16.

Drucker, P. (1990), *Managing the Non-Profit Organization*, Oxford: Butterworth-Heinemann.

Fairfield, G. Hunter, D., Mechanic, D. and Rosleff F. (1997), 'Managed Care: Origins, Principles, and Evolution', *British Medical Journal*, No. 314, pp. 1823-26.

Flynn, R. Williams, G. and Pickard, S. (1996), *Markets and Networks: Contracting in Community Health Services*, Open University Press: Buckingham.

Fox, A. (1974), *Beyond Contract: Work, Power, and Trust Relations*, Faber and Faber: London.

Gray, A. and Jenkins, B. (1995), 'Public Management and the NHS' in Glynn, J. and Perkins, D. (eds.), *Managing Health Care*, Saunders: London.

Ham, C. (1996), *Public, Private or Community: What Next for the NHS?* Demos: London.

Handy, C. (1994), *The Empty Raincoat*, Hutchinson: London.

Harrison, S. (1982), 'Consensus Decision-Making in the NHS: a Review', *Journal of Management Studies*, Vol. 19, pp. 377-94.

Harrison, S. (1988), *Managing the NHS: Shifting the Frontier*, Chapman and Hall: London.

Harrison, S. and Lachmann, P. (1996), *Towards a High-Trust NHS*, Institute for Public Policy Research: London.

Harrison, S. and Pollitt, C. (1994), *Controlling Health Professionals*, Open University Press: Buckingham.

Harrison, S, Hunter, D. and Pollitt, C. (1990), *The Dynamics of British Health Policy*, Unwin Hyman: London.

Harrison, S., Hunter, D., Marnoch, G. and Pollitt, C. (1992), *Just Managing: Power and Culture in the NHS*, Macmillan: Basingstoke.

Hoggett, P. (1996), 'New Modes of Control in the Public Service', *Public Administration*, Vol. 74, No.1, pp. 9-32.

Hood, C. (1991), 'A Public Management for All Seasons?' *Public Administration*, Vol. 69, Vol.1, pp. 3-19.

Hunter, D. (1990), ' "Managing the Cracks": Management Development for Health Care Interfaces', *The International Journal of Health Planning and Management*, Vol. 5, No. 1, pp. 7-14.

Hunter, D. (1992), 'Doctors as Managers: Gamekeepers Turned Poachers?' *Social Science and Medicine*, Vol. 35, No. 4, pp. 557-66.

Hunter, D. (1993), 'The Internal Market: The Shifting Agenda', in Tilley, I. (ed.), *Managing the Internal Market*, Paul Chapman: London.

Hunter, D. (1996), 'The Changing Roles of Health Care Personnel in Health and Health Care Management', *Social Science and Medicine*, Vol. 43, No. 5, pp. 799-808.

Hunter, D. (1997), *Health Sector Reform: Policy Formulation and Implementation: Comparing Experiences in the UK NHS and Developing Health Systems*, Nuffield Institute for Health: Leeds (unpublished).

Jenkins, S. (1995), *Accountable to None: The Tory Nationalisation of Britain*. Hamish Hamilton: London.

Klein, R. (1995), *The New Politics of the NHS*, 3rd ed., Longman: London.

Klein, R. (1974), 'Policy Making in the NHS', *Political Studies*, Vol. 22, pp. 1-14.

Larkin, G. (1993), 'Continuity in Change: Medical Dominance in the UK' in Hafferty, F. and McKinlay, J. (eds.), *The Changing Medical Profession: An International Perspective*, Oxford University Press: New York.

Lee-Potter, J. (1997), *A Damn Bad Business: The NHS Deformed*, Gollancz: London.

Maynard, A. (1983), 'Privatising the NHS', *Lloyds Bank Review*, No. 148, pp. 28-41.

Mintzberg, H. (1996), 'Managing Government, Governing Management', *Harvard Business Review*, May-June, pp. 75-83.

NHS Management Inquiry (1983), *Report* (Griffiths), Department of Health and Social Security: London.

Pollitt, C. (1993), *Managerialism and the Public Services: Cuts or Cultural Change?* 2nd ed., Blackwell: Oxford.

Rowbottom, R. et al. (1973), *Hospital Organisation*, Heinemann: London.

Royal Commission on the NHS (1979), *Report* (Cmnd 7615), HMSO: London.

Sartori, G. (1987), *The Theory of Democracy Revisited: Part One: The Contemporary Debate*, Chatham House: New Jersey.

Scottish Health Services Council (1966), *Administrative Practice of Hospital Boards in Scotland*, HMSO: Edinburgh.

Simpson, J. and Smith, R. (1997), 'Why Healthcare Systems Need Medical Managers', *British Medical Journal*, No. 314, pp. 1636-7.

Susser, M. and Watson, W. (1971), *Sociology in Medicine*, Oxford University Press: London.

Wall, A (1996), 'The NHS: Who is Attacking, Who is Defending?' *Health Care Analysis*, Vol. 4, pp. 328-31.

3 Nursing

Stephen Ackroyd

Since the early part of the present century nursing has been a highly organised occupation and nurses have protected their social standing through various periods of change since then. Over the last 100 years spokeswomen and promoters of nursing have, with varying degrees of explicitness, taken the profession of medicine as their model and, among other things, insisted on high levels of training and formal qualification for their members. By and large, this has proved to be an effective strategy. Academic commentators may differ in the extent to which they think that nurses have achieved professional organisation and standing (Jolley 1989, Melia 1987, Witz 1995). But few argue against the idea that the pursuit of high levels of formal qualification and, through this, limited control of labour markets, have been adopted by nurses as basic elements of their basic occupational strategy. As Witz (1995) argues in a penetrating recent discussion, there are obvious continuities between the elitist policies advocated at the beginning of the twentieth century and the (misleadingly named) 'new nursing' which is the focus of much debate about policy today. In practice qualified nurses, who constitute around sixty per cent of the people employed for direct patient care in British hospitals and who alone are allowed the title of nurse, have achieved a significant degree of what is usually called occupational closure (Larson 1977, Murphy 1988) (For applications of this type of analysis of nurses as an occupation see Walby et al. 1993, Witz 1995 and Ackroyd 1994, 1996a).

Taking a long view some observers of contemporary change in the NHS and hospital organisation think that there is nothing to offer a fundamental challenge to nurses. Leading members of the nursing profession are particularly apt to think that little has changed and that contemporary events do not require significantly different responses to the traditional professionalism which has served well in the past. Discussions of nursing policy feature debate over 'new nursing' and 'primary nursing' which originate from the nineteen seventies if not before (see Salvage in Robinson, Gray and Elkan, 1992). It is true that there is some limited evidence to support the point of view that professionalism, or something very like it, is still viable. Data from the 1980s, when nursing was facing the acute challenge posed by the introduction of reforms following the adoption of the Griffiths Report (1983), shows that the ratio of qualified nurses to unqualified helpers, auxiliaries and trainees steadily grew in favour of qualified nurses (Thornley 1997). It would seem that even during the testing period of the 1980s, the title and position of the qualified nurse had been effectively guarded. Certainly the formal powers of nursing institutions such as the Central Council for Nursing, Midwifery and Health Visiting (UKCC) - to advise and to be consulted even over the details of the utilisation of nurses in hospitals - are undiminished. This sort of evidence suggests to the nursing elite that business can and should be conducted very much as usual.

On the other hand, it is clear that fundamental change in the organisation of nursing is inevitable. Indeed a good deal of change has already taken place amongst nurses in the NHS hospitals, as we shall see. There is, for example, evidence from research of the weakening of vocationalism amongst practising nurses (Mackay 1990, Williams et al. 1991). Hence if pressures have been resisted by the formal organisations of nurses so far, it is less clear that the rank and file can do so successfully. The challenge to the occupation as a whole will not go away but is likely to intensify. The point to note is that the causes impelling change are themselves irresistible. The most important cause impelling change is the increased competitiveness of the world economy, and the challenge this offers to the spending activities of the nation state. For many countries, and clearly Britain is no exception here, increased exposure to global competition has produced the intensification of competitive forces in domestic markets, and placed extreme pressures on the capacity of the economy to generate wealth and bear taxation. The way in which it is appropriate to respond to this global challenge is, of course, a matter of policy. In Britain the government response has featured the distinctive policies of capping state expenditure (Hills 1993) exposing both private firms and the institutions of the state to competition, rather than thoroughly reforming and/or protecting them. In many parts of the public sector in Britain, there has been the dramatic disaggregation of the state apparatus and the introduction of quasi-markets (Metcalfe and Richards 1990, Clarke and Newman 1997).

In the NHS the application of these distinctive policies has been pushed hard in the last twenty years. Initially the most obvious change was the determination to introduce and develop a new kind of management. More recently there has been the increasing exposure of institutions to simulated market forces. In the NHS, in contrast to some other services, new policies have been backed up by effective implementation. The recruitment and development of a new management cadre has been concerted, and the development of managerial practices has also been taken further here than in many other areas. This has altered key relationships within the service, and particularly relations of authority. Thus, in this chapter the following points will be made: firstly it will be shown that the development of management has been concerted in the NHS, and secondly that the kind of management introduced has been highly distinctive but widely misunderstood by commentators. Thirdly it will then be argued that nurses have found it particularly difficult to accommodate to these changes, both at the centre in terms of creating a coherent policy for the occupation, and among the workforce which has, without appropriate leadership, failed to develop effective and practical responses. Ironical though it may be, nurses represent a group of responsible and committed employees which nonetheless is finding positive adaptation to reform a problem.

This chapter will conclude by suggesting that the new management has had only limited effectiveness. Greater efficiency in the use of resources has been secured, in that more patients are being given more treatment than before. But at the same time the ratio of productive to unproductive workers has deteriorated, the highly functional organisation of many hospitals is under threat and there is a widespread loss of vocationalism amongst the nurses and other front-line carers within the service. In sum bureaucracy has not been reduced in the NHS at any level, and the opportunity for developing nursing and the NHS in a creative ways has been substantially lost.

The new management of NHS hospitals

From 1980 or so the development of management has been a consistent outcome of the many reforms of the NHS. As measured by the numbers of managers employed, the new management hierarchy has been pushed further in the NHS than in any other area of social provision (Ackroyd 1995). Within months of taking office in 1979, the first Thatcher administration repudiated the idea of a centrally planned and administered service in favour of a declared policy of managed localism (Klein 1995, pp. 124-26, Pollitt 1993, pp. 68-9). Shortly after, the same administration set in train the processes which led to the commissioning of the Griffiths Inquiry (which reported in 1983); and, following the acceptance of its conclusions, it moved quickly to the introduction of what was called 'general management'. Since the early eighties, the kind of management which Griffiths recommended (which allocates considerable decision-making independence to managers within a framework of limited budgets), has been consolidated and developed. Such changes as the introduction of purchaser-provider splits have also allowed the development of this kind of managerialism.

What is impressive about change in the NHS is not the removal of formal hierarchy. This was highly developed in the NHS and remains so after recent reforms. Klein (1995) suggests an appropriate image for what has happened to the NHS is that of a familiar building which has been radically refurbished. The facade and basic structure has been left intact, the location of walls and floors have been preserved, but the building has been extensively reconstructed on the inside. What has changed is the personnel which staff the NHS hierarchy, together with their distinctive outlook, expertise and function. What we now see, in the place of the old administrative and political hierarchy, is a managerial hierarchy with developed executive powers over expenditure. Thus what is important is not the overall shape of the NHS structure, but its new internal organisation and functioning. Pollitt (1993) substantially concurs when he suggests that from the early 1980s, change was more significant in informal rather than formal organisation:

Instead the 1980s prescription was to avoid time-consuming statutory change, to create new types of post (general managers on short-term contracts) to reinforce their authority with a battery of new procedures (ministerial reviews, performance reviews, performance indicators, management budgeting, individual performance review) and, eventually, to introduce the competitive incentive of the internal market (Pollitt 1993, p. 67).

Thus the emphasis in understanding change must be placed firmly on the rapid development of NHS management. This is now a numerous occupational grouping with a distinctive expertise and outlook. There were 150,000 managerial and administrative staff in 1993. By contrast with this, in most other British public services, the management cadre is smaller and there was no recourse but to recruit managers largely from practising professionals (on the importance of this type of recruitment, see Ackroyd et al. 1989). In the NHS, however, the new management cadre does not have significant allegiance to professional service carers, in that they are not primarily recruited from such groups. Klein was one of the first to recognise this as an important part of the pattern of change. He suggested, as early as 1989, that what was happening was nothing short of a 'management revolution'. He writes: 'the general management revolution swept on. Everywhere at every level, new managers were appointed: some brought from industry and the armed services, but primarily they were old-style administrators reborn as managers, with a sprinkling of doctors and nurses' (Klein 1989. p. 209).

Subsequent work has amply confirmed these ideas about the pattern of recruitment to the new NHS management. Less than ten per cent of top managers in the new NHS structure are former nurses, whereas more than sixty percent are former administrative and finance staff. If we add to this sixty per cent the numbers of managers recruited from outside the NHS, it seems very clear that only a minority of the new management of the NHS are former professionals (for a breakdown of the occupational origins of NHS management appointments at the end of the 1980s, see Harrison and Pollitt 1994, p. 67).

To use the words of Strong and Robinson (1990), two of the best-known commentators on the contemporary NHS, during the 1980s the service was placed 'under new management'. To appreciate the significance of this it is important to be clear that the new management is a particular kind of management. There is a tendency for apologists and critics of the new public management alike to suggest that the new management is representative of all efficient practice, having and dealing in general managerial expertise. Certainly this new group is the first that has been willing to identify itself as management that the NHS has ever had. However it will be argued here it is a substantial misunderstanding to think of this group as somehow free of a particular identity and promoting a neutral point of view. The new management of the NHS is a distinctive form of management, in that it is concerned mainly with keeping track of the costs of hospital care, and in increasing the ratio of quantified benefits per unit of cost (Coombs and Green 1989, Nanaphiet 1992, Clarke and Newman 1997). This outlook has its origins in a combination of influences, one of the most important being the occupation from which the majority of the recruits to the management originated. This was the cadre of the administrators of the old NHS. Also important is the influence of accountancy, which profession seems to have provided the many of the techniques to assess and allocate costs which were developed for use by the new managers, as well as providing the preferred qualifications for numbers of the senior personnel themselves.

That a new and sizeable occupational group with new functions and powers has been developed within an existing structure would be a likely source of problems for any organisation. Indeed the effects of the 'management revolution' (Klein 1995, p. 148) seem to have been felt disproportionately by nurses. The reasons for this will be considered in later sections of this chapter. It might be thought that there is no great mystery why this would be so. The provision of nursing is a very large component of the costs associated with the practical delivery of hospital care. Hospital nurses are, by a considerable margin, the largest occupational group in the NHS. Despite their relatively low levels of pay, their wages constitute a large contribution to the cost of running a hospital. Salaries account for more than 75 per cent of NHS expenditure, and Thornley (1997) has recently estimated the wages bill of the nurses to be £8bn in 1996. The fact is that any managerial group, but especially one centrally interested in costs and efficiency, might also be expected to have an interest in the costs involved in the utilisation of nurses and in ways of cutting the costs of nursing provision.

But the interesting and important point to note here is that the new management has not, until quite recently, sought to control the costs of nursing by dictating the activities of nurses. Just as the new management has not sought direct control over the activities of doctors, so a similar strategy has been adopted towards nurses. The policy of the managers towards all health professionals has been in this respect much the same - it is to co-opt them rather than directly to control them. But there are also some contrasts in the way that managers have treated different groups of health professionals. Almost anything managers may seek to do, to improve the numbers of patients seen for example, requires the agreement and co-operation of clinicians to have any chance of success. The need to bring about the complicity of nurses in key decisions is much less, and for this reason they have been less often co-opted (Walby et al. 1994). It is not correct to say that nurses have been systematically excluded from decision making, but their routine involvement is now limited by comparison with the levels attained in the epoch of what is called 'consensus management' during the 1970s. These days nurses are simply expected to follow along and do what is necessary to deal with the consequences of decisions largely taken by others.

So far as the activities of managers towards nurses are concerned, there are some ambiguities bordering on paradox in what they do. As has been argued, unlike production managers in industry, the new management of the NHS has not taken responsibility for deciding the content of nursing work, but has left that to the judgement of nurses themselves. At the same time these same managers make decisions on a daily basis that have considerable consequences for the amounts and kinds of work nurses are necessarily expected to do. For nurses the ambiguous implications of the new management have involved problems. On the one hand there is apparently great concern about the need for change associated with the introduction of the new management, but the managers themselves give few indications about what appropriate adaptations might be. One leading commentator on nursing, Jane Robinson, has responded to this by postulating a 'black hole theory of nursing' (Robinson et al. 1992, pp. 5-7). According to this managers (and government) are ignorant of what nurses do and what they might wish to do, to the extent of regarding nursing with as much circumspection as they would a black hole. So far as the elite of nurses are concerned, this neglect allows them to persist with their traditional ideal of nursing as a profession. So far as the reality of work is concerned among practising nurses, however, the activities of managers have made this ideal less tenable.

The impact of the new management on the work of the nurse

The myth of Taylorism

Various commentators have recognised the development of a new management cadre as an important aspect of recent change in the NHS (Strong and Robinson 1990, Harrison and Pollitt 1994, Pollitt 1993 and Klein 1995). It is less obvious that they have understood the precise connections between the behaviour of managers and the responses of nurses. This is an area where there is much misunderstanding. Almost all writers assume that there is a standard array of techniques available to managers, and that these are what managers in all contexts invariably apply, invariably to good effect. Writers on the new public management like Pollitt (1993) and on the NHS like Walby et al (1994) have followed the lead of Cousins (1987) who developed the first effective sociological analysis of the control of the work of welfare state employees. Cousins argued that the control of these employees may be considered as an exploitative process and, as such, is similar in some ways to the organisation of work in capitalistic enterprises. However, unlike Cousins, who avoided suggesting that techniques of task control, similar to those used in manufacturing industry, are also applied amongst care workers, several writers on the management of the NHS have suggested such an application.

It is suggested with surprising frequency that contemporary public sector managers are using techniques very similar to those first developed by the so-called 'scientific management' movement. This first appeared at the turn of the present century in the USA. Nevertheless Pollitt (1993), for example, reviews the development of management thought in six stages, arguing for a degree of development in management knowledge. Yet when it comes to contemporary practice Pollitt suggests that public sector managers have usually adopted techniques based on, or very similar to, those developed by an early American exponent of scientific management, F.W. Taylor. As is well known, Taylor undertook his most influential work in the first fourteen years of the twentieth century, mainly in the American steel industry (Taylor 1911). His ideas are collectively labelled Taylorism. Pollitt in fact takes a whole chapter to criticise the supposedly neo-Taylorist tendencies of contemporary public sector managers (1993, pp. 111-46). Similarly in their analysis of the contemporary NHS, Walby et al. (1994) emphasise the importance of Taylorism both in the public sector generally, and in the NHS. After reviewing the development of management, and considering the situation of both hospital doctors and nurses, Walby et. al. come to the conclusion that 'Nurses are currently close in organisation to the Taylorist model' (Walby et al. 1993, p. 137). These are highly surprising claims. Actually the suggestion that current public sector management is Taylorist will not bear examination, and unless extreme care is taken with this sort of account, the managerialism of the NHS and its effects will be substantially misunderstood.

The basic problem with claiming that contemporary management in the NHS is Taylorist is that the core of Taylorism is the design of jobs. What Taylor suggested, and which was novel at the time he came up with it, was that there were large savings to be made by managers taking responsibility for deciding how workers go about their work, down to the smallest detail (Braverman 1974). Taylor was interested in analysing industrial tasks into constituent elements, and in reconfiguring them in ways that would make savings of time, effort and material. Given the scale and specialisation of industrial processes, there was considerable scope for applying rationalistic analysis to industrial work, so as to simplify it and make it easier to do. Taylor then added piecework incentives to ensure that output would be high. Taylor's insights are at the level of the following: a person carrying pig iron billets will move more in a day if chosen according to physical strength, if there are ramps to walk up rather than steps, if the load carried is of a particular size, if a certain number of rests are taken and if pay is awarded strictly in proportion to the amount carried. For Taylor it should be managers, rather than workers, who decide the content of jobs. Taylor was not only an engineer, he had experience of the shop floor, and so could credibly take on the redesign of industrial jobs. It is simply wrong to say that nursing work is being treated by NHS managers in this sort of way.

As we have seen managers in the NHS are not usually former nurses. Whatever expertise they have, NHS managers cannot claim sufficient knowledge of the nursing task to enable them to redesign the work even if that were a realisable objective. And of course it is not: there are many aspects of nursing that are not reducible to simple elements. Hospital treatments are not at all similar to the manufacture of products, and the work of care cannot therefore be standardised in the way that Taylor had in mind. Ironically the tendency to routinise nursing tasks, and to ensure that simpler tasks are undertaken by unskilled workers, both of which tendencies might be described as Tayloristic, were much more prevalent at an earlier epoch, when nursing organisation was securely under the control of its own membership. Making all patients follow a tight regime of sleep, rising, washing and visiting and so on, and of nurses following a strict division of task according to their qualifications, which was prevalent in the 1950s and 1960s, is the nearest thing to Taylorism that nurses have experienced. Under this sort of arrangement, all unskilled and very routine tasks were allocated to junior nurses and auxiliaries at the bottom of the care hierarchy, whilst senior nurses were freed from many routine tasks. Senior nurses developed and guarded their exclusive monopoly of highly skilled work. Even today managers in the NHS today do not attempt to be as directive to nurses as senior nurses are to their own junior members, auxiliaries and learners. In this way nurses continue to be self-managing.

Despite an historical tendency to hierarchical organisation, nursing has traditionally been understood by nurses themselves as a very inclusive role, covering not only clinical aspects of care, but all other aspects of what have been called elsewhere 'regimes of care' (Ackroyd 1995). Beyond strictly medical aspects of care, nurses also took responsibility for the psychological and social aspects of patient therapy. Indeed although it was not often formally acknowledged, the nursing role traditionally included aspects of practical organisation and management as well. Certainly it was expected that the nurse would prioritise and integrate a large number of tasks concerned with the welfare of patients, many of them having little to do with treatment as such, but which were still seen as essential to good practice. All this was included in the professional definition of appropriate behaviour. Nurses certainly became used to deciding for themselves what standards and amounts of care to devote to patients, and developed their own evaluation of standards of conduct. A compelling example of this is the care that nurses take with the terminally ill and patients with chronic and incurable conditions. In some fieldwork undertaken by the author amongst geriatric nurses for example, respondents regretted not having enough time to devote to the emotional comfort of dying patients (Ackroyd 1993). Thus nurses still regard it as important to decide on appropriate levels and types of care (Mackay 1988). In sum in many ways the work of the nurse is not an easy subject for the kind of rationalisation that is basic to Taylorism.

If the notion that the new management of the NHS is Tayloristic appears to be substantially wrong, we might well ask why commentators make this sort of error. Firstly the answer is partly a factual mistake. Accounts of practice in the NHS are often not based on detailed ethnographic study of what nurses and managers actually do. We will return to this question in the next section. However it is also true that scientific management does involve general assumptions that are in some ways similar to assumptions made by public sector managers today. Taylor did suggest, for example, that management has functions that ought to be developed: he was one of the first ideologists of management, promoting the interests of this occupation. Secondly he thought that a central task of management would be the containment of costs, and the improvement of the ratio of benefits to costs. In short he was interested in what he took to be the efficient use of resources. Thirdly Taylor did not shrink from asserting that management should impose their ideas about what should happen in order to realise cost savings and to make efficiency gains. Considered in these ways, Taylor and contemporary NHS managers do share some similar assumptions. However to focus on these assumptions is not helpful if it leads to errors in understanding of the ways in which nurses and managers actually behave.

Although it is difficult to generalise about what is happening in the relationship between managers and nurses because there are many local variations, what follows is a description of some features of the relations between managers and nurses in the NHS hospitals supported by some empirical examples.

The new management does not attempt to redesign the job of the nurse or otherwise directly affect the traditional organisation of nursing work. Much of the informal organisation of nursing is left intact. Nurses are allowed, indeed expected, to be autonomous, much as they always have been. It is difficult to imagine senior NHS managers walking around the wards to see that patients were being treated appropriately, and nursing work was being done in a satisfactory way. In industry this kind of management, called management by walking about (MBWA), is often advocated. It would be inappropriate in the NHS and probably deeply resented by nurses. Obviously managers in the NHS hospitals (unless they are among the senior nurses given a role in management) have not the expertise to see what might be going wrong on the wards. The new management therefore cannot and does not undertake supervision in this sort of way. What actually happens are processes of control that are a great deal more subtle and indirect than the supervision envisaged by Taylor and his ilk. The control being developed and extended by managers actually depends on the continuation of the autonomy of nurses to order their own work. Management relies on the sense that the nurse has that it is essential to observe high standards in the delivery of care. In short managerial control in nursing only works by trading on and using the professional self-organisation of the nurse: precisely what Taylor sought to eliminate from industrial work.

Management exerts control by circumscribing the professional autonomy of nurses - rather than by directly attacking it at its core. The control involved is therefore indirect and not achieved once and for all. It has been, and is being, progressively developed. As they have expanded their role, managers have first established their knowledge of the availability of resources (and their relative costs). Through this they influence the behaviour of doctors and nurses. Responsibility for resource provision is a function that has been habitual for NHS administrators, arising from the traditional tasks of administration which involved procurement, record keeping and crude accountancy. From this, with the benefit of accumulated experience, it is but a short step to fixing acceptable limits on the allocation and use of resources by the calculation of resource costs and through budget setting. By such means managerial responsibility for the utilisation of material resources is transformed into a tool of managerial control. However, except to note that management may impose tight budget limits, there is little in this description so far to suggest powerful constraints on nurse autonomy. Nurses may welcome having a knowledge of the costs of the materials they consume, and even for much of the time feel that this does not override their clinical judgements. But the potential here for considerable erosion of traditional professional autonomy is clear.

Managers in the NHS developed a serious level of strategic control of hospital activities in the 1980s when they began to promote innovations in organisation and treatment based on their estimated costs. In such cases management agendas can often be seen to dictate significant aspects of the conditions of work for clinicians as well as nurses. If for example, hospital bed-occupancy rates can be improved, a significant improvement in cost to benefit ratios might also be achieved in accordance with managerial priorities. Developments of this kind must find some support in the willingness of clinicians to increase treatments levels. However, given this, managers can convert responsibility for costs into the strategic control of service development. Thus knowledge of costs and the power to control expenditure through budgeting, may be constructed into key mechanisms through which managerial control is exerted. This example also suggests that management activity can indirectly, but nonetheless significantly, affect the work of nurses, without in the least interfering with their jobs directly; and by leaving their professional autonomy apparently intact. Such an innovation is the equivalent of altering the speed of a production line in industry, without retraining personnel or re-allocating roles. In short the management control of nurses works not by directing their activity, but by setting new parameters and limits within which they must undertake their supposedly autonomous activities.

In one of the few recent reports of the interaction of hospital managers and other health service workers based on close study, Green and Armstrong (1995) have analysed the interactions between managers, doctors and nurses which took place over hospital admissions. According to these authors, the ability to claim complete knowledge of the 'beds state' in their hospital (itself a distribution strongly influenced by prior budgetary decisions) was a key factor shaping the (supposedly objective and clinically-based) decisions casualty doctors made about the priority attributed to a case for admission to the hospital. Although the decisions made by doctors are at no time seen to be dictated by management, it is difficult to avoid the conclusion, and these authors certainly do not, that it was knowledge of resources (in this case the physical availability of beds) which frequently shaped clinical judgements. In these circumstances the nurses have two masters, and have to adjust their activities to support the outcomes of negotiations between managers and doctors.

Finally it is the case that in many localities, management has translated its responsibility for costs into control of aspects of the allocation of nursing work. The logic underwriting this is straightforward. As has been argued, managers have responsibility for costs, and nursing labour is itself a considerable contribution to costs. Hence, in principle, managers have some sort of claim to control the utilisation of nurses as a resource which contributes to the delivery of care. However such a logic conflicts directly with ideas that nurses have about their professional autonomy, and this contradiction is a potential limitation to managerial authority. What is interesting, therefore, is the extent to which managers have not pressed this logic to its conclusion and claimed direct control of all aspects of nursing labour. However, in many hospitals today, there is a good deal of direct allocation of nurses to particular wards and tasks being made on a day to day basis.

In a large city hospital in which fieldwork was recently undertaken, local managers were actively tailoring resources to patient needs by increasing patient throughput with the compliance of clinicians. The innovation of new arrangements for the provision of hospital services such as new day care clinics, new arrangements for rapid turnaround after surgery and the flexible use of remaining conventional wards were all in progress. Such activities greatly increased the scale and complexity of patient flows into and out of the hospital, and between different parts of the hospital. They also made the demand for the services of nurses unpredictable at times. The result was frequently a need to reallocate nurses between wards at short notice.

In this case, as in that of many similar hospitals, the impact of managerial allocation of nurses was softened by the use of nurses to handle these aspects of management direction. The organisation of management in hospitals today commonly includes people called 'clinical nurse managers'; these are almost without exception former nurses who now manage nurses. There are two ways of looking at such roles, and the job title reflects this ambiguity. One possibility is to see these people as specialist managers, responsible for a key management resource. This is the way practising nurses tend to regard them. Another possibility is to see them as nurses who buffer the impact of managerial activities on their professional colleagues. This is the way managers tend to regard them. In many ways the latter view is more accurate. It is seldom that nurse managers are seen as likely recruits to the senior management levels. As we have seen, few nurses make the transition to general management. They are held to lack general managerial knowledge and skill. The nurse manager is a senior nurse shorn of the authority that a position in an extended professional hierarchy used to confer. At the same time they lack access to the sources of power managers have acquired from their general control of resource allocation and budgeting.

In summary it is clear that some remnants of the old professional nursing hierarchy are necessary to handle the potentially divisive issue of the how much nursing womanpower and manpower should be used as a factor of production in hospital care. In their own interests managers have been content to leave the professional autonomy of nurses substantially intact, and they do not attempt to break it down directly as Taylor suggested should be done. This is, however, highly unsatisfactory from the point of view of the nurses, as will now be discussed.

Why nurses feel the effects of the new management so deeply

Much that is needed to understand the impact of new NHS management on the experience of the nurse has now been set out. Although management has not undertaken direct control of nursing work, it has nonetheless gradually extended control over key parameters of the activity of nurses. Nurses have been left with the capacity to organise themselves, but under conditions that are not in their control and which are becoming increasingly problematic. As we have seen, managers have greatly increased the amounts of work nurses have to do in several ways. The most obvious general point is that management has increased the numbers of patients passing through hospitals. At the same time, managers have become increasingly vigilant about the use of resources and insisted that nurses become so too. There is another indirect effect of management activity which has also tended to increase nursing workloads in significant ways. This is the emphasis on customer care, which has been an ideological accompaniment of managerialism. Nurses these days have to spend a great deal of time simply reassuring patients or dealing with their queries and complaints. Given the increased numbers of patients treated against a background of increased controls on expenditure such additional work is testing. Whatever its merits from other points of view, the kind of consumerism which suggests that the opinions of the 'customer' must always be taken seriously, is hardly helpful to hard pressed nurses. Fieldwork in hospitals these days suggests that the need to give attention to the voice of the patient makes a substantial contribution to the demands placed on nurses.

These factors contribute to work intensification, but do not amount to direct control of nursing activities by managers. There are other recurrent concerns about possible ways in which managers might attack the costs of nursing care. One of these is that managers will adopt a policy of 'dilution' in which they will reduce the traditional proportions of qualified nurses, and replace them with untrained workers (Thornley 1997). But there is very little evidence that this is being undertaken as policy. It seems from current research work that only a tiny minority of managers have become interested in introducing schemes for quantifying the necessary amounts of nursing work, and on this basis determining for themselves the numbers of qualified nurses to be employed. The proportions of qualified nurses are still mainly set by traditional criteria over which the nurses' professional institutions retain influence. Ideas about policies of dilution, greatly over-estimate the extent to which the de facto powers of managers have developed. Much, much more common is under-staffing by inadvertence, where failures of recruitment necessitate excessive movements of nurses between locations, and/or the employment of large numbers of agency nurses to preserve the required proportion of qualified nurses at given locations. Such managerial failures add unpredictability of work location to the other burdens of nurses. This severely limits their capacity to treat patients as they would wish by exercising their full range of skills.

The tendency for work to be more demanding is probably not, however, the most important factor in determining the response of nurses to new management. Nursing is an occupation born out of adversity, and the view, which many nurses have, that problems are only to be expected, is an enduring part of the values of the occupation. A notice recently observed on a busy nursing station effectively sums up the attitude: 'The difficult we do at once, the impossible takes a little longer'. Such fulsome commitment must be a handicap for any occupation faced by increasing demands and workloads. However, the levels of commitment that nurses traditionally exhibit do have practical limits if not emotional ones. Thus, although they have an extraordinary capacity to make do and mend, the real problem is not that there is more work to do, but that it is actually becoming impossible to produce satisfactory outcomes - as they are assessed in their own terms - much of the time. The professional autonomy of nurses cannot magically solve all the problems with which nurses are daily confronted. Caught as they are in a vicious crossfire of competing demands - from management to give care to more patients in increasingly adverse circumstances, and from patients themselves to respond more quickly and effectively to their individual needs - huge demands are placed on their capacity for self-organisation. Nurses compromise their own standards on a daily basis, and this is the real problem of nurse morale (Ackroyd, 1993).

This last point is crucial. Authoritative accounts of what nursing is about are still recognisably trying to adapt and develop a professional model. Proponents of the 'new nursing' suggest that nurses should take over some of the routine therapeutic functions of the doctors. Even the widely approved 'project 2000', makes the qualified and multi-functional nurse central to nursing policy. And yet the reality of the work of many nurses is that they are faced with too much work on a daily basis, and are often obviously unable to make professional ideals fit their actual work experience. The result is widespread dissatisfaction, loss of vocationalism and the falling away of recruitment. Lurid accounts of the work situation of NHS nurses, such as those presented by the *Daily Mirror* over two days in the run up to the election in 1997, when this chapter was first being drafted, are doubtless greatly exaggerated. But they do contain a grain of truth. There is now a good deal of evidence for the widespread deterioration of the conditions of work of the hospital nurse, and also that these nurses are reacting adversely to this. It would appear that morale amongst nurses has been precarious for some time (Whitson and Edwards 1990, Ackroyd 1993), that nurses are leaving the profession in large numbers (Price-Waterhouse 1988, Soothill et al. 1991, 1994) and that those remaining at work are losing their traditional vocationalism and increasingly treating their occupation as 'just a job' (Williams et al. 1991, Peelo et al. 1994, Bagguley 1994). It is suggested here that the new managerialism in the NHS has a good deal to do with this.

Are we beyond bureaucracy in NHS hospitals?

The unreformed NHS before 1970 exhibited some of the classic features of bureaucracy. If we bear in mind the model of the tall hierarchy with numerous levels of authority identified in organisation theory (Weber 1968, Albrow 1970), then the centralised structure of the NHS before reform was a highly developed bureaucracy. There are quite a few reservations to make about this general diagnosis. In addition to the administrative structure, which formed the main element of the hierarchy and extending beyond the hospital connecting local hospitals with district authorities and ultimately the central government, there were significant political influences. Political power was used to influence policy and some major decisions in the administrative arena, and the structure was to some extent pervious to influences exerted by political parties and elites at different levels. There is some evidence also that professionals, who were employed at all levels in the NHS structure, acted independently of administrative authority. It is not, of course, a criticism of the classic model of bureaucracy to suggest that it contained professionals. Weber was quite clear that qualifications and expertise (usually defining attributes of professions) are also essential features of bureaucracy. Subsequent studies have amply confirmed that bureaucracy and professionalism are compatible (Hall 1968). But it is a departure from the pure model of bureaucracy if professionals have policies of their own, independent of those imposed by the controllers of the organisation. The employment of professionals in the general NHS structure bolstered their influence at the local level.

Clearly it might plausibly be argued that professionals had too much power in the post-war NHS, impeding rational decision-making and compromising political direction. There are research reports which confirm this sort of view of the NHS hospital prior to reform. Writing in 1976, Davies and Francis (1976) suggest that the post-war NHS hospital had three elements or subsystems within it: a professional system and a political one both supplementing the administrative hierarchy. Thus there are arguments which suggests that the NHS hospitals in particular were not inflexible bureaucracies prior to reform. Certainly, at the hospital level, the administrative cadre was especially weak and largely subordinated to the authority of the professionals. Administrative staff did not have significant managerial powers. Indeed the presence of powerful professional groups, as well as the continuing influence of local political networks, were among the reasons put forward as to why costs were supposedly spiralling out of control, and why right-wing governments after 1979 sought the reform of the service devising the new public management as their instrument. Be that as it may, Klein (1995) suggests that a good description of the actual organisation of the NHS for much of the post-war period is a 'workers' co-operative'. In this arrangement power was in the hands of the health professionals. Such management as there was, was not undertaken by a separate cadre of managers, but discharged by doctors and nurses as an adjunct to their professional roles. Many hospitals were not at all classic bureaucracies, but informally organised and exhibiting quite different features of organisation.

It seems very clear that, in many ways, before the introduction of reform, nurses were themselves effective managers without being self-conscious about the matter. Nurses organised the management of patients, of junior nurses and other carers, not to mention the arrangements of all aspects of patient care. It is a considerable irony in view of this, that nurses were neither able to recognise their practical managerial expertise nor to defend their position as managers when faced by a concerted external challenge. It is hardly surprising that the legacy of self-management (which was surprisingly effective) was not preserved. What happened is that, with a government committed to limiting costs and improving accountability, a new kind of managerialism was seen to be appropriate, and was, without very much effective challenge, put in place. Obsessed with inappropriate professional models, nurses are basically incapable of recognising both that the new management is a threat to their de facto power in the workplace and that, in the longer run, it will be a threat to their status too. Despite the fact that nurses have traditionally undertaken a good deal of practical management in the course of their work, their particular professional values did not allow them to acknowledge the fact, let alone give the idea emphasis. Nurses have been unable or unwilling to change their values so as to be able to make a successful claim to managerial expertise. A new kind of professional (the public sector manager), armed with a different kind of professional rhetoric (new managerialism), has proved better placed to take advantage of the opportunities offered by shifts in national policy.

It is difficult to sustain an argument that the adoption of new management has reduced the bureaucracy of the NHS. As we have seen, various pundits have argued that the same scale of structure is in place. It may not be a classic bureaucracy in the manner that the unreformed NHS was. It is much more like the bureaucracies associated with large and monopolistic firms, with their large numbers of accountants managing large regional divisions. But it is the case that the numbers of managers and clerical staff have grown considerably over the last two decades. There has been little scope for diminished overheads in these circumstances, for the new managers command large salaries. Although they have undoubtedly improved efficiency in the utilisation of NHS resources in some ways, the number of unproductive staff it has been necessary to continue to employ is too large. Taking the entire staff of the NHS into consideration, it can be calculated that there is now one manager or administrator to every two carers treating patients. In the heyday of the unreformed NHS this ratio was close to one to five. Hence the New Labour claim that substantial savings can be made in the NHS by cutting bureaucracy, seems prima facie, very plausible indeed. The whole apparatus is expensive for what it does. Also some other facts are worth quoting. There are 50,000 fewer nurses now employed in the NHS than at the beginning of the 1980s, and the supply of good recruits to nursing has all but dried up. The new hospital trusts are collectively more than £200 million in debt. And there are currently more than a million people waiting for routine surgery. Hence not only has the NHS failed to escape from bureaucracy, in broad terms, it is difficult to see this as an effective use of public money.

So far as the hospital nurse is concerned, there is still a good deal of bureaucracy, in the mundane meaning of the term, to cope with day to day. If we take by bureaucracy, following routines and keeping records which are not required by the needs of patients, but are required by the managerial control system, then the work of the nurse today is highly bureaucratic. It is an obvious point arising from participant observation, and indeed almost any nurse will tell you, the work of nursing still involves a good deal of record-keeping and form filling which seems to bear little relation to the curative task. Such features of the work are sometimes onerous, but they pale into insignificance by the side of other factors. Here the most significant points can be summed up as the increase in work intensity and the challenge of work which involves continuing to necessitate the exercise professional discretion in circumstances which make this very difficult if not impossible to be effective.

Finally perhaps the matter for most regret in this picture is the fact that alternative ways of responding to the challenge of global competition were not considered when reforms of the NHS were (rightly) first deemed necessary in the early 1980s.

There was no consideration given to the possibility of building on the new forms of management that had been developing in the NHS hospitals for some time. There is a deep irony in the fact that this type of participative management - to which nurses were key contributors - feature many of the attributes of team working and customer orientation which are now actively promoted by leading private sector human resource managers. The combination of obsolete management ideas and too much concern accountancy which characterises the 'new' management seems to be the worst of all worlds.

References

Abbott, A. (1988), *The System of the Professions*, University of Chicago Press: Chicago.

Ackroyd, S. (1993), 'Towards and Understanding of Nurses' Attachments to Their Work', *Journal of Advances in Health and Nursing Care*, Vol. 2, No. 3.

Ackroyd, S.(1994), 'Nurses, Management and Morale' in Mackay, L. et al. (Eds), *Inter-Professional Relations in Health Care*, Edward Arnold: London.

Ackroyd, S. (1995), 'The New Management and the Professionals', *Work, Organisation and Economy Paper Series* No 24, Department of Sociology, University of Stockholm, Sweden.

Ackroyd, S. (1996a), 'Nurses and the Prospects for Participative Management in the National Health Service' in Soothill, K. et al. (eds.), *Themes and Perspectives in Nursing*, London: Chapman and Hall.

Ackroyd, S. (1996b), 'Organization Contra Organisations: Professions and Organisational Change in the United Kingdom', *Organisation Studies*, Vol. 17, No 4.

Ackroyd, S., Hughes, J. and Soothill, K. (1989), 'Public Sector Services and Their Management', *Journal of Management Studies*, Vol. 27, No. 6 .

Albrow, M. (1970), *Bureaucracy*, Pall Mall Press: London.

Bagguley, P. (1996), 'Nurses and the New Industrial Relations' in Soothill, K. et al. (eds.) *Themes and Perspectives in Nursing*, London: Chapman and Hall.

Braverman, H. (1974), *Labour and Monopoly Capital*, Monthly Review Press: New York.

Clarke, J. and Newman, J. (1997), *The Managerial State*, Sage Publications: London.

Collins, R. (1990), 'Market Closure and the Conflict Theory of the Professions' in Burrage, M. and Torstendahl, R. (eds.), *Professions in Theory and History*, Sage Publications: London.

Coombs, R. and Green, K. (1989), 'Work, Organisation and Product Change in the Service Sector: The Case of the U.K. National Health Service' in Wood, S. (ed.), *The Transformation of Work?* Unwin Hyman: London.

Cousins, C. (1987), *Controlling Social Welfare*, Brighton: Wheatsheaf.

Davies, C. and Francis, A. (1976), 'Perceptions of Structure in N.H.S. Hospitals' *Sociological Review Monograph*, No. 22, University of Keele: Staffordshire.

Griffiths, R. (1983), *N.H.S. Management Enquiry*, London: D.H.S.S.

Green, J. and Armstrong, D. (1995), 'Achieving Rational Management: Bed Managers and Emergency Admissions', *Sociological Review*, Vol. 43, No. 4.

Hall, R. (1968), 'Professionalisation and Bureaucratisation', *American Sociological Review* Vol. 33, No. 1, pp. 92-104.

Harrison, S. and Pollitt, D. (1994), *Controlling Health Professionals,* Open University Press: Buckingham.

Hills, J. (1993), *The Future of Welfare*, Joseph Rowntree Foundation: York.

Jolley, M, (1989), 'Current Issues in Nursing' in Jolley, M. and Allan, P. (eds.), *Current Issues in Nursing*, Chapman and Hall: London.

Klein, R. (1989), *The Politics of the National Health Service*, Longmans: London.

Klein, R. (1995), *The New Politics of the National Health Service*, Longmans: London.

Larson, M. (1977), *The Rise of Professionalism: A Sociological Analysis*, University of California Press: Berkeley.

Mackay, L. (1988), 'No Time to Care', *Nursing Times*, Vol. 84, No. 11.

Mackay, L. (1989), *Nursing A Problem*, Open University Press: Milton-Keynes.

Mackay, L. (1990), 'Nursing: Just Another Job?' in Abbott, P. and Wallace, C. (eds.), *The Sociology of the Caring Professions,* Falmar Press: Basingstoke.

Melia, K. (1987) *Learning and Working: The Occupational Socialisation of Nurses,* Tavistock Publications: London.

Metcalfe, L. and Richards, S. (1990), *Improving Public Management,* Sage: London.

Murphy, R. (1988), S*ocial Closure: The Theory of Monopolisation and Exclusion*, Clarendon Press: Oxford.

Nanaphiet, J. (1992), 'Decision-Making and Accounting: Resource Allocation in the N.H.S' in Gowler et al. (eds.), *Case Studies in Organisational Behaviour*, 2nd ed., London: Paul Chapman.

Peelo, M., Francis, B. and Soothill K. (1996), 'N.H.S. Nursing: Vocation, Career or Just a Job?' in Soothill, K. et al. (eds.), *Themes and Perspectives in Nursing,* London: Chapman and Hall, pp. 14 -30.

Pollitt, C. (1993), *Managerialism and the Public Services*, 2nd ed., Oxford: Basil Blackwell.

Price-Waterhouse, *Nurse Retention and Recruitment*, Price-Waterhouse: London.

Salmon Report (1966), *Report of the Committee on Senior Nurse Staff Structure*, London: H.M.S.O.

Salvage, J. (1992), 'The New Nursing' in Robinson, J.; Gray, A. and Elkan, R. (eds.), *Policy Issues in Nursing*, Open University Press: Milton-Keynes.

Soothill, K., Henry, C. and Kendrick, K. (1996) (eds.), *Themes and Perspectives in Nursing*, Chapman and Hall: London.

Strong, P. and Robinson, J. (1990), *The N.H.S.: Under New Management*, Oxford University Press: London.

Taylor, F. (1911), *Scientific Management*, Harper and Brothers: New York.

Thornley, C. (1997), 'Restructuring Employment Relations in the N.H.S', paper given to the Labour Process Conference, University of Edinburgh.

Walby, S., and Greenwell, J. (1994), *Medicine and Nursing*, London: Sage.

Weber, M. (1968) *Economy and Society*, London and New York: Bedminster Press.

Whitson and Edwards (1990), 'Managing Absence in an N.H.S. Hospital', *Industrial Relations Journal*, Vol. 21, No. 4.

Williams, C., Soothill K. and Barry, J. (1991), 'Nursing: Just a Job', *Journal of Advanced Nursing*, Vol. 16, No. 2.

Witz, A. (1995), 'The Challenge of Nursing' in Gabe, J, Kelleher, D, and Williams, G. (eds.), *Challenging Medicine*, Routledge: London.

Acknowledgements

The author would like to thank the following people for their comments on earlier drafts of this paper: Dr Rosie Tope, Professor Martin Laffin (as well as the other participants in the Glamorgan seminar), Professor Keith Soothill and Ms. Sharon Bolton.

4 The accounting profession in local government

Linda A. Keen and Michael P. Murphy

This chapter examines the changing role of the public sector accounting profession with particular reference to local government. Local authority management and service delivery systems have been dominated by a strong professional ethos since the inception of modern local government in the nineteenth century. However a key element of the new managerialism, adopted by an increasing number of local authorities during the 1980s and 1990s, has posed a challenge to this professional hegemony - a challenge to which the accounting profession has had to adapt. Beginning with a discussion of accounting in general, this chapter then goes on to examine the particular role of the accounting profession in local government and the ways in which it has changed over recent years in relation to developments at national, organisational (local authority), and practitioner levels.

An overview of the accounting profession

The major impetus for the development of accounting as a profession was the emergence of the joint stock company as the predominant business form in the mid nineteenth century and the requirement for such companies to prepare annual audited accounts. The consequent demand for practitioners with the necessary expertise to prepare and audit these accounts, and to provide other services such as insolvency work, was the initial stimulus for the development of the accounting profession whose members sought through the formation of legally sanctioned professional associations to 'define, licence and monopolise the market for 'professional' accounting labour' (Wilmott 1986, p. 556). Since the nineteenth century the accounting profession has grown significantly, both in scale and in scope, to the point where today it is one of the largest in the UK represented by six professional bodies.[1] Each of these professional accounting bodies has its own specific specialist expertise and interests. The Chartered Institute of Public Finance and Accounting (CIPFA) represents accounting within the public sector.

Historically accounting's status as a profession has been given substantial statutory reinforcement, for example the exclusive right to carry out a statutory audit of company financial statements and the requirement that a local authority chief finance officer belong to one of the 'chartered' bodies. However clear differences in activities and interests exist between those practitioners engaged in the supply of professional services via public professional practice to clients on a fee paying basis as independent practitioners or as part of larger professional practices such as the 'big six', [2] and those employed by public and private sector enterprises, commonly members of the Chartered Institute of Management Accountants and CIPFA.

Accounting is a highly segmented profession in terms of the different knowledge claims, professional associations and their political strategies, and practitioners' workplaces. Where accountants enjoy a legal monopoly and use this as a basis for the development and marketing of other services to clients, they equate to Johnson's (1972) 'collegiate' (traditional professional) model of occupational control where the practitioners exercise a significant degree of control over a client's problem definition and service needs. However as the market for all professional accounting services has become more competitive over recent years with clients, particularly the larger ones, seeking to define the services they need and to obtain the best value for the fees they pay, the balance of power has shifted somewhat and is more akin to Johnson's 'patronage' model, or Reed's (1996) 'knowledge workers'.

Given this shift, practitioners - whether organised into professional accountancy practices ranging from small local firms to the 'big six', or employed directly by the 'client' organisation as 'organisation professionals' (Reed 1996) - may experience tensions or conflicts between their 'cosmopolitan' orientations to the wider professional community standards and values and their 'local' orientations towards the contracting or employing client organisation's requirements (Gouldner 1957). Given that a fundamental requirement for an auditor, including auditors of local authorities, is that of independence from the auditee, the tensions between these orientations - exacerbated by the increased reliance of professional practices on the discretionary allocation of non-audit work for their fee income - have led to much debate about the propriety of practices providing a significant amount of non-audit services to their audit clients, and the incorporation of limits to this in professional ethics statements (ICAEW 1992). Similar conflicts, between meeting their statutory, their professional and their employing organisation's requirements, are experienced by public sector accountants.

During the competitive environment of the 1980s and 1990s 'organisation professional' accountants in the public sector have become threatened by the 'predatory' nature of those accountants engaged in public practice. The extent to which professional accounting practices (such as the 'big six' and their predecessors), as well as the professional institutes dominated by these practices, have seen the public sector as an area 'ripe for the plucking' should not be underestimated. The value of public sector consultancy and audit assignments awarded to such practices over the last two decades is undoubtedly significant (although little reliable data is available given the range of public sector organisations awarding such contracts). At least in part such practices were brought in because they were perceived as having the 'commercial' expertise and values which the government was keen to introduce into the public sector. The importation of private sector accounting concepts into the public sector has culminated in the plans for the introduction of essentially private sector financial reporting principles in the Resource Accounting Initiative (HM Treasury 1995).

The accounting profession is segmented vertically as well as horizontally. Clear hierarchical lines separate the higher level and more complex work from the lower level and more routine work. These lines are reflected in differing levels of professional expertise, qualifications, status, remuneration and job security. At the lower levels of organisations, both public and private sector, many people have long carried out accounting work (for example keeping the 'books of account', acting as cashiers and cost clerks). Such people would typically be engaged in routine work under the supervision of higher-level practitioners with recognised professional qualifications.

Despite this segmentation, the accounting profession as a whole has sought to maintain its status and rights to self-regulation via the professional bodies (including CIPFA) by emphasising their claims to particular expertise, to ethical practice and the responsibility of individual members of the profession to maintain its reputation. The professional bodies emphasise training in the workplace allied with academic study and have continuing professional development schemes. They sponsor research into accountancy and financial management issues, and seek to influence policy and practice by initiating and responding to policy proposals.[3] They emphasise the service they provide - to their clients and to society as a whole - portraying themselves as disinterested purveyors of their professional expertise. To some extent this has been achieved by collaboration through the Consultative Committee of Accountancy Bodies (CCAB), and the Joint Disciplinary Scheme (JDS). But these have not always been entirely happy collaborations, in part because of the dominance of the interest of those members engaged in public professional practice. Equally there have been a number of failed attempts to merge the various professional bodies: if accounting is a generic area of professional expertise, albeit applied in different contexts, it is unclear why there need to be so many different professional associations. Given these turf wars the professional bodies have not always had an easy task to maintain the status of the profession, particularly given recent accounting and auditing causes celebres.

Accounting professional bodies, like those of other professions are: '*primarily*, but not exclusively, political bodies whose purpose is to define, organise, secure and advance the interest of (their most vocal and influential) members.' (Wilmott 1986, p. 556). Recent CIPFA developments aptly illustrate this perspective. CIPFA is the primary professional body for public sector accountants - 95 per cent of local authority chief financial officers are members of CIPFA (CIPFA 1997a), although local government legislation only requires that they be members of one of the 'chartered bodies'. Originally founded in 1885 as the Corporate Treasurers' and Accountants' Institute (from 1901, the Institute of Municipal Treasurers and Accountants, and from 1973 CIPFA), in 1979 the association sought to increase its membership by widening its charter to encompass the whole public sector. By 1994 only about half of its members were employed in local government. It issues guidance and advice on all aspects of financial management to local authorities - including a comprehensive code of accounting practice which defines proper (local government) accounting practice, and a code for treasury management (following the BCCI collapse and the interest rate swap debacles of late 1980s/early 1990s) - and participates in the process of devising central government legislation as well as advising members on the implementation of such legislation. CIPFA strives, together with various other organisations representing local government chief financial officers, to construct a unified image of the profession: 'partly because they bring together education, recognition, and guidelines on accounting methods' (Clarke and Cochrane 1989, p. 44).

CIPFA has faced several difficulties in recent years in maintaining its influence and status. Since 1979 central government has threatened CIPFA's dominance of local authority finance by playing a greater role in this area (Cook 1993). The Audit Commission, launched in 1983, has become an authoritative source of advice and admonitions to public organisations. The rise of 'creative accounting' in the 1980s, as public authorities responded to central government controls by using the inherent flexibilities in accounting to portray organisational realities favourably, has weakened the professional claims to disinterested expertise.[4] Under these pressures accounting practices reflected local political choices and moved away from CIPFA's 'universal' accounting rules. CIPFA, usually perceived as the weakest of the 'chartered' bodies, has responded by re-examining its role and has twice attempted to merge with the much larger Institute of Chartered Accountants in England and Wales (ICAEW). These mergers failed largely from the unwillingness of ICAEW members to vote for merger, apparently from fear of compromising the established status of their association.

These difficulties have led CIPFA to revamp itself, in common with most other UK professional bodies (Watkins et al. 1996). The Institute is emphasising continuing professional development, professional ethics and standards, and the provision of more focused services and regional branches (Hepworth 1996). A good example of CIPFA's revamped role was the 1993 launch of the advanced diploma in business and financial management aimed at primarily non-financial senior managers to extend its membership coverage: 'The advanced diploma, by attracting senior managers from every segment of the public sector... enhances the standing and influence as CIPFA as a body of influence in the public sector for financial management' (Brown 1996, p.14). In 1997 it reorganised extensively to facilitate a more focused service provision to members and ensure that its 'activities remain relevant and competitive', particularly in co-operation with other bodies, such as the Audit Commission and the National Audit Office (CIPFA 1997b).

What is accounting?

One of the most influential definitions of accounting is: '... the process of identifying, measuring and communicating economic information so as to permit more informed judgements and decisions by the users of the information' (American Accounting Association 1966). This definition provides a purist's view - that the practice of accounting is inherently neutral, being simply about providing information on which others will base their decisions. In some ways it is a Judas-like view of accounting and accountants, accepting no responsibility for the use of the information in real world decisions. Nor does this definition reflect the different areas of accounting activity.

The first of these areas, the most public face of accounting, is the preparation and publication of the annual financial statements of enterprises, both public and private: 'The objective of financial statements is to provide information about the financial position, performance and changes in the financial position of an enterprise that is useful to a wide range of users in making economic decisions' (International Accounting Standards Committee 1989). The second area relates to the main focus of this chapter - the activities of accountants, professionally qualified and other, within organisations - what is classically called management accounting. This has been defined as: '... the process of identification, measurement, accumulation, analysis, preparation, interpretation and communication of information (both financial and operating) used by management to plan, evaluate and control within an organisation and to assure use of an accountability for its resources' (International Federation of Accountants 1987). Within the overall ambit of management accounting there is the subset of cost accounting which has been defined as: 'Cost accounting is a technique or method for determining the cost of a project, process or thing.... . This cost is determined by direct measurement, arbitrary assignment or systematic and rational allocation' (Institute of Management Accountants 1983). These definitions demonstrate the diversity of accounting and the importance of useful and reliable financial information in decision making. They emphasise the neutrality of accounting but deny any managerial role for accountants. Yet in many organisations accountants obviously do exercise a managerial role, not least in the area of financial management which has been defined in the following terms: 'It is the task of those involved in the finance function to plan, raise and use funds in an efficient manner to achieve corporate objectives' (Pike and Neale 1996).

Similar task requirements apply in the public sector and in local government. CIPFA quotes Surrey County Council: 'The aim of the finance function is provide corporate management with accurate and timely financial information and advice; in order that the maximum financial resources are made available; and thus enable timely decisions to be taken; which facilitate the economic, efficient and effective delivery of public services within the resources set.' (CIPFA 1995, p. 4). This control over financial information and claimed expertise in financial matters, together with their usual role as 'gatekeeper' to the corporate treasury, ensures that they do play a broad managerial role. The apocryphal phrase 'the accountants won't allow it', implying that they act as 'obstacles to profligacy and sticklers for procedure' (Cochrane 1993, p.31) illustrates this role. This phrase reflects the historically core role of the treasurer in local government - to ensure that all expenditure was for legal purposes and fell within budgetary constraints.

The third field of activity with which accountants are commonly associated is that of audit. Traditionally audits have been of two types. Firstly accountants have attested to the reliability of the financial statements of organisations (the external audit) and secondly they have verified compliance with the organisation's internal procedures (internal audit). More recently performance audits have been added, giving accountants a role in ensuring that enterprises, particularly in the public sector, are achieving 'value for money' with the three component elements of economy (in the price paid for the necessary resources); efficiency (in the use of these resources) and effectiveness (of the outputs achieved from the use of the resources).

The changing role of local government accountants

Public sector accounting rests on the assumption that those entrusted with public funds must be required to demonstrate that those funds have been spent in accordance with their delegated authority. The precise requirements have varied over time and among public functions (Glynn 1993). But there has always been a strong emphasis on ensuring accountability through the regularity and probity of all expenditures (Audit Commission 1993, 1994 and 1995a). The constitutional status of local authorities, with all expenditure requiring authorisation by statute or by subordinate legislation, has given rise to very explicit accounting and financial management obligations. These are illustrated in the requirement, under the Local Government Act 1972 and the Local Government Finance Act 1988, that authorities must have a chief accounting officer (whether called Treasurer or Finance Director or Chief Finance Officer) who is appropriately qualified (a member of one of the chartered accountancy bodies). This chief finance officer (CFO) has responsibilities for preparing published accounts, providing an internal audit service, ensuring the collection of council revenues and ensuring that the council does not engage expenditure which is illegal or beyond its resources.

The accounting function within local authorities has traditionally fallen into three main categories. Firstly corporate functions - financial planning and management, budgeting, auditing responsibilities, treasury management; secondly support services - payroll, cashiers, management accounts and maintaining records of debtors and creditors; and thirdly revenue collection - council tax collection, benefits administration, national non-domestic rates (Audit Commission 1995b).

Historically the corporate function has acquired the most importance. Professional reputations have been made in this rather than the other two functions. The finance function itself was highly centralised with lower level service professionals being permitted little or no control over financial resources. Similarly traditional finance departments were rarely sensitive to what those in the 'customer' service departments required by way of financial information, and they placed little emphasis on 'value for money' or the cost and standard of the financial services provided (Audit Commission 1995b).

The achievement of the Conservatives was to introduce a new ethos into the public sector, ostensibly at least drawing on private sector values and practices. Their overarching aim was to make the public sector deliver 'value for money' (Farnham and Horton 1993, Ferlie et al. 1996, Gray and Jenkins 1995). They introduced market and quasi-market mechanisms into the public sector, including the privatisation of a number of public utilities, compulsory competitive tendering, the NHS internal market, Next Steps agencies, and delegated accountability across the public sector, based on devolved budgets and clear performance measurement. Local government was particularly targeted. It was subjected to ever tighter financial controls, beginning with the Rates Act 1984 which 'capped' local authority rates and limited central government funding.

What were the implications of these changes for the accounting profession in local government? Obviously the accountants were necessary for the implementation of these changes. Yet as the scrutineers, the accountants, at least initially, escaped such investigation, although all other activities in the public sector had to be scrutinised through 'value for money' criteria (Humphrey and Scapens 1992). Accounting and power are intimately related: 'Power and accounting are clearly intertwined. In particular information is power, hence accounting control and information systems are closely associated with and can affect the distribution of power in organisations ... . In this respect, accounting and information systems staff have the ability to acquire power for themselves and affect a re-distribution of power among their users' (Koh and Low 1997, p.51).

Tighter finances increased the need for financial planning by local authorities thus enhancing the power of the centralised finance departments responsible for ensuring balanced budgets within legal constraints. The traditional emphasis of the finance department was reinforced: '...on the corporate: the preparation of budgets, guardianship of the authority's finances (S. 151 responsibility) and the control of expenditure' (Audit Commission 1995b, p. 3). The ability to budget accurately and to control expenditure became increasingly important as the budgetary squeeze continued, entailing a switch from demand-led to resource-led budgets (Cochrane 1993, Elcock 1993). The emphasis was on the size of the cake with less on how efficiently and effectively the cake was being used. In the words of one CFO: 'morale... has never been higher in the Finance Department because we feel we have at last got control of you lot [other service professionals]...' (Cochrane 1993, p. 33). The power of the central finance department vis-à-vis elected members was also strengthened by the increased complexity of local government funding systems.

However efficiency and effectiveness could not long be ignored. The Local Government Finance Act 1982 established the Audit Commission for Local Authorities in England and Wales and required that 'An auditor shall... satisfy himself... that the body whose accounts are being audited has proper arrangements for securing economy, efficiency and effectiveness in the use of its resources'. The external audits and the 'value for money' studies conducted under the auspices of the Audit Commission, particularly their comparative aspects, undoubtedly helped to reinforce the hand of the finance departments, particularly the internal audit functions, as they sought to achieve 'efficiency gains' at a local level. Despite the rhetoric around 'value for money', given the manifold problems in measuring the 'value', greater emphasis fell on the 'money'. Many finance departments were quick to take advantage of this and get involved not just in monitoring the overall level of expenditure but questioning the activities on which such expenditure was being made. To sum up:

> The post-1979 concern with financial responsibility and economic efficiency has generated an endless stream of financially orientated initiatives: efficiency scrutinies, value-for-money audits, cash limits, performance indicators, delegated budgets, and internal markets. Such initiatives have served to promote the language of accountancy as the basis for discussions over public sector organisational reform and provided accountancy with a unique status. Indeed, it would perhaps appear to be the only profession which is now able to use its criteria to assess the performance of other professions. (Humphrey and Scapens, 1992, p. 142).

Competitive tendering further strengthened finance departments. The Local Government Planning and Land Act 1980 and the Local Government Act 1988 required a range of services to be put out to competitive tender. Initially the requirements related principally to manual services (e.g. refuse collection, catering services and maintenance services) but white collar services were later included. The problems associated with competitive tendering, such as service specifications and quality assurance procedures, have been well documented (Walsh 1992, Stewart 1993, Walsh 1995, Stewart 1996). Not least of these problems is that of costing the tenders of in-house direct labour organisations, and the financial evaluation of tenders received. Both these processes require a sophisticated level of financial expertise - thereby reinforcing the dominant role of the accountant.

The 1980s became an era when: 'Treasurers, their departments and the local authority accounting profession took on an increasingly visible and powerful role in local government' (Cochrane 1993, p. 37). Yet the utility of the information being provided by accountants was increasingly questioned both by academics and private sector organisations (Johnson and Kaplan 1987, Kaplan and Norton 1996). Accounting was not the holy grail for ensuring efficient and effective management as many in the public and private sectors began to realise. Rhetoric started to give way to the reality that costs in the public sector were not uniquely and incontestably identifiable (Ellwood 1996).

Indeed the ascendancy of the accounting profession carried within it the seeds of its own destruction. The Audit Commission (1995b) describes how the traditional finance function in local government was very centralised with a strong focus on corporate rather than departmental issues, and with senior staff in finance functions who came from accounting, rather than service delivery or broader managerial, backgrounds. The spread of devolved budgets and heightened accountabilities meant that service delivery departments needed their own departmental and locally available financial expertise. The major source of such expertise, at least in the first instance, was the central finance department. Many departments made explicit service level agreements with the central finance function and accounting staff were appointed to service departments, either by the departments hiring their own or by central staff being seconded and ultimately appointed to departments (Keen 1995, Keen and Murphy 1996, Audit Commission 1995c). These changes have widened accountants' role from pure accounting to financial management, partly mirroring the general public sector move from administration to management (Audit Commission 1995b, CIPFA 1995, Cochrane 1993, Rawlinson and Tanner 1990).

This is not the whole story. From the late 1980s finance functions have been subjecting themselves, or been subjected, to the same sort of appraisal as they previously inflicted on other departments. In the words of the Audit Commission: 'managers and members should review the purpose of the accountancy function in a modern authority' with a move away from an emphasis on detailed control to the provision of 'high level management accountancy services' and 'medium term financial planning' (1995b, p.10). Consequences have included detailed 'service level agreements' between user departments and finance departments; a considerable amount of 'market testing' of the 'value for money' offered by finance departments; and outsourcing of what were traditional finance department responsibilities but are not longer core to the 'modern vision'. These changes are well illustrated by the trend to sub-contract or privatise functions such as payroll and information technology, and the previous government's requirement that at least thirty-five per cent of local authority finance services should be the subject of compulsory competitive tendering (Watt 1996). A recent survey of professional support services indicates that by 1997 the outsourcing market for financial services had already reached over £63 million per annum (LGMB 1997). The Labour government plans to abolish the compulsory element of competitive tendering in 1999, replacing it with a duty on local authorities to demonstrate that they are providing high quality and value-for-money services through whatever organisational form they wish (Vize 1997).

The finance function is itself coming under challenge as a service provider. Individual departments are querying the value of the services they receive from their accountants. Moreover as accounting work (at least at the basic level of budgetary management) becomes more diffused through the organisation following delegated budgets, other professionals are acquiring the necessary skills to design and implement their own financial management and control systems. These professionals are likely to incorporate into their own professional competences some elements of the accountant's expertise to defend their own professional boundaries against the accountants. Service professionals are in some cases using such new competences to provide not only more efficient, but also more effective, services more responsive to local community and client needs (Ferlie et al. 1996). In addition the value of the language of accounting is under challenge as service departments look for the 'value' and not just the 'money'. They are making more use of the 'broad scorecard' approach which integrates non-financial information with financial information, and may even exclude financial information, in the design of performance management and appraisal systems (Kaplan and Norton 1996). The financial management initiatives of the 1980s are now seen as resting on 'outdated methods of management which have frequently been shown to be inadequate and, at best, to have only a very loose relationship with organisational effectiveness' (Humphrey and Scapens 1992, p. 146).

The traditional organisational place of accounting within local government has come under increasing challenge. Competitive tendering and allied outsourcing arrangements such as management buy-outs and/or facilities management arrangements have already been adopted in some, mostly Conservative, authorities. Private sector accountancy practices such as the 'big six' are already heavily involved in the private sector provision of services for councils such as Bromley, Westminster, and Kensington and Chelsea. By 1995 some 39 companies had been awarded 77 financial services contracts worth some £772,930 (Shaw et al. 1996). Although most white-collar contracts are won in-house (Wilde 1996), the pressures on internal finance functions of such outsourcing possibilities, together with the new government's continuing commitment to quality and value-for-money, will continue to focus attention on minimising the cost of financial services, setting service standards, and continuing to focus on reviewing 'the purpose of the accountancy function in a modern authority' (Audit Commission 1995, p.10). Certainly these processes encourage the separation of core accountancy functions from the 'mundane' collection of council tax, pensions work and payroll administration functions, which are easier to separate out from the corporate functions, and which are more likely to be outsourced (Cook 1993, Shaw et al. 1996). Revenue collection has also encountered significant changes as a result of the changing nature of the revenues themselves, most notably the recent moves from rates to community charge to council tax, and the removal of the business rate from local control. To some extent this has meant that the finance function and the professionals within it have found themselves without a clear sense of purpose. However the central tasks remain (overall budget management; ensuring legality of expenditure, a focus for professional development) and new ones focusing on strategic financial management are emerging. Thus the accounting function is not going to wither away - but it does need redefinition. Both the Audit Commission (1995b) and CIPFA (1995) urge elected members and managers to review the role of their accounting functions along the lines of:

1   Core (central) accounting functions should be clearly specified and separated from the provision of support services. Less emphasis should be placed on detailed day-to-day control by the central function of service department activities and more on using corporate frameworks to set common ground rules and standards to ensure that departments have sound control systems reinforced by audit coverage and risk assessment.

2   Support services should concentrate on 'providing service managers with expert advice on financial issues (including high-level management accountancy services) and help with the financial aspects of change' (Audit Commission 1995b, p.11). Particularly within the context of CCT requirements for both financial and other services, careful attention is required to setting and monitoring the standards of financial services to service delivery departments, minimising costs and developing procedures to govern the relationship between support financial services and the departmental 'customers'.

65

3   Similar concerns apply to redefining the role of the internal audit. Audit should acquire a more strategic role under the guidance of an audit committee not accountable to the finance department but to a broader constituency within the senior management of the authority and its elected members (Audit Commission 1996). The change is one from an accountancy dominated audit with great emphasis on regularity of expenditure (although this must of course remain an element) to an audit process which focuses on the effectiveness of management and the achievement of performance - a management audit (Murphy 1996).

4   The focus should be on helping authorities to identify and achieve their strategic objectives through the use of the professional skills of the accountants in tandem with those of other professions.

Changing practitioner roles

The impact of the changes outlined above on CFOs and other senior accountants suggests a move away from the historically neutral role of the accountant associated with traditional hierarchical and bureaucratic local authority management systems. This role involved little or no 'client' orientation, other than formally to the chief executive and elected members. The emphasis was on professional or collegiate forms of occupational control, used by senior practitioners to 'legitimate their exercise of hierarchical authority over subordinates, including public service professionals, and influence over policy in relation to those in positions of, at least formal, power over them, in particular the elected politicians' (Laffin 1986, p.23).

From the mid 1970s local authority expenditure constraints, plus the statutory functions of the CFO role, enabled these officers to: '... gain professional recognition for their ability both to manipulate central rules and the financial markets to the benefit of their local authorities, and for their ability to encourage those authorities in the ways of careful financial control' (Clarke and Cochrane 1989, p. 46). CFOs could ignore the impact of spending constraints and the required efficiency savings on service outcomes during the annual 'budgetary game' (Clarke and Cochrane 1987, Cochrane 1993), and were able to make significant incursions across the professional boundaries of their service departmental colleagues. However CFOs have had to adapt as new criteria of effectiveness and 'quality' have moved into the ascendancy. These criteria embody elected members' policies and service departmental chief officers' professional concerns, and these criteria challenge the accounting language of the new managerialist approaches (Humphrey and Scapens 1992). This development, together with the new importance attached to the finance support function both at senior and lower level devolved business units in the context of CCT, has meant that the CFO and other senior practitioners have adopted more 'client-centred' or local forms of service orientation. These orientations represent an intensification of the patronage form of occupational control exercised more directly by not only elected members but other departmental senior officers in their new 'client' role vis-à-vis the CFO as a provider and overseer of financial advice and support geared more specifically towards meeting corporate and departmental service policy and development requirements. Even so the extent of such incursions into the professional autonomy boundaries of finance practitioners should not be overstated. Firstly chief officers, including CFOs, probably continue to exert considerable influence over elected members in relation to policy-making in many authorities (Young and Mills 1993). Secondly central departments, including finance, appear to continue to exercise considerable control over front-line service departmental activities (Audit Commission 1995c). Thirdly and perhaps most importantly significant variations in the way in which CFOs and central finance departments operate within individual local authorities are likely to persist.

The operating style of senior support service professionals, including finance, will continue to be affected by their local authority's choice of strategic management style (Earl and Vivian 1993, CIPFA 1995). Some local authorities may continue with a more traditional direct service provision role for the centre - where the CFO acts as a referee or mediator over a budgetary process focused on bargaining rather than the pursuit of strategy, and where control over resource utilisation remains relatively centralised. Other authorities may adopt slimmer, more strategically orientated commercial, neighbourhood and/or community governance approaches with a correspondingly different CFO style (LGMB 1993, Leach et al. 1994). For example within the predominantly commercial approach adopted by Kent County Council in the early 1990s, the role of the CFO focused on the three key functions of quality assurance through the 'head of profession' role, corporate financial adviser and statutory officer (Glynn 1993).

Nevertheless any consequent shrinking in the size of finance departments is unlikely to affect adversely the professional status and authority of senior finance staff. The finance services most likely to be affected by CCT are discreet and peripheral functions such as payroll administration and council tax collection. Indeed senior finance officers are likely to support any moves towards a smaller core accountancy function as this 'allows them a greater say in shaping their departments and budgets to advance their interests in the same direction as key business and political elites' (Shaw et al. 1996, p. 27).

Such moves and associated cost-cutting may involve job losses and poorer conditions for the lower level, and frequently unqualified rank and file staff, as well as produce a status divide between those in the 'purchaser' core and the 'provider' periphery, imposing lower status and job security on the latter (Langan and Clarke 1994). For example Lambeth's finance function has recently completed a 'comprehensive assessment programme testing people's competence for jobs. There will be no compulsory redundancies... but some people have been downgraded and early retirement issues still have to be resolved' (Wild 1996, p13). The split within white collar services into core 'purchasers' and peripheral 'providers' also produces the well documented public accountability problems inherent in attempts to separate policy from implementation (Glynn and Murphy 1996, Stewart 1992 and 1996, Walsh 1995). This process can deny elected members direct involvement in the management of services and can actually enhance the power of senior finance professionals now insulated from the public through the loss of the direct service provision link. This loss not only threatens to 're-enforce the insularity of the service, but will separate it from important countervailing pressures to produce a more public-centred approach' (Shaw et al. 1996, p.27).

The roles of devolved finance managers are also being changed by the moves towards smaller and slimmer central support service departments, the devolution of finance support staff to service department business units, and changes in financial control systems from detailed centralised control to less detailed, decentralised but tighter overall control (Stoker 1989). Under the pre-devolutionary, more centralised system, finance practitioners' sources of role identity and job satisfaction, were derived primarily from their traditional cosmopolitan professionalism and professional accounting expertise: 'performing technical aspects of their work efficiently together with some vague sense of public service' (Rosenberg et al. 1982, p. 127). Devolution requires a new local orientation by these devolved practitioners to meet the needs of their service department/business unit manager 'customers' using a broader set of higher order analytical skills rather than basic bean-counting ones. These changes tend to reduce finance staff's reliance on their traditional professional/expert public finance skills and knowledge (probably exercised previously within a central finance department of fellow professionals) and require a greater understanding of general management and business context within which service department/business unit managers operate (Rosenberg et al. 1982, Keen 1995, Keen and Murphy 1996).

To illustrate Keen and Murphy (1996) report how finance managers interviewed stressed their shift away from the 'ivory-tower' accountant or 'old-fashioned' auditor type roles towards a role of enabling and facilitating budget-holding line managers to control their devolved budgets. The new role meant designing financial systems to meet the needs of their service line managers. The term 'customer', used freely by these managers throughout the interviews held with them, symbolised the significance of this change. Yet the line managers themselves doubted that they had become true 'customers' of the finance department although they did accept that relationships had changed in this direction, leading them to develop some accounting skills to enable them to be effective 'customers'. However the extent of this skills development should not be overstated, being limited largely to lower order budget management skills.

These changes mean that finance managers are experiencing new vertical and horizontal tensions in their relationships with, and accountabilities to, two different corporate clients - the line managers and the central finance section of the new corporate service department. Departmental line managers expect the devolved finance managers to be flexible in terms of the specific finance systems and procedures they require for their business needs, and yet the finance managers themselves have to reconcile these expectations with adherence to the standards and systems set by the central finance function to meet statutory requirements for financial probity and integrity, as well as to monitor overall spending levels. Thus devolved budgets create considerable scope for debate between senior service departmental and finance managers over the design of particular departmental financial planning control systems. Similarly, at lower management levels, the exercise of the middle line managers' devolved financial responsibilities (and the achievement of their budgetary performance targets) involves them in negotiations with their finance manager or advisors over the extent of the line manager's powers to deploy their resources creatively whilst at the same time operating in accordance with the (sometimes conflicting) requirements of the departmental financial control systems, and their own 'cosmopolitan' orientations to national professional standards and values.

Central finance managers were aware of the potential threat posed by devolution to their previous professional autonomy vis-à-vis departmental financial planning and control systems. They made several, only partly jocular, comments, about the way in which, under the new devolved system, they adopted a variety of diplomatic strategies to limit the potential dilution of their professional control over such matters by departmental finance and line managers: 'we try and make it [the financial system] look as though it was something they [the departmental managers] have complete control over, whereas, in fact, it was something that still required central direction' (Central Finance Manager). Similarly the Audit Commission found that sixty per cent of the users of financial services experienced low levels of control over these services: 'most users felt that the nature and level of the services which they received was very much determined by the providers' (Audit Commission 1995c, p.16). The finance managers devolved to the departments commented on the way in which, as under the previous system, they exercised ultimate authority over this producer/consumer relationship in terms of their powers to insist that line managers' resource deployment activities followed the laid down financial procedures and regulations: '....you still have to say NO! - although you try and do it more nicely; you try and persuade them and talk it through' (Devolved Finance Manager, Highways). The line managers also identified the reality of the balance of power behind the rhetoric of devolution: '... the financial standing orders are fairly strict.... . If I step out of line, I'll be told that I can't do that ... ' (Highways Services Manager).

Although the finance managers were very aware of these devolutionary threats to their professional autonomy, they appeared to have access to sufficient expert-based power to maintain a high degree of control vis-à-vis other occupational professional groups. They could depend on the heavy reliance by the non-financial-expert middle managers on financial sources of help to ensure they met their budgetary targets (a key performance measure) and maintained high standards of probity and integrity. Their position was also strengthened by the new addition, to their traditional cosmopolitan technical expertise, of the local management skills and knowledge required to help them work effectively with, and understand the business needs of, their devolved manager customers or clients. Overall the devolved finance managers considered that this broadening out of their roles to encompass a wider and more general management orientation had enhanced their professional standing and improved their career prospects (although Rosenberg et al. 1982 raise concerns about the possible negative impact of devolution on professional status and career progression). These managers also considered that devolution had improved the general overall effectiveness of financial management within the authority (including a greater and beneficial level of integration between the service and specialist finance functions) at a time when increased resource constraints placed even more emphasis on efficient and effective resource utilisation.

Conclusions

Professional accountants have experienced major changes under the new managerialist approaches adopted by local authorities. Initially these changes involved switching from a role based on traditional bureaucratic controls, largely based on 'bookkeeping' principles, to a more enhanced resource management role. Latterly devolved management systems have involved operational managers more in the resource management process. They and the elected members have questioned the role, status and values of accountants. So that although the New Public Management initially reinforced the status and authority of the accounting professionals in local government, the changing focus of managerialism towards the end of the 1980s and into the 1990s resulted in a questioning of the neutrality of accounting language and the 'absolutism' of accounting information and the demystification of, at least parts, of accounting as service line managers started to acquire budget management and other accounting related skills.

Consequently the previously largely formalised and institutionalised tensions between support service organisational professionals such as the accountants and the service delivery professionals have become more fluid. CFOs can no longer detach themselves from direct involvement in the service policies and objectives of their elected members and direct service provider chief officer counterparts. Whilst the statutory obligations to ensure the legality and probity of spending remain, CFOs have been drawn into the more general management side of service delivery, and conversely, service professionals have become more involved in the finance management. This shift is mirrored at the lower levels by more junior accountants in the support function who owe divided *cosmopolitan* loyalties through their professional hierarchy to corporate finance and, ultimately, to the national professional body, and to their *local* service line manager 'customers'. The accountancy technobureaucrats are having to learn, like their direct service professional counterparts, to provide services 'with' rather than 'to' their organisational clients. They are having to develop a very specific individual corporate client focus at all levels in the local authority hierarchy, resulting in a strengthening of corporate patronage forms of control. Accountants, at all levels, are having to develop more general management competences, especially organisational political skills. The indications are of a partial convergence, within both the accountancy and service professionals, between accounting and general management expertise.

Yet the extent to which service professionals can make incursions into the higher realms of more complex accounting procedures should not be exaggerated. The financial management terrain is contested in ways unthinkable at the beginning of the 1980s, yet limits still exist on how far lay service officers and most elected members can question the intricacies of accounting information. Financial regularity remains a statutory obligation on local authorities and CFOs are statutory officers with defined responsibilities. As such they must remain influential members of the senior management team of a local authority. Even so significant variations exist among local authorities in terms of strategic planning styles and organisational forms, including the role of the centre and support services and considerable room for manoeuvre remains in terms of the precise role and organisation of the finance function.

Within the finance departments the vertical segmentation between the higher level professional elite in the corporate 'purchaser' roles and the lower level in 'provider' roles, both within devolved budgetary units and within specialised central functions, such as: payroll, revenue collection and pensions administration. This has been, and may well continue to be, exacerbated by requirements for applying CCT to 'white-collar' departments, and even the government's plans to replace CCT with 'value' based assessments. Thus, in terms of the four possible future scenarios posed for local government professionals in the introduction to this book, the higher echelons of professional accountants within local government are likely to experience limited change and demonstrate a degree of professional elitism; more junior, and less qualified staff are likely to encounter the de-professionalisation scenario; those possessing transferable professional skills may opt for, or be driven to, professional flight, as Reed's (1996) entrepreneurial knowledge workers, to maintain autonomy, professional influence and career paths. Well-qualified professional accountants who have been devolved from central service departments to service delivery departments may well find themselves in the most difficult situation in career terms, particularly if they are CIPFA qualified and are not readily employable outside the public sector, except insofar as they might be attractive to private sector professional practices seeking to develop their capability to tender for public sector work under the CCT and other initiatives.

Notes

1   The UK accounting profession comprises six institutes: The Institute of Chartered Accountants in England and Wales (ICAEW), 109,200 members; The Institute of Chartered Accountants of Scotland (ICAS),14,000; The Institute of Chartered Accountants in Ireland (ICAI), 9,500; The Association of Chartered Certified Accountants (ACCA), 50,000; The Chartered Institute of Management Accountants CIMA), 42,000; and The Chartered Institute of Public Finance and Accountancy (CIPFA), 12,000. Source: GCAS (1997).

2   The range of services a large professional practice might offer nowadays includes: audit and accountancy, taxation advice, forensic accounting, insolvency work, corporate recovery, due diligence work, financial advice, and a whole range of management consultancy services. The 'big six' are: Coopers & Lybrand, Price Waterhouse, KPMG, Deloitte & Touche, Arthur Andersen, Ernst & Young; although some of these are currently considering mergers with each other.

3　The historical tendency in the UK has been for the legislature to leave much of the responsibility for the development of 'generally accepted accounting practice' to the profession rather than, with some exceptions, laying down detailed statutory requirements although there has been some change in this attitude in recent years. Legislation has concentrated on laying down overall 'quality' requirements for 'proper' accounts rather than detailed accounting regulation.

4　There is an extensive body of literature on the inherent difficulties of trying to devise a completely standardised and uniform set of accounting bases to cope with the contingencies inherent in organisational realities. A useful insight into the issues involved can be gained from the publications of the Accounting Standards Board which is trying to address these issues in a private sector context, in the same way as CIPFA is attempting in a public sector context. It is at least arguable that a valuable higher level accounting skill is that of using the flexibility of accounting to achieve organisational gain.

References

American Accounting Association (1966), *A Statement of Basic Accounting Theory*, New York.

Association of Graduate Careers Advisory Services (1997), *Accountancy, Taxation and Financial Management*, CSU Publications: Manchester.

Audit Commission (1993), *Protecting the Public Purse - Probity in the Public Sector: Combating Fraud and Corruption in Local Government*, HMSO: London.

Audit Commission (1994), *Protecting the Public Purse: Ensuring Probity in Local Government*, HMSO: London.

Audit Commission (1995a), *Protecting the Public Purse: Ensuring Probity in Local Government*, HMSO: London.

Audit Commission (1995b), *From Administration to Management: The Management of the Finance Function in Local Government*, HMSO: London.

Audit Commission (1995c), *Opening the Doors: A Review of the Audits of Central Support Services*, HMSO: London.

Audit Commission (1996), *Called to Account: The Role of Audit Committees in Local Government*, HMSO: London.

Brown, S. (1996), 'CIPFA's New Diplomacy', *Public Finance*, 14th June, 1996, p.14.

CIPFA (1995), *The Changing Role of Financial Management in the Public Services: A Perspective*, CIPFA: London.

CIPFA (1997a), Information provided by CIPFA.

CIPFA (1997b), *Press Release*, 12th May, London.

Clarke, A and Cochrane, A. (1989), 'Inside the Machine. The Left and Finance Professionals in Local Government', *Capital and Class*, Vol. 37, pp. 35-61.

Cochrane, A. (1993), 'From Financial Control to Strategic Management: The Changing Faces of Accountability in British Local Government', *Accounting, Auditing and Accountability Journal*, Vol. 6, No. 3, pp 30-51.

Cook, P. (1993), *Local Authority Financial Management and Accounting*, Longman: Harlow.

Earl, M. and Vivian, P. (1993), *The Role of the Chief Information Officer*, London Business School: London.

Elcock, H. (1993), 'Strategic Management' in *Managing the New Public Services*, in Farnham and Horton.

Elcock, H. (1996), 'Local Government', in Farnham and Horton.

Ellwood, S. (1996), 'Full cost pricing rules within the National Health Service internal market - accounting choices and the achievement of productive efficiency', *Management Accounting Research*, Vol. 7, No. 1, pp. 25-51.

Farnham, D. and Horton, S. (1993) (ed), *Managing the New Public Services*, Macmillan: Basingstoke.

Farnham, D. and Horton, S (1996) (ed), *Managing the New Public Services*, Macmillan: Basingstoke.

Farnham, D. and Horton, S. (1993), 'The New Public Service Managerialism: An Assessment', in Farnham and Horton.

Ferlie, E., Pettigrew, A, Ashburner, L. and Fitzgerald, L. (1996), *The New Public Management in Action*, Oxford University Press: Oxford.

Gaster, L. (1995), *Quality in Public Services*, Open University Press: Buckingham.

Glynn, J. (1993), *Public Sector Financial Control and Accounting (2nd Ed)*, Blackwell: Oxford.

Glynn, J. and Murphy, M., (1996), 'Public Management: Failing Accountabilities and Failing Performance Review', *International Journal of Public Sector Management*, Vol. 6, No. 5/6, pp. 125-137.

Gouldner, A. (1957), 'Cosmopolitans and Locals: Towards and Analysis of Latent Social Roles', *Administrative Science Quarterly*, Vol. 2, pp. 281-306.

Gray, A. and Jenkins, W. (1995), 'From Public Administration to Public Management: Reassessing a Revolution?', *Public Administration*, Vol. 3, Spring, pp. 75-99.

Hepworth, N. (1996), 'Strength in difficult times', *Public Finance*, 26th July 1996, pp 10-12

HM Treasury (1995), *Better Accounting for the Taxpayer's Money: The Government's Proposals*, (Cmnd 2929), HMSO: London.

Humphrey, C. and Scapens, R. (1992), 'Whatever Happened to the Liontamers? An Examination of Accounting Change in the Public Sector', *Local Government Studies*, Vol. 18, No. 3, pp. 141-147.

Institute of Chartered Accountants in England and Wales (1992), *New Guide to Professional Ethics*, London.

Institute of Management Accountants (1983), *Management Accounting Terminology: Statement on Management Accounting No. 2*, Montvale NJ.

International Federation of Accountants (1987), *Preface to Statements on International Management Accounting*, New York.

International Accounting Standards Committee (1989), *Framework for the Preparation and Presentation of Financial Statements*, New York.

Johnson, T. (1972), *Professions and Power*, Macmillan: London.

Johnson, H. and Kaplan, R., *Relevance Lost: The Rise and Fall of Management Acounting*, Harvard University Press: Boston.

Kaplan, R. and Norton, D. (1996), '*Translating Strategy into Action: The Balanced Scorecard*, Harvard Business Press: Boston.

Keen, L. (1995), 'Organisational Decentralisation and Budgetary Devolution in Local Government: A Case of Middle Management Autonomy', *Human Resource Management Journal*, Vol. 5, No. 2, pp. 79-98.

Keen, L. and Murphy, M. (1995), 'Devolved Budgetary Management in Local Government: Lessons from a Shire County', *Financial Accountability and Management*, Vol. 12, No 1, pp. 37-52.

Koh, H. and Low, C. (1997), 'The Effects of Power Bases on Subordinate Compliance and Satisfaction: An Empirical Study of Accountants', *British Accounting Review*, Vol. 29, No.1, pp. 49-65.

Laffin, M. (1986), *Professionalism and Policy*, Gower: Aldershot.

Langan, M. and Clarke, J. (1994), 'Managing in the Mixed Economy of Care', in J. Clarke, A. Cochrane and E. McLaughlin (eds.), *Managing Social Policy*, Sage: London.

Leach, S., Stewart, J. and Walsh, K. (1994), *The Changing Organisation and Management of Local Government*, Macmillan: Basingstoke.

Local Government Management Board (1993), *Fitness for Purpose: Shaping New Patterns of Organisation and Management*, LGMB: Luton.

Local Government Management Board (1997), *Survey Report on Professional Support Services*, LGMB: London.

Littleton, A. (1966), *Accounting Evolution to 1900 (2nd Ed)*, Russell and Russell: London.

Murphy, M. (1996), 'Management Audit', in Glynn, J.J., Perkins, D.A and Stewart, S. (eds.), *Achieving Value for Money in the NHS*, Saunders: London.

Pike, R. and Neale, W. (1996), *Corporate Finance and Investment*, Prentice Hall: Hemel Hempstead.

Rawlinson, D and Tanner, B. (1990), *Financial Management in the 1990s*, Longman: Harlow.

Reed, M. (1996), 'Expert Power and Control in Late Modernity: An Empirical Review and Theoretical Synthesis', *Organisation Studies*, Vol. 17, No. 4, pp. 573-597.

Rosenberg, D., Tomkins, C. and Day, P. (1982), 'A Work Role Perspective of Accountants in Local Government Service Departments', *Accounting, Organisations and Society*, Vol. 7, No. 2, pp, 123-37.

Shaw, K., Snape, S. and Hind, K. (1996), 'Protecting the Core Business: Local Authority Responses to Compulsory Competitive Tendering for Financial Services', *Local Government Policy Making*, Vol. 22, No. 5, pp. 22-9.

Skelcher, C. (1993), *Managing for Service Quality*, Longman: Harlow.

Stewart, J. (1993), 'The Limitations of Government by Contract', *Public Money and Management*, July/September, pp. 1-6.

Stewart, J. (1996), 'A Dogma of Our Times - The Separation of Policy Making and Implementation', *Public Money and Management*, July/September, pp. 33-40.

Stoker, G. (1989), *New Management Trends*, Local Government Training Board: Luton.

Tonge, R. and Horton, S. (1996), 'Financial Management and Quality', in Farnham and Horton.

Vize, R. (1997), 'Labour Set to Scrap CCT April 1999', *Local Government Chronicle*, 2nd May, p.1.

Walsh, K. (1992), 'The Extension of Competitive Tendering', in S. Leach et al, *The Heseltine Review of Local Government*, Institute of Local Government Studies, University of Birmingham.

Walsh, K. (1995), *Public Services and Market Mechanisms*, Macmillan: London.

Watkins, J., Drury, L. and Bray, S. (1996), *The Future of the UK Professional Associations*, Bristol University: Bristol.

Watt, P. (1996), 'Compulsory competitive tendering for the finance service in local government', *Local Government Policy Making*, Vol. 23, No. 3, pp. 15-21.

Wilde, P. (1996a), 'Life in the Line of Fire', *Public Finance*, 5th April, pp. 10-13.

Wilde, P. (1996b), 'Compulsory Competitive Tendering: Reasons Behind the Changes', *Public Finance Supplement*, 15th November, p. *vii*.

Wilmott, H. (1986), 'Organising the Profession: a Theoretical and Historical Examination of the Development of Major Accountancy Bodies in the UK', *Accounting, Organisations and Society*, Vol. 11, No. 6.

Young, K. and Mills, L. (1993), *A Portrait of Change*, LGMB: Luton.

5 Planning

Huw Thomas

This chapter discusses the changing nature of professional practice in planning in the 1980s and 1990s. In particular it considers the extent to which the organisation and practice of local government planners might be said to conform to the post-bureaucratic model as outlined, for example, by Hoggett (1991). The defining characteristics of this model are taken as follows. Firstly a breaking down of local government departmentalism, as problem-solving increases in importance and carrying out statutory functions becomes less so; one aspect of this is a growing concern for results, not methods. Secondly the flattening of hierarchies, and 'down sizing', within departments as a clearer distinction emerges between (centralised) strategy and decentralised operational work, the latter conducted with considerable discretion. Middle management is cut out. Thirdly the contracting out of certain functions (for Hoggett this is one kind of 'decentralisation') so that the local authority ceases to be an 'all singing all dancing' organisation.

The causes of these changes are said to be a combination of public finance crises/cutbacks, central government hostility to a burgeoning local government which constitutes a locus of political opposition and lobbying by private sector interests with a direct interest in bidding for contracted out local government functions (for example Stoker 1990, 1991). At times these accounts can make local government appear somewhat passive or, at least, purely reactive. Yet the experience of planning suggests that professionalised occupations may have had some part to play as independent generators of change. However this chapter is somewhat speculative - partly because it is intended as a series of thoughts for discussion, and partly because there have been no large scale examinations of professional practice in planning over this period and the available evidence tends towards the anecdotal.

The chapter begins with a sketch of the history of the planning profession and some characteristics of its membership and working environment. The point is made that planning may never have fitted comfortably into the 'bureaucratic' model of local government which presumably preceded the current post-bureaucratic phase. Successive sections then consider changes in planning at national and local governmental level including in the latter some speculative remarks about the changing experiences of street-level planners. The chapter concludes that while professional practice in planning may never have been captured comfortably by the bureaucratic/post-bureaucratic dichotomy, its day to day practice has always been extraordinarily sensitive to the relationship between senior officers and senior councillors - great variations in organisational culture have existed which make sweeping generalisations peculiarly difficult. Finally the fact that the core regulatory functions of planning - notably, the control of development - have remained within local government means that strong elements of continuity exist within any planning office.

The planning profession

Town planning became professionalised during the twentieth century. The Town Planning Institute, later the Royal Town Planning Institute (RTPI), was founded as a qualifying association in 1914 by the so-called 'parent professions' of architecture, engineering and surveying, each of which laid claim to a new area of work which was beginning to be defined by statute; the first modern town planning legislation usually being taken to be the Housing and Town Planning Act 1909. But the new policy area, and hence employment opportunities within it, did not really begin to establish itself until the Town and Country Planning Act 1947 and sundry post-war legislation relating to New Towns (Healey 1985). The 1947 Act established a planning system which in essence remains in place today. The core of the Act was the requirement placed on those proposing most kinds of development to apply to local authorities for planning permission, and a requirement on local authorities that in considering such applications they should take into account (though not be bound by) the relevant development plan. In brief local authorities had to draw up development plans and consider planning applications (development control). After 1948 they began to set up divisions, typically within Engineer's or Surveyor's departments, to undertake the new tasks.

From the late 1940s onwards the RTPI institutionally, and its members in their various workplaces, began a struggle to raise the status and importance of the profession within local and central government and de facto to control entry into certain classes of jobs. The growth and status of the profession came to depend in practice on its fate in local government. By the early 1960s about 20 per cent of the RTPI's members were in the private sector and, having dipped in the interim, by the early 1990s the proportion was back at much the same figure (Coombes 1992, Faludi 1972). But by the 1990s the Institute has close to 14,000 corporate or full members as opposed to just 2,300 in 1962 and so the gap in absolute terms between public and private sectors has grown. Moreover of those in private practice in 1992, forty per cent had previously worked in local government and forty-eight per cent were sole practitioners (Coombes 1992). For much of its recent history, then, the experience of professionalism in planning has been shaped by the dynamic of the public sector, particularly local government, which in 1990 employed two thirds of members of the RTPI (Nadin and Jones 1990). It is reasonable to ask whether this dominant culture position has changed in recent years given contracting-out in local government and a small, but discernible trend, in the employment of planners in public organisations outside local government as local governance fragments (Nadin and Jones 1990, Stoker 1991), and this question will be addressed below.

For the moment, then, the focus will be on planning as a profession largely based in local government. The story of the last fifty years is one of the profession's ostensibly doing rather well out of the bureaucratic model in as much as by the late 1960s 'stand-alone' planning departments were commonplace, membership of the RTPI, or eligibility for membership, was a standard (though not universal) requirement for a post as a local authority planner. As a vital component of the professionalisation strategy town planning had also established itself as a subject for undergraduate and postgraduate study. The success of this strategy is illustrated by the fact that in a 1990 survey of the RTPI's membership fewer than two per cent had entered the profession by taking the Institute's own exams, that is membership for the vast majority has long been via higher education courses offering exemption from taking the RTPI's exams (Nadin and Jones 1990). In addition to their core development control and development planning functions, most planning departments in local government had managed to capture some new responsibilities assigned to local authorities in the 1960s and 1970s, notably the designation of improvement areas under the Inner Urban Areas Act 1978 and urban programme issues and their successors more generally.

Yet if the story of planning's professionalisation by carving out a niche in a burgeoning local government bureaucracy has a familiar sound to it, it should be qualified by noting some features which do not fit easily into the bureaucratic model. For example there is some evidence that working practices within planning departments have never been hierarchically organised quite in the way required by the bureaucratic model. Certainly there have been tiers of seniority within planning departments, yet there has also been scope for wide-ranging discussions not simply of how to undertake certain tasks but also of even what those tasks should be. The degree of discretion allowed planning authorities in drawing up development plans, for example, meant that there could be extended discussion among professional planners in which all levels participated (see Underwood 1980, on Haringey). Keeble's text books from 1952 onwards stressed the value of informality in the professional working environment, and I have personal experience of a planning department where formal hierarchies were regarded as having only a passing relationship with professional expertise, that is there was an informal status hierarchy based on perceived professional competence.

Even in development control, where bureaucratic systems are an essential component of an efficient operation and some researchers have found a generic administrative mentality (McLoughlin 1973), Keeble (1952) recognised that a high degree of operational discretion for case officers was inevitable. Indeed his discussion resonates with more recent references to the strategic/operational distinction in post-bureaucratic management (e.g. Hoggett 1996). Finally though the core activities of local planning authorities have always been plan-making and development control, planners have also been involved to varying extents at different times and places in what can loosely be termed 'implementation', that is making things happen. The New Towns programme was one example of this, post-war and 1960s city centre redevelopments were another. Typically these kinds of activities involved planners in multi-professional team work, in problem-solving and one suspects very often in a semi-detached relationship to the 'mainstream' planning functions (Holliday 1973). In all these respects there are more than intimations of post-bureaucratic practices. Nevertheless it would be ridiculous to suggest that planning has somehow been isolated from the enormous changes in the economy and government of the last twenty years. The economic context will not be rehearsed here, but the next section reviews central government's activities in relation to planning. This is useful for two reasons: firstly it allows us to chart the fate of the political-professional relationship at national level; secondly the national policy context, it will be argued, provides one key element in any understanding of the changing nature of town planning activity, including its organisation and management, at local level.

Planning and central government

Central government actions have influenced the manner in which town planning is organised and conducted at a local level in broadly two ways. Firstly planning has inevitably been influenced by the remarkable changes in the organisation and functions of local government in general promoted by Conservative governments of the 1980s and 1990s, such as compulsory competitive leadership (CCT) (Stewart and Stoker 1995a). Secondly central government policies specifically relating to planning have heavily influenced the nature of planning locally.

The purpose of this section is to set out and discuss the latter, that is the national planning policy framework(s) of the last twenty years or so, drawing particular attention to the rather fragile presence of professional influence at central government level. The ways in which planning might have been affected by the huge changes in local government will be considered in the next section.

It is not too much of a distortion of a complex reality to say that over the last thirty years or so the stock of town planning in national government has consistently fallen under both Labour and Conservative administrations, reaching a particularly low point in the Thatcher years. In the mid and late sixties town planning was seen as an essential tool for modernising towns and cities through urban renewal, thereby improving living standards, as in slum clearance, and economic performance for example, by constructing urban motorways. Only a reorganised and effective planning system, it was argued, could cope with anticipated economic and demographic growth (PAG 1965), and securing effective town and regional planning was one of the prime considerations behind local government reorganisation in the early 1970s (Recliffe-Maud and Wood 1974). An indication of the congruence at that time in what Solesbury (1993) has termed policy frames between central government, local government and the profession was the career of Dr Wilf Burns, who became the government's chief planning adviser in 1967 having served as the first chief planning officer for Newcastle-upon-Tyne in its ambitious (T. Dan Smith) heyday and, before that, in Coventry, one of the examples of what a strong, comprehensive, interventionist planning system could offer post-war Britain (Ward 1994). In sharp contrast by the mid 1980s the government's chief planning adviser was a career civil servant who was not a member of the professional institute; and the subsequent short-term appointments - Peter Hall and David Lock - have stood outside the professional establishment. So much for the future, as Francis Amos (1984) put it, the 1960s were 'the years of abundance' and the professional institute benefited, with corporate membership increasing by two-thirds over the decade, and student membership increasing over threefold.

By the mid 1970s the relationship between the profession and various tiers of government was becoming strained. Within local government town planning was split between the two tiers, and though this created a bonanza of new well-paid jobs, it also created in a number of places bureaucratic and political minefields for those planners charged with drawing up integrated, co-ordinated development plans in two spatial scales for different political and professional bosses. Progress in plan-making was slow, and the products often seemed irrelevant to the day to day management of the built environment. Moreover intellectually and politically town planning was coming under fire. There were two related kinds of critique which, in retrospect, can be seen as especially significant.

The first was largely focused on the planning profession itself and challenged the claims of planners to have an intellectually sound expertise. A succession of sociologists highlighted the intellectually naïve and unreflective conceptions of key notions, such as 'community', 'neighbourhood' and 'public interest', which planners employed. Some critics argued that even when planners sought a credible intellectual base for their expertise (such as systems theory), they were operating with notions of society as being based on consensus, whereas in practice it was characterised by conflict (Simmie 1974). This critique often led on to a second, which emphasised that planners' intellectual naïveté meant that they drifted into an uncritical conservatism, supporting the societal status quo.

Others argued that planners' crassness served the interests of their own profession, which could inject its own values and prejudices into judgements labelled as 'objective' and 'technical'. These critiques of planning were similar to the demystification and debunking of other professional claims; and intellectual doubts about the value of professionalism, and the precise extent and nature of professional expertise, were to link up, by the 1980s, with more widespread public scepticism about authority in general (Giddens 1990). Politically town and country planning was deeply suspect to Thatcherites. In 1982 the Adam Smith Institute published a pamphlet by Robert Jones, later to be a minister in the Department of the Environment, accusing the post-war planning system of presiding over 'Town and Country Chaos' and advocating its abolition and greater reliance on restrictive covenants as ways of securing sensible patterns of development (Jones 1982).

Though he was no Thatcherite ideologue, her first Secretary of State for the Environment, Michael Heseltine, was also happy to voice these kinds of criticisms, and a vision of the proper role of planning, which were to set the tone for relations between government and the planning system, and the profession, in the 1980s. There were regular references to the 'need for a speedy and efficient planning system ...[and] ... the need for relevant planning which delivered decisions quickly' (Heseltine 1982, p. 11).

However while the Conservatives might be suspicious of planning, they came to recognise its important role in underpinning the quality of life of many Conservative voters in leafy suburbs and rural shires. Suggestions of modifying green belt policy in the mid 1980s, for example, were quickly dropped in the face of uproar from the NIMBY minded middle classes. Later in the 1980s and in the early 1990s there was widespread, if sometimes grudging, recognition even among Conservatives that some mechanism was necessary to co-ordinate the provision of infrastructure with the granting of permission to develop and particularly in areas of development pressure such as London Docklands (Brownill 1993). It should be noted that development interests such as the British Property Federation (1986) were established supporters of development plans if they introduced certainty into markets and were sensitive to market trends, that is limited to light-handed market management. The complete dismantling of the planning system established in 1947 was never likely, therefore, but it still had quite a shake-up (Healey 1985). Thornley (1993) has argued that there were three aspects of a distinctive Thatcherite central government approach to the '1947' planning system.

Firstly a number of modifications of the system were introduced, usually with the aim of speeding up bureaucratic processes and reducing the amount of regulation; the value of producing plans at all was questioned in particular. Secondly parts of the 1947 system were by-passed, notably by setting up urban development areas in which local authorities did not exercise planning control (though urban development corporations did but in a market sensitive way). Thirdly there were (generally unsuccessful) attempts to pilot simplified alternatives to the existing planning system - as in Enterprise Zones.

These policy innovations structured the ways in which local government planners responded to the local peculiarities of their circumstances. Firstly suggestions for simplification, streamlining and 'speeding up' implied that existing procedures were needlessly complex; planners responded by arguing that speed and simplicity could improve the quality of decision-making and of outputs (e.g. Thompson 1987). Their arguments cut little ice, though the Audit Commission (1992) became interested in improving the quality of planning. In the early 1990s the RTPI commissioned a study designed to provide practical guidance for local planning authorities keen to create an 'effective' planning service (Elsworth Sykes Planning 1991). One particular source of pressure on local authority personnel was never exerted on planners, namely compulsory competitive tendering (CCT). Competitive tendering has not been imposed on local planning authorities. There seem to be two reasons for this. The private sector in planning and related professions is too small to cope with the potential workload created by successful tendering, so any tendering would not involve realistic competition. In addition because planning is a regulatory activity which can create or destroy the possibility of great financial rewards for developers and land owners there is always concern over the potential for conflict of interest. Any scheme for contracting out planning functions would have to include clear safeguards against conflicts of interest, which would probably include restrictions on the private sector clients consultancies could take on. As a result there might be little financial incentive for the private sector to tender for core planning functions.

Secondly another way in which the central government context structured planners' responses as professionals in local government related to the clear rationale for central government's pressure for streamlining - the desire to make planning more market-oriented (Thornley 1993) and to make it more of a service for developers (Underwood 1981). Because planning is actually delivered at local level by elected local authorities with some discretion over the precise content of plans and decisions on planning applications, central government could never force or guarantee that changes in the outlook of planning authorities would take place. Indeed there is evidence of great variation in local planning practice in the 1980s and 1990s (Brindley et al. 1989, Healey et al. 1988). Nevertheless the national policy context, relentlessly reinforced in circulars and speeches, did alter the framework within which every planning authority made its day to day decisions.

Thirdly and finally these innovations made planners uneasy and insecure. Eventually enterprise zones, simplified planning zones and urban development areas were not to prove to be models of a plan-free Britain, but in the mid to late 1980s it did not always seem that way. As a profession planners needed to prove their worth symptomatically another of the RTPI's commissioned studies argued that town planning was central to 'Caring for Cities' (Fleming 1990).

Some have argued that Conservative policy towards planning in the 1990s, under John Major, differed sufficiently 'in leadership style and policy approach... [to]... warrant a sensitivity in any analysis.' (Allmendinger and Tewdwr-Jones 1997, p. 100). A new concern for the environment is touted as one reason for a rehabilitation of the development plan as an important locally produced tool for managing urban and rural change. Suddenly planning, in the sense of making plans, has come back into fashion in central government, even if the plans are still market sensitive and are to reflect central government policy guidance. To be sure the nature of planners' insecurities have changed. They are now more concerned about threats to their livelihoods from local expenditure cuts than being made redundant because of their irrelevance to public policy. But the idea of planning as a service and the need for market sensitivity are likely to remain significant for many years to come.

Planning in local government

The previous section considered some ways in which central government attitudes and policies relating to planning as a policy area might have influenced the standing of the profession. In so doing it also touched upon some of the general organisational changes in the local government, such as CCT, which were part of Conservative central government efforts to change the face of local government.

If the outline of the changing status of town planning within central government since the 1970s is relatively straightforward to discern, the picture is considerably more complex and hazy at local government level. Two things are clear. Firstly that from the mid 1960s to the early 1970s town planning became established as a separate department in very many local authorities, especially the larger urban areas, the spur appearing to be comprehensive redevelopment and urban renewal schemes in the larger towns and cities and the need for structure plans, often using sophisticated methodologies, in the shire counties. Secondly, by the late 1970s, and through the 1980s, the variations in the day to day practice of planning in different kinds of authority, which one presumes must always have existed, had become so pronounced as to encourage contemporary commentators to talk in terms of planning's 'fragmentation' (e.g. Davies 1981).

Brindley et al. (1989) argue that the fragmentation was not random, and that the key factors influencing its pattern were: the variations in local economic circumstances and, in particular, the dramatic spatial implications of the economic restructuring in the UK from the early 1970s, and variations in local political responses to this economic restructuring.

We would expect, therefore, some variation in the way the planning profession operates in local government. However there have also been significant national political, and governmental forces seeking to influence the nature of local government in the 1980s and 1990s. Stewart and Stoker (1995) identify three key directions in which these have operated. Firstly the institutional changes, in particular a fragmentation of responsibilities for services which had been major local authority concerns (e.g. the management of social housing), meanwhile organisations outside local authorities were often the ones given responsibilities for all (or part of) new policy areas - such as some environmental concerns. These developments certainly affected planners for, as Thomas (1984) has argued, in the late 1970s and early 1980s, before the shake up of local government became as forceful as it was later to be, local authority planners became involved in new policy areas such as economic development and tourism promotion. He argues that this expansion of areas of concern was a move by a profession worried about job losses (actual or threatened) and eager to be seen to be responding to local political priorities. Other examples of this broadening of the interests of planners are their roles in the new function of town centre management, the promotion of the 'environmental agenda' (for example working out the implications of Local Agenda 21), and involvement in urban policy initiatives (such as grant giving under the Urban Programme, or urban development grants; in urban development corporations, and, latterly, in Single Regeneration Budget (SRB) projects, City Challenges or Community Revival projects). A sample survey of its membership conducted by the RTPI at the end of 1988 found that about a third of respondents' current workload involved development control or development planning; about twenty per cent worked in implementation or project management; with a further third working in economic development, urban design and conservation. When invited to write in the area in which they currently worked, seven per cent wrote tourism. We see here an indication of the significance in employment terms of non-core planning activities.

This involvement in new kinds of activities has had three consequences, each of which - in different ways - could have implications for the practice and standing of planners as professionals. Firstly they have often involved modes of operation which fit uneasily with the bureaucratic procedures of local government. The author has personal experience of the growth of economic development as a new activity in a local authority planning department; the officers engaged in this pioneering work soon chafed at conventions such as the chief officer's signature being used for every letter leaving the department or the need for every agreement to be in writing. They saw as their 'clients', local small firms, whom they could not regard as potential antagonists, as people who might try to embarrass them or report them to the ombudsman. Similar findings have been reported in tourism development (Thomas and Thomas, forthcoming) and in the environmental field, where, again, relations of trust and co-operation must be developed which can be constrained by too much of the traditional local government formality.

Secondly these new areas of policy on the fringes, as it were, of traditional planning concern have been the ones most open to being undertaken by new kinds of agencies often at arms length or even further away from local authorities. Thus urban development corporations and various kinds of other agencies have been promoted by central government as vehicles for urban regeneration, Groundwork trusts have been supported as one kind of environmental agency and so on. However there is little evidence that the operations of arms length agencies have opened up dramatically new vistas for professionals working in planning authorities for two reasons. The actual involvement of planners in these agencies, either as employees or through partnership arrangements with local authorities, is extremely variable. SRBs for example appear to be housed in a variety of departments, while the breadth of City Challenge organisations' remits mean that local authority economic development, education and housing departments can have more contact with them than planning, though physical development is still an important part of the strategy of most City Challenge organisations (Russell et al. 1996). The other reason for speculating that these new kinds of agencies have hardly revolutionised the practices of planners is that there is some evidence that local authority practices tend to be the exemplars for the agencies rather than the other way around (Davoudi and Healey 1995, Robinson 1997, but see also Russell et al. 1996).

Thirdly a major implication of the partial capture of new policy areas by planners has been that planners have been working in fields where they cannot claim sole possession of all relevant expertise, and it might be argued, are actually engaged upon the development of new realms of knowledge and expertise with other professions. Multi-professional working in planning is not new. In the 1960s the RTPI was torn apart by arguments over what such team working meant for planners' professional standing. Bitter debates took place but nobody doubted that urban renewal, comprehensive redevelopment and the like required co-operation among planners, many kinds of engineers, surveyors, environmental health officers and so on. This kind of boundary dispute continues. Lately the most contentious has been the move by some transport planners to set up a new transport planning organisation complementary to the existing professional institutions (Headicar 1995, p. iii). As Healey (1985) has pointed out in the 1960's the influence of local authority employees within the RTPI meant that the Institute rejected the idea of planning as a collection of specialisms - this would have endangered the push for stand alone planning departments in local government. There remains a reluctance in the RTPI to acknowledge the fragmentation of practice and real tension between its traditional professional rhetoric and the increasingly fluid circumstances in which its members work.

However it is arguable that the 1960s and 1970s style of team working is rather different from the kind of activities which economic development, town centre management and the like involve. For in the latter new, allegedly holistic understandings of particular phenomena are being developed. It is not a case of having a group of experts, each claiming to understand a single dimension of a problem and then agreeing to share their expertise. Rather some of those involved suggest that 'the problem' cannot be adequately captured, or defined, within the terms of their existing expertise, but they do have techniques, skills, knowledge which may be of some relevance to the task of trying to understand, and influence, the phenomenon under consideration - and they agree to pool these intellectual resources, to merge them with those of others, to see if a new and more powerful synthesis can be developed. It is plausible to suggest that the growth of significant professional forums outside the Royal Town Planning Institute to discuss these new concerns is an indication of the extent to which existing professional boundaries and knowledge are seen as irrelevant. Meanwhile the RTPI has responded by setting up specialist panels to try to capture the increasing variety of work within which its members are engaged.[1]

Stewart and Stoker (1995b) identify 'a revolution in management' as the second key area of change in local government. The main driving force for this has been the split between the local authority (or part thereof) as a client and the local authority (or part of it) as a (potential) contractor. As has been pointed out earlier CCT has not affected planning directly, and very few local authorities have voluntarily contracted out all or part of their planning function (CPOS n.d.). It is plausible to speculate, therefore, that the internal management of local authority planning services has not been changed as radically as that of, say, the housing or leisure services. However anecdotal evidence suggests that the most senior levels of local authority planning have been affected by the knock on effects of CCT on the overall departmental structures of local authorities. In very many, amalgamation of departments has occurred and planning departments have been caught up in this. Senior planners who wish to lead a department in which planning is only one function alongside (say) environmental health and street cleansing, will need to familiarise themselves with the management challenges of CCT, even if it does not affect planning itself. Inevitably this encourages professional planners of a certain seniority to see themselves as local authority managers rather than senior professional advisers.

In any event it would be misleading to suggest that the core functions of planning departments have been conservatively organised and managed. Many or even most local planning authorities have reconsidered the way in which they undertake their core planning functions. The RTPI commissioned study on delivering planning services mentioned above and the number of senior planners undertaking MBAs, are two indicators of how widespread this interest in service delivery is. The defensiveness of these concerns is rather well captured by a quotation by a recent president of the RTPI in the introduction to an Institute publication on quality assurance: 'The planning profession is under a great deal of pressure to demonstrate its ability to perform against criteria set by Central Government. We could continue to merely respond to these pressures, but I believe the profession will be better respected if it adopts a proactive approach' (McKay 1993, p.7).

Not surprisingly these management orientated reviews have not generally questioned the role, status or competence of planners as professionals.

The third of Stewart and Stoker's key dimensions of the revolution in local government has been the attempt to increase central control over local government activity. Fundamental to the hobbling of local authority initiatives has been the increase in budgetary controls. However this central thrust has been complemented by specific initiatives in individual policy areas and planning is no exception. Of particular relevance to the nature of planners' work, and their professional standing, has been the attempt by government to reduce local political involvement in decision making in development control. The publication of 'league tables' based on speed of decision making in development control, for example, has put some pressure on authorities to delegate some decision making powers to senior officers and/or senior councillors.

The background to this concern is the fact that local planning policies and decisions tend to attract considerable local political attention because they often make immediate differences to people's quality of life. In addition in the highly politicised local government context of the 1980s and 1990s many local councillors have seen planning policy as an area for making local political capital. DoE guidance that in public inquiries on planning appeals costs be awarded against local authorities which ignored their officers' recommendations can be interpreted as strengthening professional influence vis-à-vis the political; but it can as plausibly be construed as strengthening central government's hand, as one of the primary tasks of the planning officer is to relate relevant governmental guidance to decisions and issues facing local authorities (Tewdwr-Jones 1995).

It is difficult to be confident about generalising in this area, but it is certainly plausible to suggest that in many areas politicians have tried to promote a notion of civic pride which is intended to bridge social and political divides, and have seen big projects; in other cities planning has been one vehicle (among others) for expressing a more strident 'civic' political philosophy (e.g. GLC 1985). The planning system on this view, is there to be used to promote a very specific political agenda, and, if necessary, used as 'creatively' as, say, local government finance was. This can and has placed planning employees in a difficult position if they feel/felt that they once were being asked to compromise their professional integrity (such as by departing from standards or procedures they would otherwise have followed). Crawley's (1991) discussion of his response as a planner working for a radical right-wing council is one of very few in the literature; his response was pretty robust and self confident - he would not thwart his employers but he would seek to persuade them of, and steer them towards, his own, rather different, outlook. However interesting as this response is, Crawley is probably unusually reflective about and critical of the intellectually discredited ideology of the planning profession which portrays it as operating in some kind of value free manner to promote the public interest. Similarly Crawley's employing authority might also be portrayed as unusually clear about its political direction, and unusually decisive and vigorous in intervening in those local bureaucratic processes it wished to influence.

Conclusion

The bureaucratic/post-bureaucratic distinction has never fitted planning very comfortably. The profession's growth and status has depended upon local government departmentalism, but its working practices have at the very least approximated to post-bureaucratic flexibility (especially perhaps as graduate entry has become the norm). These practices have been set up and consolidated by the profession itself rather that being foisted upon it, and they illustrate the importance of keeping in mind professional agency in discussions of post-bureaucracy. Planning also has a history of task orientation and creative problem solving which, to be sure, has become more prominent in recent years but has always been a genuinely, professionally valued component of professional practice. Despite a few scares in the 1980s, the profession's core activities of development planning and development control remain securely within its local government domain. Indeed professional standing in relation to local political influence in these processes is perhaps increasing, though the RTPI was disappointed that the recent Nolan report on local government did not go further in bolstering it (Nolan 1997). The professional Institute's problem is, and has been for some time, that these core activities offer nowhere near enough employment opportunities for the rapidly expanding membership and still growing numbers of graduates from accredited planning schools. For reasons of crude material interest, as well as personal and professional kudos, planners have to be concerned about the kinds of issue areas which increasingly are exercising the multiplicity of agencies engaged in local governance. These issues - economic development, creating safer cities, creating sustainable towns and cities - rather than new statutory obligations are where national and local political interest is focused and where exciting new employment opportunities exist. The story of planning in the 1990s is one of individuals, and some planning departments, throwing themselves into these activities while trying to redefine spheres of competence and potentially exclusion. It is a fruitless task, and it can surely only be a matter of time before the profession realises it must share its concern and responsibilities with non-planners in perhaps the majority of areas in which its membership is employed. This may precipitate the development of a new non-exclusionary model of professionalism in planning, but its dynamic will be related only obliquely to post-bureaucratic trends in local government.

Note

1 Town centre managers, economic development officer, tourism officers and environmental assessors all now have professional or proto-professional institutions. For its part, in 1997 the RTPI had the following specialist panels with remits to inform Institute policy: Design and Conservation in the Historic Environment; Countryside and the Natural Environment; Development Control; Development Planning; Urban Regeneration and Economic Development; Environmental Education; Equal Opportunities (Race Relations); Equal Opportunities (Women); Information Technology and GIS; Housing Development and Renewal; Management Development; Minerals, Waste Management and Environmental Protection; Planning Aid; Research; Scottish Planning Policy; Students and Young Members; Transport; Welsh Planning Policy.

References

Allmendinger, P. and Tewdwr-Jones, M. (1997), 'Post Thatcherite Urban Planning and Politics: A Major Change?' *International Journal of Urban and Regional Research*, Vol. 21, No. 1.

Amos, F. (1984), 'The 1960s: The Years of Abundance', *The Planner*, Vol. 70, No. 9.

Audit Commission (1992), *Building in Quality*, HMSO: London.

Brindley, T., Rydin, Y. and Stoker, G. (1989), *Remaking Planning*, 1st ed., Unwin Hyman: London.

British Property Federation (1986), *The Planning System - A Fresh Approach*, BPF: London.

Brownill, S. (1993), *Developing Londons Docklands*, 2nd ed., PCP : London.

Coombes, T. (1992), *Planning in the Consultancy Sector*, RTPI : London.

County Planning Officer's Society (n.d.), *Planning in a Competitive Environment*, CPOS: London.

Crawley, I. (1991), 'Some Reflections on Planning and Politics in Inner London,' in Thomas, H. and Healey, P. (eds.), *Dilemmas of Planning Practice*, Avebury: Aldershot.

Davies, L. (1981), 'The Future of Practice', *The Planner*, Vol. 67, No. 1.

Davoudi, S. and Healey, P. (1995), 'City Challenge: Sustainable Mechanism of Temporary Gesture?' in Hambleton, R. and Thomas, H. (eds.), *Urban Policy Evaluation*, Paul Chapman Publishing: London.

Elsworth Sykes Planning (1991), *Planning - Is it a Service and How Can it be Effective?* RTPI: London.

Evans, B. (1995), *Experts and Environmental Planning*, Avebury: Aldershot.

Faludi, A. (1972), *The Specialist versus Generalist Conflict*, Oxford Working Papers in Planning Education and Research No. 12, Oxford Polytechnic: Oxford.

Fleming, P. (1990), *Caring for Cities - Town Planning's Role*, RTPI: London.

Greater London Council (1985), *The Future of Planning: London's Proposals*, GLC: London.

Headicar, P. (1995), 'What Position do Town Planners Merit in Transport Planning?' *Town Planning Review*, Vol. 66, No. 3.

Healey, P. (1985), 'The Professionalisation of Planning in Britain', *Town Planning Review*, Vol. 56, No. 4.

Healey, P. et al. (1988), *Land Use Planning and the Mediation of Urban Change* Cambridge University Press: London.

Heseltine, M. (1982), 'Secretary of State's Address', *Town and Country Planning Summer School Report of Proceedings*, RTPI: London.

Hoggett, P. (1991), 'A New Management in the Public Sector', *Policy and Politics* Vol. 19, No. 4.

Hoggett, P. (1996), 'New Modes of Control in the Public Service', *Public Administration*, Vol. 74, No. 1.

Holliday, J. (ed.) (1973), *City Centre Re-Development*, Charles Knight: London.

Jones. R (1982), *Town and Country Chaos*, Adam Smith Institute: London.

Keeble, L. (1952), *Principles and Practice of Town and Country Planning*, 1st ed., Estates Gazette: London.

McKay, H. (1993), 'Introduction' in RTPI *BS5750 Quality Assurance for Planners* RTPI: London.

McLoughlin, J. (1973), *Control and Urban Planning*, Faber: London.

Nolan, Lord (1997), *Standards in Public Life. Third Report of the Committee on Standards in Public Life*, HMSO: London.

Planning Advisory Group (PAG) (1965), *The Future of Development Plans*, HMSO: London.

Robinson, F. (1997), *The City Challenge Experience*, Newcastle City Challenge West End Partnership Ltd: Newcastle.

Russell, H. et al. (1996), *City Challenge - Interim National Evaluation*, HMSO: London.

Simmie, J. (1974), *Citizens in Conflict*, Hutchinson: London.

Solesbury, W. (1993), 'Reframing Urban Policy', *Policy and Politics*, Vol. 21, No. 1.

Stewart, J. and Stoker, G. (eds.) (1995a), *Local Government in the 1990s*, Macmillan: London.

Stewart, J. and Stoker, G. (1995b), 'Fifteen years of Local Government Restructuring, 1979-1994' in Stewart, J and Stoker, G (eds.), *Local Government in the 1990s*, Macmillan: London.

Stoker, G. (1990), 'Regulation Theory, Local Government and the Transition to Fordism' in King, D. and Pierre, J. (eds.), *Challenges to Local Government*, Sage: London.

Stoker, G. (1991), *The Politics of Local Government*, 2nd ed., Macmillan: London.

Tewdwr-Jones, M. (1995), 'Development Control and the Legitimacy of Planning Decisions', *Town Planning Review*, Vol. 60, No. 2.

Thomas, H. (1984), 'British Town Planners Under the Thatcher Government', *Plan Canada*, Vol. 24, No 1.

Thomas, H. and Thomas, R. (forthcoming), 'The Implications of Changes in Local Governance for Tourism Development', *Progress in Tourism and Hospitality Research*.

Thompson, R. (1987), 'Is Faster Best? The Case of Development Control', *The Planner*, Vol. 73, No. 9.

Thornley, A. (1993), *Urban Planning under Thatcherism*, Routledge: London.

Underwood, J. (1980), *Town Planning in Search of a Role*, University of Bristol: Bristol.

Underwood, J. (1981), 'Research Review: Development Control' *The Planner*, Vol. 67, No. 4.

Ward, S. (1994), *Planning and Urban Change*, PCP: London.

Acknowledgements

I am grateful for the comments on an earlier draft by Ian Crawley, Neil Harris and Martin Laffin.

6 Social services

Roger Clough

Social services: disputed territory

'Don't use the word *welfare*', someone said at a meeting the other day, 'it has a ring of the 1950s'. A word with an honourable lineage acquires new nuances. A part of the uncertainty as to ways to govern social services derives from the uncertainty, at times disparagement, as to their task. In this chapter I examine the government of social services, the arrangements in place for the control, accountability and management of the service together with the organisational structure for its production.

Social services departments: hopes and dreams

Social services departments (SSDs), created after the Seebohm Report and the Local Authority Social Services Act 1970, were given responsibilities for a cluster of activities that had formerly been under the separate welfare, mental health and children's departments. One department was to provide access to social services for all children and adults.

The years that followed witnessed an expansion of SSDs in real terms. The identification of social problems repeatedly led to calls for more social services staff. There was a belief that SSDs had the potential to improve people's life circumstances. In part this view followed an analysis of people in society: the new social sciences provided streams of evidence of inequality, disadvantage and inadequate provision; there was a strongly held view that staff in social services could play a part in compensating for these. Today there would be more debate about analysis and outcome.

Ambivalence to welfare

The government of social services cannot be understood without recognition of the changing perception and the uncertain definition of its task. Nowhere have the debates been played out more completely as to the nature of society, or the responsibility of one person to another and of state to citizen. SSD services are provided for people who themselves find difficulties in managing their lives or are thought to do so by others. They focus on practical aspects of living (capacity to look after oneself as an adult or to be looked after as a child), on people's psychological states (their sense of self and identity, their attitudes to others) and on the interplay between the practical, social and psychological. By definition they are residual services. Thus immediately we are in the territory of differing explanations as to whether people are in their current position on account of societal structures, genetics, environmental factors or personal choice of life style.

Social services for older people illustrate the intense discussion over levels of provision, methods of rationing, systems for provision and access, and methods of payment. Questions are raised as to the contract between state and citizen. Increased attention is being paid to the financing of services for older people: should what has been termed 'long term care' be paid for by state or individual? Of course the contrast is false: individuals as citizens are the people who pay for state provided services. Nevertheless the fact that the two are posited against one another is of immense significance. The matter is seen not as 'How is this service to be paid for?' - for example by taxation, state managed insurance, private insurance or by payment at time of need - but as 'Who should pay - state or individual?'

Services for younger adults raise a different question: how to provide access to the sorts of life experiences enjoyed by others? Services for children and young people are the most disputed area of social service activity. Arguments include: the rights of the state to intervene in the lives of private citizens; the basis of the judgement of adequacy of parental care; the extent to which those who face problems or who are thought to have been disadvantaged should have access to services which in some way may seem better than those available to those who do not get social service help. Immediately the Victorian concern that what was provided in poor relief should be 'less eligible' than that available to the poorest person in work comes to mind. The consequence for social workers is well recognised: they are to intervene to protect; they are to leave people to manage their lives; they are to focus on those 'at most risk'; they are to provide services to support people to manage better.

The ferment I have described has significance for those who are potential service users and those who provide services. While a generalisation, there is a large measure of truth in the statement that by and large people do not want to use social services. It is thought that the use of social services indicates a failure to manage independently, with 'independence' being a prized state; indeed social services may be called in to help, but may end up exerting statutory control over one's life.

Thus the key themes emerge of responsibility, control, justice and equity. These precede debates as to the types of service which are needed and the systems for their production. The point is central to an understanding of social services organisation: among the different stakeholders of service users and potential users, workers, managers, government at central and local levels and citizens, there is little of shared values or shared understanding of task.

The first part of the debate is on the need for welfare, its ends. Secondly there have been substantial questions as to effectiveness: have social services achieved what they claimed or others expected of them? Again this is not the place to pursue the question, but recognition of the doubts about both the quality of the services and their consequences has been considerable.

Social services are designed to provide for people who are not coping. In doing this social services staff have seen themselves, and been seen by others, as being on the side of the people with whom they are working as well as on the side of the state. The struggle of social services staff to represent others, to account for their situation and to challenge discrimination has led to their being identified as 'loony lefties'. In this version of events it becomes the staff who have to be controlled.

My statement is not to endorse all activities of all social services staff, some have made naive responses which ignored complexity. Yet at their best they struggle to work well in situations which others ignore. The 'impossible task' view of welfare work is set out by Cheetham and colleagues (1992). Commenting on the types of 'troubles' which are the subject of welfare activity they write:

> Since the responses to such troubles are often both contentious and ill resourced, social work by its association with them, can reap the whirlwind. Thus, when care management falls apart and old people deteriorate in residential care or their daughters collapse from overwork or anxiety, when children are killed by their parents or removed from them, amid cries of protest, when supportive systems fail to prevent deterioration or disaster, so will the storms break around the world of social work. (1992, p.145)

Social work within social services departments

I have been writing, deliberately, about *social services staff* and *social services work*. By these terms I have meant those who work in *social services activity*. The fact that it is difficult to find words that capture what goes on in this type of social welfare work is in itself significant. There are two parts to the confusion. The first relates to the variety of tasks which are undertaken: can the different types of work activity within social welfare be defined? Secondly are the factors related to the organisation in which people work? are there differences in the tasks of those who work in private, voluntary and local authority organisations such that there is a justification for the use of different terms to describe their functions and tasks?

It is not appropriate here to produce long lists of social services work. In brief *social services work* includes: *direct care* (that is the tasks in home care, day centres or residential homes which have a practical, tending or caring component, such as helping people top get dressed, bathe or get meals); *the environment* in which direct care is provided (in a residential home or day centre, the organisation has responsibility for the management of the buildings and much of the structures and systems in which people will live); and assessment, service planning, advice, counselling, negotiation with others for service development, liaison with other professionals, statutory responsibilities, particularly in the fields of children and young people and mental health; this cluster of activities may all be undertaken by qualified social workers; however, some may not. Finally other professions, for example occupational therapists and education welfare officers, may also be employed in SSDs.

The term *social care* has become widely used but its meaning is imprecise: some use it to cover the full range of social welfare activities including direct care and social work while others use *social care* to define most of the work of SSDs which is not social work. I shall stick with *social welfare* and *social services* work to describe the overall activities and *direct care* and *social work* to distinguish the key tasks. The main focus of this chapter is on social work.

Increasingly social services work is undertaken outside SSDs, that is by voluntary and private organisations. This applies in particular to the provision of residential homes and increasingly various aspects of care to people in their own homes. Nearly all statutory social work is undertaken within SSDs although the National Society for the Prevention of Cruelty to Children (NSPCC) does undertake some statutory child care work in England.

After 1970 the welfare departments, which had largely unqualified staff, merged with children's and mental health departments which had larger numbers of qualified staff. Differing routes to qualification were brought together into a generic qualification for social work rather than the former specialist branches. Social work became the dominant occupational group in the new departments, and before long nearly all directors of the new organisations (known as departments of social service in England and departments of social work in Scotland) were social workers. In Northern Ireland social service work was placed under a combined Health and Welfare Board. Yet social work was only a small proportion of the total work of the new departments. Thus from their foundation direct care services existed alongside social work. The pattern is different from the other public sector services discussed in this book. Social work became the dominant profession in part because of the fact that by and large, social workers were the only qualified staff and the only workers with aspirations to be a profession.

Two main consequences followed from this situation. Firstly social workers established themselves as the high status profession and others who wanted such status trained as social workers. The title of a Central Council for Education and Training in Social Work (CCETSW 1973) working paper made just such a case for residential work: *Residential Work is a Part of Social Work*. Secondly social work itself has endeavoured to establish itself as a very new profession alongside others with whom it comes into contact: medical and nursing staff, teachers, police and the magistracy.

In the process social work has had to try to identify its nature as a profession with distinctive characteristics and skills. There are occasions when too much has been claimed in terms of authority, expertise and skills, and there have been attempts, as with other professions, to exclude non professionals from related activities. There are several significant points. The first is that the designation 'social worker' in general usage is not reserved for qualified staff. Many people claim for themselves or are viewed by others to be doing social work; sometimes the term is even used dismissively by police, teachers, medical or nursing staff: 'I seem to end up doing nothing but social work'. Thus the phrases 'social work' and 'social workers' are used both technically to describe a range of activities undertaken by qualified staff demanding certain values, knowledge and skills (CCETSW 1994) and as a loose term for activities which try to help people, perhaps listening to people's account of their circumstances.

Jordan writes: 'Social workers are trained to respond in difficult circumstances in ways which are not natural, to use human methods of resolving conflict or alleviating suffering; social workers do not possess high status and power - have to learn to work in unpromising situations, pay respect to people's values' (1987, pp. 207-8). He argues that social work should eschew the exclusive claims of other professions. Its task, in his terms, is to work in ways which are open, sharing knowledge with service users and even exposing the limitations of its own knowledge in ways which other professions would not allow. Social workers work with people who are marginalised and stigmatised - and it is inevitable that they in turn will be marginalised and stereotyped.

It is important to note that, given the comparatively recent bringing together of various activities under the banner of 'social work', there is a debate internal to social work as to task and skills. This debate differs from that in other professions which have a firmer hold on what is core activity and what are the professional boundaries. Social work remains uncertain as to its core. Is social work to include counselling; advocacy, welfare and information rights, assessment; community work and community development?

In summary of the first part of this chapter, we have reached a position where there is a recognition of the problems inherent in: defining the tasks to be undertaken by SSDs on behalf of society, determining the way in which provision should be made and deciding who is to provide the service. Looking further at the last of these, the key issue is not only whether a qualified worker is needed for certain activities (the lay-professional debate), but also what are the merits and costs to services being provided by volunteers, voluntary societies, probably with paid staff, privately owned or public sector organisations.

The criticisms of social services

The background is well rehearsed elsewhere but must be noted as a prelude to the argument to follow. In brief several themes have been running in parallel. I am listing criticisms made, not in any way evaluating or endorsing. Firstly uncertainty exists over the justification for SSD provision. Secondly the effectiveness of SSD provision is widely questioned and its failures recognised, whether shown by poor practice or workers abusing service users, in particular whether SSD provision has made people dependent? Thirdly social service professionals are said to get in the way of people receiving the services they want; this is a specific aspect of a wider theme about the arrogance or abuse of power by SSD staff, in particular social workers as service users have had too little choice. Fourthly it is argued that the state should leave people to manage their own lives. Fifthly public sector provided services, it is claimed, are costly and inefficient.

Comments, perhaps couched in different language, have come from all parts of the political spectrum. The solutions have been those of the Conservative government from 1979-97. We have yet to see how Labour in government will make a difference. Again briefly summarising a complex scenario, those on the left of the political spectrum had tended to counter the attacks on SSDs by defending what had been in existence. There was insufficient willingness to examine the concerns, for example about the quality of practice or the power of professions.

The Conservative solution

The Conservative government saw SSDs controlled by local government as a part of a challenge to central government. Its solutions were: to seek tighter control over the spending of local authorities, to move to greater specificity over what is to be done and how, and to limit the scope for SSDs to provide services directly.

The chosen organisational mechanism as in health was to attempt to mimic the market. The phrase needs a more precise definition than there is space for in this summary but is used as if it has a readily understood meaning. It has been a particular type of 'market' that is used as a model. In business and industry the Conservative government presumed that less external regulation and planning would lead to efficiency and competitive advantage. There must be substantial doubts as to whether this analysis is sound in relation to economics and industry. Hutton (1996 and 1997) is one of many critics of the analysis on the very grounds of efficiency, competition and growth which were the intent of reforms.

There seem to be two key assumptions on which the market analogy is based. Firstly the merits of competition are assumed to be increased efficiency, effective challenges to restrictive practices and greater value for money. Secondly individual service users, described as consumers or customers, are to have their powers enhanced to select services. The power of the professional is to be challenged by consumers choosing what they want. Building on these two assumptions various planks were put in place to ensure change. Many services were put out to compulsory competitive tendering. In SSDs restrictions were placed on the use of specified parts of the community care funding: eighty-five per cent was to be used to purchase services from voluntary and private providers. Individuals were to be informed of their rights and provided with procedures as to how to complain.

The market talk filtered down to systems for management and organisation: particular styles of management were presumed to be efficient in the public sector, styles which were challenged by new wave management theorists in industry. Staff, it was assumed, were unwilling to be managed. The answer was to be found in a more directive style of management which assumed that the key motivation for workers is money and that people will not work in line with organisational demands unless tasks are specified in detail and workers are closely supervised. 'Managers must be allowed to manage' rings the rhetoric.

It is worth noting that the professions which have been most attacked by government have been those which have claimed the competence, perhaps exclusive competence, of the professional to assess and work with individuals. Those professions whose skills have been seen as technical and furthering the ends of governments seeking greater control over the public sector, such as accounting, have gained new territory.

My argument is that the market model and its mechanisms are not appropriate for social services. Potential welfare users may be vulnerable and dependent, perhaps in crisis, at times when they are being asked or required to act as rational entrepreneurs. Their choices, and their capacity to choose, are limited. Further quasi or social markets cannot be allowed to expand when people value the service and want more of it.

The incoherence at the heart of social service activity

The amount and rapidity of governmental and organisational change, together with the fact that they have not been tested or piloted but have been imposed, have had significant consequences for SSDs. Harding (1992, p. 13) contends that 'change should be slow and evaluated'. It requires an 'active leadership' and a 'learning organisation'. I have argued the same elsewhere (Hadley and Clough 1996, pp. 198-205). With Roger Hadley I have summarised the pre-1990 criticisms of practice as tendencies for:

a   professionals to impose their view of what people needed and the services that should be offered;

b   users to be slotted into existing services, rather than services to be developed in response to their needs;

c   the availability of funds to direct where both users and workers looked for solutions to problems.

If we examine those three elements in 1995, the emerging evidence from our own and others' studies suggests:

a   there has been significant reduction in the authority, status and control of professionals;

b   there is limited evidence of new services being developed;

c   funding systems continue to dominate the provision of services (Clough and Hadley 1996).

Further Harding (1992) analyses the effects of change on SSDs at that time. She claims that there has been 'the destabilisation of an entire service' (p.4) and that there has been 'a tendency to consider costs in terms of economy and efficiency, not effectiveness' (p.5). There has been a move in the personal social services 'to central direction, from being locally governed to locally administered' though she recognises the requirement to work out locally what is wanted. She notes the interrelationship of services with the inadequacies of one affecting demand on another.

Three key points follow in Harding's review. Firstly bureaucracies defend themselves by systematising and regulating activity such as the assessment of clients. Assessment by its very nature needs to remain personal and human and not lose its soul in a jungle of procedures and checklists (p.11). Secondly she argues that the targeting of services creates a smaller and marginalised band of service users, preventative work has also been cut back and the tendency under pressure is to ration rather than innovate. Thirdly there are the effects on staff. In summary she argues:

> Major changes in policy are making heavy demands on staff. Changes in services, (cutbacks, changing priorities) along with increased demand (homelessness, early discharge from hospital, unemployment, changing aspirations of service users) mean front line staff and managers are under constant stress as they face the public. There are departmental reorganisations. There are real tensions between professional and managerial cultures within departments, the two having different concepts of accountability. Skills are no longer valued ... . (1992, p.12)

Perhaps most significant is the effect on staff. I contend that to work well with people who may be disturbed, vulnerable or confused, staff themselves must have a firm hold on the purpose and value of their work. The evidence that staff are despondent and disillusioned is persuasive. In the main this is based on small studies but they ring true to the experience of many workers. At the root is a combination of frequent changes to systems and practice, work pressures and a management style which is based on distrust.

The implications for staff are borne out in the study already quoted (Hadley and Clough 1996, pp. 163-83). Interviewees noted the following points:

> The work environment is *incoherent*. There is little or no sense of direction within agencies: this affects all participants - local politicians; senior management; middle management; front line workers; relationships between statutory agencies and with voluntary and private sectors; relationships between aspects of different policies. And in turn this influences relationships between users and staff.

There is an over-riding management and political interest in *survival*, shown in a defensive style where what matters is presentation, not quality, of information; in deed, there is increasing mistrust of information and statistics.

At the heart of the current work environment is pervasive mistrust. ... In the main, [staff] no longer feel trusted to get on with their work and are themselves increasingly mistrustful of the intentions of their managers.

The objective of giving users in the system more power is fatally weakened by the unwillingness to examine or acknowledge the service deficit. Users are not given a straightforward assessment: it is hedged by what the organisation may be able to provide and by considerations of the liability of the organisation.

Thus a significant change for staff has occurred in their understanding of the nature of their accountability: accountability to whom? for what? The notion of accountability to professional ethics has been threatened. For our interviewees at least, previously the ultimate test of theirs and others' actions was the congruence of actions with their ethics, at the heart of which lay the well being of the user. At best, those working in the public sector, now are confused; at worst, they have been informed that their primary loyalty is to the organisation and that in undertaking their work they must first take account of how the matter will be viewed by the nebulous organisation.

There are many staff who are ill at ease with the way in which they are required to undertake their work. ... The dominant picture is of workers and managers alienated from their work environment, from the requirements of the organisation, from the systems that are imposed to achieve those requirements and from the way in which they are expected to carry out their work with users. They do not understand the worlds in which they have to operate nor even their own parts in them. Not surprisingly, workers are not free to give of their best in the sense of being able to be creative and flexible. Indeed, as a result of the changes they are unwilling to use initiative.

The shrinking base of social work

In the 1980s and 1990s the power and authority of social workers, as of many other professional groups, have been challenged. There are clear trends towards loss of authority, status and autonomy.

There is uncertainty. What is the professional base, the identity and the training needs for those working in direct care? Earlier I made the point that the qualification recognised for residential work has been the same as that for field social workers, the Diploma in Social Work. Yet few residential workers are qualified. I am one of an increasing number of people who now argue that training for residential work is not best placed within social work: it has not led to many staff working in residential homes being qualified and the training has not been sufficiently related to the work undertaken (Clough, forthcoming).

There has also been a debate as to whether probation officers should be trained as social workers. The Conservative government in 1996 decided that a social work qualification was no longer to be recognised as the appropriate qualification for probation officers though there are still discussions as to what is to be the appropriate training. Probation officers have been as alarmed at the downgrading in academic terms of the prospective qualification as they have been over the split from social work.

From the earlier description of social work it will be apparent that it is a somewhat ill defined activity. Indeed social work could be defined almost by stating that it was what social workers did. The splitting of functions has allowed a review of the territory. The question changes from: 'Is this cluster of activities best undertaken by a social worker?' to 'Which of these tasks is best performed by a social worker?'

It is difficult at this stage to gauge the extent of change. The separation into purchaser and provider has meant that a substantial amount of direct care work is now provided by the private and voluntary sectors rather than the local authority SSD. However most of this work was not in any case undertaken by social workers, so this in itself has changed SSD but not social work activity.

Many professionals argue that they can no longer do the job in the way that they were trained and as they understood it. This is true for social workers, in particular those working with adults. Social work with children and young people, and with adults who have mental health problems, has had higher status than work with older people and those with learning disabilities. A significant development following the generic training for field social workers has been the recognition of the complexity of work with older people who may face complex changes in ability and role, loss and, for surprisingly large numbers of people, depression (Rowlings 1981, Clough 1981, Marshall 1990, Hugman 1994).

In most SSDs work with adults, and in some work with children, has been split into purchaser and provider branches. In the main social workers are placed with purchasers. The social work role is seen as that of assessment, working out a cluster of appropriate services known as a care package and monitoring the effectiveness of the care provided. Some SSDs have acknowledged that one of the services which might need to be provided is social work, in the sense of counselling, but the views of many staff are that older people in particular are being treated once again predominantly as if they have only practical problems, not ones that potentially are as complex as those of any one else.

Some SSDs are appointing non qualified staff to undertake assessments for community care services, perhaps using qualified staff for complex work. Again some SSDs are using non qualified staff to undertake part of the monitoring work. The territory of the qualified social worker is no longer clearly defined.

It is easy to present the debate in absolute terms, for example that formerly social workers undertook assessments and that now in some SSDs these are undertaken by non qualified staff. The reality is far more complex. The task of assessment never was a once-and-for-all activity by one person. Others such as reception staff have always been involved in determining whether someone should be calling on health or social security rather than the SSD.

So there is a move towards reducing rather than enlarging the scope of the activity called social work. One of the clear trends over the last 25 years has been a dramatic increase in the proportion of social work staff who are qualified, rising to above ninety per cent in 1997 (Boateng 1997). We know too that Department of Health repeats year on year that an insufficient number of social workers are being trained to meet the demand and further that 90 per cent of students who qualify for the Diploma in Social Work get jobs within six months. What we do not know is the number of social work qualified students who are taking jobs in social services work but in posts which were not designated for Diploma in Social Work qualified staff, nor indeed the number of posts in the UK which are designated as social work posts. The probability is that newly qualified students are a marketable commodity, but that the total number of social work posts is reducing year on year.

The boundary of social work is being redrawn. In addition I argue that social workers are less autonomous and have reduced authority. The managerialist style referred to earlier, which has developed in many SSDs, has imposed specification not only of what is to be recorded on forms but of ways of working. This impinges on the freedom of staff to work as they think best. In 1971 King, Raynes and Tizard in a study of children's residential units linked to mental handicap hospitals (as then described) argued that in those units where staff had more authority for the purchasing of goods, setting the staff rota and establishing the routines within the home, children had more control of their lives.

Twenty five years later a 'nurse-manager' described a move to work in an SSD to set up houses for people with learning disabilities. Initially the finance and administrative staff had been willing to work with him to set up systems that he deemed appropriate:

> The promising start was not to endure. It was followed by a reorganization which basically wiped out all that we'd done. New administrative systems were imposed, managed from a town which was far more remote, and negotiations were with someone far more senior who had been a personnel manager in industry.

> Locally we had an ethos based on 'Trust your staff and they'll do their job'. I think we were thought of as really naive. Several practices that I thought of as good practice, they thought of as wishy-washy with the staff taking us for a ride. (Hadley and Clough 1996, p.108)

One aspect of the former system had been that staff ate their meals with residents, and got their meals free. The idea was that this was a better way of supervising than staff hovering around and that it would be a more homely atmosphere. The management insisted staff should not get free meals. Not surprisingly staff took their formal meal breaks, did not eat with the residents and there was a return to the former supervisory practices.

The most marked formal intrusion into the field of social workers has been in the case of probation officer training. Once probation officers were no longer trained as social workers, it was made clear that they had to focus their work on the reduction of offending behaviour; notions of helping probationers manage their social circumstances or dealing with personal problems were to be excluded from the work unless it could be argued that they contributed to a reduction in offending behaviour. Even in work in probation hostels staff talk about having to define the work in terms of 'reduction in offending behaviour' not the very obvious housing and care components of providing a residential base.

The formal, statutory authority of social workers, in particular in child care and mental health, has not been reduced. In both areas social workers have maintained their significant powers in relation to the lives of others. In our recent study of workers and managers in community care, several people described the difference in expectations placed on staff (Hadley and Clough 1996). Staff feel less sure of their professional authority and accountability. Previously, however nebulously, many people thought of their overriding loyalty as being to a professional ethos. Now they also have to take into consideration expectations that they should be good employees. One staff member described to me what this meant: 'When undertaking assessments for community care we are expected to take account of what money the department has available in setting out what are a person's needs.' 'Loyalty' comes to mean 'being helpful to the organisation'. The position is further complicated by the tension in Department of Health guidance and judicial interpretation of that guidance. At present it is not clear whether authorities have a duty to provide services once an individual has been assessed as needing them.

I want to draw out from this example of community care one further subtle, indeed insidious, change. One of the planks of the separation of purchasing from providing functions has been that staff at local level should be given increased responsibility for the management of the budget, which could be seen as an increase in delegated responsibility. In fact passing down to face workers and first line managers responsibility for budget management in times of pressure on resourcing may be simply passing the authority, and with it the stress and the blame, but give little in the way of power.

Controlling access to the profession

The Central Council for Education and Training in Social Work (CCETSW) is the body authorised by statute to oversee the training of social workers. It has responsibility for the oversight of the qualifying award (the Diploma in Social Work) and for approving consortia to run the qualifying programmes and so controls the shape of the training for qualified workers. It is also involved in the development of Scottish/National Vocational Qualifications (S/NVQ) which are the tests of competence being developed for different levels of staff in social service work. Thus the requirements for qualification and the approval of courses providing entry to qualified social work are controlled by an organisation accountable to government, not by the profession itself through a professional association.

CCETSW is not expected to enter the sort of debates discussed above as to which posts in an organisation should be for qualified social workers: that, it would be argued, is for employers to determine. There is no equivalent of a national association for doctors or nurses which represents the interests of its members to ensure that all such activities are undertaken by qualified staff. The British Association of Social Workers (BASW) is a professional association which represents its members. There is no obligation on social workers to be members and, in spite of more or less vigorous attempts at different times to represent the interests of qualified social work, it has had comparatively little influence.

One proposal has been floated to set up a system to register staff. Known as the General Social Services Council (GSSC) the function of this body would be to keep a register of all staff employed in social care. The Labour government is considering whether to adopt the proposal. If approved the probability is that the Council would start with the registration of senior staff and proceed to other staff at a later date. The GSSC would be an independent statutory body with a primary task to protect the public who use social services, and it would publish and enforce standards. It would be self financing, having to collect money for its operation either from employers or from individual staff. Brand (1997) notes: 'Individual staff will be personally accountable for their own conduct and practice; but employers will be involved in the process of setting the standards, and will be expected to support their staff in complying with them.'

The GSSC would hold the list of registered staff and therefore, very powerfully, be able to strike a person from the list. The terms of reference are likely to include staff working in the areas of social care and social work. Such a register would have oversight of individual staff. However it would have no influence over which tasks should be undertaken by which staff.

It should be borne in mind that for the vast majority of staff working in social services work there is no requirement to have any training. To occupy a post designated by an employer as one for a qualified social worker an appointee needs a Diploma in Social Work or equivalent. For all other posts, for example in home care or residential care with adults, no training is required.

Whither social services work?

The structures under which social services work is provided have shifted significantly. The Conservative government both encouraged and required a shift in the provision of services away from the local authority to the private and voluntary sectors. Labour has yet to set out its strategy for social services.

SSDs maintain their responsibility predominantly to assess the need for services in their area and to plan with others (voluntary bodies, health authorities, education, private sector) a broad strategy for service planning and development. This is the policy core, described by Laffin in chapter 1. To a large extent there has been a move to devolved service delivery.

However SSDs also have a responsibility for assessing the needs and wants of individuals, and for working out with service users the cluster of services to meet needs, in community care described as a care package. This is 'disputed territory' (Clough 1996) in that much guidance put out by SSDs would suggest that the process is one of negotiation of services needed between services user and social worker. While such negotiation may well, and certainly should, be integral to the tasks of assessment and provision I contend that the social worker maintains the authority to exercise judgement, which frequently is glossed over.

Having determined which services are to be provided, the SSD has responsibility for monitoring the impact of the services. It is at the next stage in the process, the production of the services, that there has been a substantial shift in SSD activity. Thus it may be helpful to analyse social welfare activities in a different way as follows:

1   Policy development

2   Policy review: reviewing complaints; regulation

3   Individual assessment for service eligibility and service planning; monitoring of effectiveness of services for the individual

4   Purchasing of services from others: setting contracts, monitoring

5   Provision of services: a) statutory social work; b) non statutory social work; direct care.

Consequences of changes

It is too early to do more than highlight trends. Firstly those in policy development and senior management in SSDs are not necessarily social work qualified. There have been two trends in recent years relating to senior management. One has been to create different groupings of departments within a local authority so that, for example, some local authorities are combining social work and housing in one department. There has to be a named individual responsible for social service work but that person does not have to be a qualified social worker. The other trend has been towards a growing number of appointments of non social work qualified staff, and indeed staff with no experience of social services work, to posts of director and assistant director. There is no accurate, current information on the background of all senior staff in SSDs in the UK.

Secondly there remains an ambiguity about people's entitlements to services. Given that it is a 'person in his/her social setting' which is being assessed, it is not surprising that there is a lack of precision and consistency. The problem for service users is that they still have no measure of whether they have been assessed as eligible for a service. In child care it is common for much work to be described as 'preventative' and for the SSD to state that it is unable to undertake such work. In community care the focus of services on those in greatest need may mean that early intervention for users and carers may not be feasible, even though we know that one of the key factors in helping carers to maintain their work is early support (Levin et al. 1994).

Thirdly in community care the formal powers for negotiating about services have been passed largely to purchasers of services, that is other SSD staff, not to individuals themselves. The system and the model on which it is based varies little whatever the capacity of the service user.

Fourthly there is abundant evidence that people find it difficult to negotiate with those providing services to have the service provided in the way they want. Even when going to a hotel or restaurant people are more likely to exercise their consumer power by not going back to a place we dislike than putting their case for better service. It is more difficult to negotiate when they are more dependent on the service provision for their basic welfare and when they feel less confident. Technically the service user may move from a residential home or find a different home carer. However making such a change is complex - it is uncertain whether there are other places - difficult and emotionally costly.

Fifthly it is no longer clear what is the core domain of social work. Social work has exclusive control on categories 5a and 5b above, the statutory and non statutory social work, and plays a major but not exclusive part in policy development, review, purchase and individual assessment.

Sixthly we have no sound evidence on the impact of community care legislation and guidance. Research has tended to examine the extent to which various policy intents appear to have been realised, for example whether or not users are empowered. Little has been done to chart what actually happens and what service users and carers think about this. I would expect it to be the case that users do have substantially greater choice in service provision if they are selected as eligible for a service.

Regulation

Regulation raises many of the central debates about service provision: control of standard setting; consistent yet flexible implementation; judgement of risk; authority to take action.

Residential homes, that is places defined as providing residential care, for children and adults are subject to registration and inspection; the same applies to day services for children under five (childminders, play groups, day nurseries, and play groups and activities). The authority of regulation is found in the Registered Homes Act 1984, the Children Act 1989 and the National Health Service and Community Care Act 1990. Regulation is the responsibility of local authorities and nearly all have placed this with the SSD. There are moves to transfer this to the Chief Executive of the authority on the basis that this would separate further those regulating from those in the SSD purchasing and providing service.

Residential schools are subject to inspection but not registration from the local authority inspection unit but at less frequent intervals. Nursing homes are regulated by health authorities. Direct care for people in their own homes is not yet subject to external regulation.

The Conservative government vacillated in its attitudes towards regulation. Initially reluctant to give local authorities and SSDs the responsibility, the government decided that it would be more efficient to use the existing structures of the local authority rather than create new ones. More recently, under pressure from providers, there have been comments about a lighter touch and placing them outside local authorities. Interestingly providers in the main want regulation. Their concerns are to be assured that all sectors are treated the same and to achieve consistency (not subject to changing demands as inspectors produce new standards).

Conclusion - future scenarios

The debate is not just about alternative groupings of particular functions but whether the Seebohm dream of a generic service for all will be changed. There are five central questions: should work with different groups of users be split into specialisms? should any such re-organisation involve re-groupings with other departments or agencies (for example a child care service to include social services child care work and education *or* adult community care to be passed to health authorities)? what is to be the territory of qualified social work? what training is there to be for staff in direct care? which body is to control regulation?

Many of these questions concern organisational shape. I want to conclude by focusing on the function of social workers. This book, and this chapter, examine the changing nature of professionalism within changing organisations. Of course change, in the words of glib management gurus, can pose opportunities as well as threats. The test in social service provision is whether users and potentials users of services are getting a better deal.

My concern is less about the future of an activity that currently is called social work than about the function that at its best it fulfilled. Social work has contributed an immense amount to an understanding of the structural, social and psychological dimension of what otherwise are defined as medical, educational or personal problems: people's circumstances affect their lives and their responses. I have no doubt that at times some people will want others with the skills which were inherent in social work to help them find or recover their own coping strategies. Nor have I any doubt of the need for people to make judgements about others' circumstances, whether for assessment for community care, child care competence or state of mental health. There is a danger that not only will the profession of social work be diminished but with it the functions which it fulfilled in and for citizens.

References

Boateng, P. (1997), Speech at CCETSW 's twenty fifth jubilee.

Brand, D. (1997), *General Social Services*, CCETSW: London.

CCETSW (1973), *Residential Work is a Part of Social Work*, Central Council for Education and Training in Social Work: London.

CCETSW (1994) *Rules and Requirements for the Diploma in Social Work*, CCETSW: London.

Cheetham, J. et al. (1992), *Evaluating Social Work Effectiveness*, Oxford University Press: Oxford.

Clough, R. (1981), *Old Age Homes*, Allen and Unwin: London.

Clough, R. (1996), *Assessment in Community Care: Disputed Territory*, unpublished research paper.

Clough, R. (forthcoming), NISW: London.

Hadley, R. and Clough, R. (1996), *Care in Chaos: Frustration and Challenge in Community Care*, Cassell: London.

Harding, T. (1992), *Who Owns Welfare*, Social Services Policy Forum Paper No. 2, National Institute for Social Work: London.

Hugman, R. (1994), *Ageing and the Care of Older People in Europe*, Macmillan: London.

Hutton, W. (1996), *The State We're In*, Vintage: London.

Hutton, W. (1997), *The State To Come*, Vintage: London.

Jordan, B. (1987), *Rethinking Welfare*, Blackwell: London.

King, R., Raynes, N. and Tizard, J. (1971), *Patterns of Residential Care*, Routledge and Kegan Paul: London.

Levin, E. et al. (1994), *Better for the Break*, HMSO: London.

Marshall, M. (1990), *Social Work with Older People*, Macmillan: London.

Pollitt, C. (1993), *Managerialism and the Public Services. Cuts or Cultural Change in the 1990s?*, Blackwell: Oxford.

Rowlings, C. (1991), *Social Work with Elderly People*, London: Allen and Unwin.

7 Social housing management

Richard Walker

The extent to which social housing organisations have moved away from bureaucratic forms of organisation and control will be explored in this chapter. A range of predominately government-led reforms have brought market mechanisms and networks into social housing though hierarchical forms of organisation and control remain prominent through housing association and local authority provision and management. In many senses this is to be expected as it takes substantial time for new organisational paradigms to be established.

Although the focus of this chapter is social housing and its professional body, the Chartered Institute of Housing (CIH), the range of occupational and professional groups that work within the social housing sector is large. However as the owner occupied sector has become the dominant tenure, in part through the transfer of public sector stock through the Right to Buy, most people's contact with the housing profession now comes through estate agency, surveying and the legal profession. Within social housing tenants will be in contact with housing officers and, in more recent times, with a range of other occupations and professions including community development, local economic development, social services and social workers, the police and planners who play a role in the provision of services. Cross occupational working is historically established within housing, for example with environmental health, though it has increased in extent over recent years. Increased diversity, delegation and devolution in the social rented sector also means that whilst in the past when the majority of provision was through local authorities the range of actors has now increased to include housing associations, tenant-led organisations, various government agencies, voluntary organisations and the private sector. This complex milieu of organisational and occupational group interaction within social housing has created historical problems over the boundaries of housing management - a debate which has been given renewed importance through processes of rationalisation and the role given to social housing organisation in the discharge of community care responsibilities. Of interest is the peculiar British nature of these issues. For example within Europe housing management services are clearly defined as property based or facilities management and no social housing profession exists.

Though many aspects of these changes relate to social and economic restructuring, government policy and reform programmes have had a substantial impact on the social housing sector through the introduction of market-led systems and the associated networks they have spored. However, although central-local government conflict typified housing under the Conservative administrations of the 1980s and 1990s, social housing organisations have themselves developed new responses to the changed environment such as opting out. The Institute has also found a new voice and policy role and has been instrumental in the promotion of local housing companies. Housing organisations and housing staff have also championed new ways of working and organisation including decentralisation and 'housing plus'.

To interpret this milieu and understand the extent to which housing has moved towards post-bureaucratic forms of organisation and control and to address the specific questions of this book, this chapter examines three eras of social housing and its professionalisation. Firstly the historical form of organisation and control in social housing and the role and development of the profession. Secondly the Conservative government's rationalisation of the sector, increased control over stock and management and the growth of the social housing profession during a period of hostility. Thirdly the reform process from the late 1980s onwards which is leading to new forms of organisation and production. Within this section the development of the housing association sector and the variety of opt out housing organisations is explored in more detail. Within this framework attention is paid to the actions of government and professional bodies at the national level, individual organisations at the institutional and of individual housing staff at the practice level. Conclusions indicate that the interaction of government, organisations and individuals has left the housing profession and the nature and form of the housing organisations facing an uncertain future.

The bureaucratic organisation of housing management and the emergence of the housing profession

Social housing has historically been based around bureaucratic forms of organisation and control. The traditional providers of social housing, local authorities, were hierarchically organised. Control was exercised from the centre by mechanistic and standardised co-ordination with formal procedures or, if not formally written procedures, formal rules of behaviour, and impersonal regulation and objectivity. In essence they were typified by a process of administration rather than management. Officers had little freedom in decision-making and needed to refer problem solution up the hierarchy to senior officers and to members. Indeed examples of members making detailed decisions in relation to the allocation of homes continues, though such practices have been restricted in the 1996 Housing Act. Many of these organisations were of substantial size, particularly after the reorganisation of local government in 1974 which increased the size of housing departments by ten fold and led to the creation of some organisation which managed over 100,000 homes.

Many local government departments were highly professionalised leading to a conflict between bureaucratic and professional forms of control in local government. However the professionalisation of housing has been slow and recent indicating the ascendance of bureaucratic forms of control - centralisation, formalisation, specialisation, hierarchies of legitimated authority - as against professional control - self-regulation, collegiality, credentialism and semi-autonomy. Indeed bureaucratic forms of control have been promoted and adopted over professional forms of control through the historical domination of housing by other professions

The ascendancy of bureaucracy can, in part, be explained by the contested nature of housing management (Franklin and Clapham 1997, Franklin, forthcoming) which can be traced back to the last century. The first model developed out of the state's initial regulation and intervention in the housing market, leading to the provision of the first council housing in the 1880s, and the dominant property based and profitable management of properties seen in the private rented sector and the model dwelling companies. Though a model which has subsequently predominated during this period an alternative model of housing management emerged. This model was associated with the social reform movement and with Octavia Hill, often attributed to be the founder of housing management (Clapham 1992). Hill promoted a highly welfare interventionist form of housing management combining property management and social work, though one which was paternalistic and was associated with improving the moral standards of working class households.

These two approaches to housing management found their formal expression in two professional bodies within housing - The Society of Women Housing Estate Managers registered in 1932 and The Institute of Municipal Estate Managers (IMEM) registered in 1938. The Society of Women Housing Estate Managers (created by the amalgamation of a number of women's housing organisations, including the Association of Women Housing Workers formed in 1916), argued for an interventionist, welfare focussed and small scale approach. Building on the ethos of Octavia Hill they believed in the role of education and training and drew membership from largely middle class graduates. Their work was in a range of organisations including societies, trusts, the private sector and on a limited scale in the public sector. The origins of the profession are then outside the public sector, concerned not with the aims of regulating public servants and addressing issues of corruption, but from the voluntary sector where concerns were centred rather around social reform and moral improvement.

The Institute of Municipal Estate Managers philosophy developed out of the technical, functional, public health and financial approach. This reflected the background of predominately male local government officers drawn from a broader social spectrum, who typically had functions beyond housing. Thus housing was built and maintained by the engineer's department, designed by the architects, financed by the treasurers and administered by the town clerk. This situation led to housing decisions being taken at the top of other departments. The Institute's philosophy was to separate rent and social welfare functions, seeing their role as necessarily being in different departments. Training focused on the technical functions and did not involve supervised placements as in the case of the Society. Despite conflicting approaches the development of these two bodies indicated that by the end of the 1930s there was an emerging will to create a profession centred around housing management.

These two approaches have ebbed and waned over time reflecting in part the prevailing ideology towards housing, public or private, and prevalent circumstances. For example the welfare approach reasserted itself during the process of rehousing slum dwelling occupants during the 1930s and again during the 1980s and 1990s which have seen the residualisation and marginalisation of the public housing sector. However the two approaches remain in tension as the sector is subject to new business pressures involving a stress on 'core business' and property or asset management. The administrative and property based approach promoted by the IMEM gained ascendancy following the substantial housing shortages created by World War Two and the subsequent population growth. In 1965 the Institute of Housing was created from a merger between the two competing professional bodies. The IMEM dominated, though it exerted little influence on housing work and policy while training and education remained concentrated within the Institute drawing on experienced housing officers to educate the less experienced with a techno-bureaucratic emphasis on skills development rather than education and specialist knowledge.

Alongside these conflicting housing management philosophies local authorities were historically given limited advice through their professional associations, from other agencies on the organisation and functioning of housing management services, on what constituted either effective or efficient structures or policies; while legislation set down only limited statutory requirements, such as to maintain a waiting list or assess housing needs. This left the organisation of the sector to the range of professional actors involved. One can suggest that though at its height local authority housing management was looking after a third of the UK population, 6.5 million homes, the ways in which it was organised were until recently the product of local circumstance and very rudimentary exchanges on best practice as the profession did not work to effectively promote itself (Walker and Williams 1995).

Central government did take some interest and offer advice to the emerging housing profession. For example the 1938 Central Housing Advisory Committee inquiry into the running of municipal housing estates in the context of rehousing former slum dwellers heard arguments from the two societies for their respective approaches, accepting the need for social work functions but not seeing the necessity for staff to have this training (CHAC 1938). In 1959 CHAC also called for greater decentralisation to develop cost accounting and uniform accounts and an increased property focus (CHAC 1959). Issues of housing management and organisation only received more sustained and systematic interest from government, professionals and academic circles once the local authority housing departments' role as developers of new homes declined, though substantial questions still exist about the most efficient and effective ways to organise and manage social housing (Walker and Williams 1995, Williams 1997). A lack of guidance on how to control and organise housing work can also be attributed to the view of housing work as mundane administration associated with the collection of rents and the allocation of homes.

When more substantial advice came it was from outside the housing profession. The Cullingworth Report (CHAC 1969) argued for comprehensive housing departments to co-ordinate and plan services as part of the corporate management fad. In the period following the 1974 reorganisation of local government, this model was promoted alongside the social housing management role to act as a counterweight to the technical professions' domination of council housing which was seen as leading to a range of management problems, most notably 'difficult-to-let' estates (Laffin 1986).

However such advice was not uniformly adopted even following the reorganisation of local authorities in Wales in 1996. More recently some local authorities and professionals have rejected the idea of comprehensive housing services in response to compulsory competitive tendering. Instead they have broken up housing departments to meet the basic criteria based on housing activity within the housing department, once again fragmenting the profession and recreating it as a ragbag of functions. Thus it is possible to suggest that the range of arguments presented to create comprehensive housing departments worked against the historic professional organisation of local authority housing services around the more established professional areas such as engineering and law and has now become the norm (Walker and Williams 1995). Alternatively it indicates the dominance of other professions and their ability to stop a unified housing service and housing profession from emerging with the specific aim of resolving housing problems (Proven and Williams 1991).

The lack of guidance or strong professional (housing) control with different professions exerting control over housing management led to a variety of organisational forms within local authorities, most notably the coordination of housing activity across a range of departments. This raised issues about interdepartmental working, communication and responsiveness (Walker and Williams 1995) and to relatively limited innovation which was primarily centred around differing approaches to housing management. The lack of a strong profession, and a sector based around responding to immediate needs and pressures, such as the numbers of homes built, resulted in very limited planning. Although the introduction of Housing Investment Plans in the late 1970s did lead to better quality planning and strategy. However this legacy left the sector ill prepared for the rationalisation reform programme which was initiated by the late 1970s Labour government but which took hold under the Conservative (Williams 1997). This can partly be attributed towards the historical lack of training and education within the sector - skills and knowledge were not specialist and could be codified and learnt through communication - leading housing officers to be blamed for all the ills of local authority housing (Proven and Williams 1991).

Consequently by the early 1980s the local authority housing sector was typified by a bureaucratic form of organisation. Large, and in some cases very large, housing departments managed and provided new homes through direct control to around a third of the British population without substantial central government or professional housing intervention. However an early strand of consumerism was seen in the 1980 Housing Act which introduced the Tenants' Charter which primarily standardised tenancies on common legal footing but also provided for a range of rights. The longer term impact of the Charter has been to allow tenants to shape aspects of housing management through their rights to consultation and involvement.

At this time alternative forms of social housing provision were insignificant with housing associations playing a relatively minor role. Local authorities did work in partnership with housing associations which built homes for specialist groups of people often with local government finance, and housed people from local authority waiting lists. Local authorities also worked in partnership with builders, owner occupiers and private landlords to improve and provide housing whilst market forms of organisation have also played an important role in housing provision (Reid 1995).

Privatisation, rationalisation and the emergence of the housing profession

The bureaucratic model of directly co-ordinating, controlling and managing capital and revenue services was eroded during the 1980s. Central government control over stock was seen to be increased through the Right to Buy policy, the introduction of low cost home ownership activities to housing associations, while central government support and finance was reduced. More substantial changes in organisational form and control did not occur until the late 1980s. These changes resulted from government reform and a questioning of the nature, purpose and form of housing organisations and housing management which has led to greater central government control over housing management. Such changes galvanised the development of the profession and its training and education programmes and simultaneously upgraded the skills and knowledge of housing staff, giving them the capacity to manage and introduce change within the sector, becoming what Ackroyd (1996) calls a 'new model' profession. Franklin (forthcoming) notes that it is ironic that since 1979:

> ... the Institute has emerged with a more powerful identity, has become more adroit and influential in addressing policy issues, and has established a professional qualification. It is as if, having recognised what could be the writing on the wall, the Institute has galvanised itself into action on behalf of those it represents, hoping perhaps to salvage both purpose and some sense of dignity for its members.

Notably the profession has not sought closure in the labour market. Despite an increasing expectation that housing officers should be qualified, only 12,000 of an estimated 100,000 plus people working in social housing belong to the professional Institute. To expand its membership the Institute has started to develop occupational self-organisation and informal organisation through the promotion of standards and good practice to develop common cultures, knowledge and ways of working.

The contemporary process of public sector reform really originated in the mid 1970s when the then Labour government introduced an austerity programme in response to economic crisis. New policies also emerged then such as the Right to Buy, then introduced by some Conservative local authorities, and small scale decentralisation through the Priority Estates Project (PEP), part of the government sponsored recreation of housing management. After 1979 the Thatcher government's popularist support for home ownership was most clearly expressed through the Right to Buy which partly contributed to its success in the 1979 and 1983 elections. Indeed this ideological support for home ownership was the cornerstone of Conservative government housing policy aimed at creating a 'property owning democracy' and shifting responsibility to individuals for their housing provision, though supported by state subsidies. This in turn led to a strongly anti-municipal housing standpoint.

However the implementation of the Right to Buy was not smooth and formed the basis of continuing central-local government conflict during their term in office. It was opposed in many areas, on principle or on the grounds of outstanding needs (see the case of Norwich in Malpass and Murie 1994) and subsequent legislation was introduced to overcome problems whilst increasing discounts. Even so some housing officers felt that it would enhance their social welfare role and hence their standing. The Right to Buy has led to the sale of 1.7 million homes substantially reducing the size of the sector and leading to its residualisation and marginalisation (Forrest and Murie 1991). A variety of policy initiatives continue today which either sell homes to sitting tenants or offer reduced entry costs in to the home ownership market.

Tenure restructuring has led to fundamental changes in the social composition of households within the sector - seventy-two per cent of local authority and housing association households are now economically inactive and the proportion of local authority and housing association tenants in full-time work fell from about forty-six per cent in 1981 to twenty-one per cent in 1994/95. In addition central government control has been extended to financial resources. This extension has led to substantial reductions within the housing sector and increasingly stringent rules on revenue funding and capital funding, notably the limited reuse of capital receipts from the Right to Buy.

Consequently social housing now houses the poorest and neediest members of society. The concentration of deprivation in housing estates has renewed the debate about the nature of housing management. Government pressures during the 1990s, for example compulsory competitive tendering or efficiency drives, put pressure on housing management to be focused around a bricks and mortar administrative approach. Simultaneously welfare approaches to housing management have gained increased importance as social landlords have had to respond to an increasingly deprived tenant population by adopting decentralisation and tenant participation strategies. Furthermore the Institute has turned full circle and now argues for a welfare based housing management approach in response to changing circumstances amongst tenants and initially as a strategy by the profession to counteract the Conservative government's hostility (Franklin and Clapham 1997).

This process of privatisation has led to a welfare dependent tenantry and a tenure of last resort. It has been imposed on a weak housing profession whose members were unable to defend their position and has reduced the professional standing of the occupation. The NHS and education system may be unrecognisable compared to what they were like twenty years ago, but the NHS is still free at the point of delivery and state schools still educate the mass of children, though some people have chosen to opt of this system. However social housing is now for those who cannot compete in the market place for housing and in the majority of cases even for employment.

Alongside tenure restructuring and rationalisation processes government control has extended to housing organisations. Questions were asked about the nature and effectiveness of housing management services in the mid 1980s with the primary aim of reducing the costs of the sector (Audit Commission 1986, Maclennan et al. 1989). These concerns stemmed from the government's desire to understand better performance within the sector and built on criticism that local authorities are necessarily bad and inferior managers (Coleman 1985) or that they are too large to be effective (Power 1987, Clapham 1989). Although the outcome of this research has been to emphasis continually efficiency and effectiveness within the sector (Walker, forthcoming) and to provide performance information to tenants (Walker and Symon 1995), research findings have not been conclusive in indicating that one form of organisation and management of housing is more effective than another (Maclennan et al. 1989, Bines et al. 1993). This is in part a product of the complexity of the task. Performance is dependent upon local policy and practice and tenant population, while the condition of the housing stock is often be the product of historical circumstance. In particular the environments in which social housing landlords work result in wide differences in performance. For example urban local authorities have the worst performance scores but the highest levels of tenant involvement (Bines et al. 1993). And the difficulties associated with measuring the context of performance to establish peer groups for housing association performance have led to the abandonment of such attempts and the substitution of simple size comparisons (Walker 1994). The initial and continuing impact of these research studies has been to force housing organisations and individual officers to pay more attention to the costs of service provision, how services should be provided, organisations structured and what should be provided. However there is much that we do not know about performance, for example how tenants determine their satisfaction with housing management services, particularly if they have limited experiences of other landlords or forms of tenure, and how housing organisations have responded to performance regimes.

The outcome of these studies has been the development of a complex performance regime in both the housing association and local authority sector. Within the local authority sector the Report to Tenants regime provides performance information to tenants (Symon and Walker 1995). This regime was ostensibly developed to increase tenants' involvement in housing management services by providing them with information to question and challenge local policy and practice. The outcome of the regime has been rather different as central government has collated the data to derive league tables of the relative performance of authorities and influence resource allocations decisions, though this has now been superseded by the Citizen's Charter regime. However tenants still receive two differing performance reports with different information or the same information derived from different definitions! Performance data has become key to housing associations and is used by the regulators and private financiers to judge management competence. Within Wales comparative league tables of the performance of association and authority are now produced. The creation of a performance culture, which extends through organisations and drives front line housing officers' work also signals the adoption of a private sector ethos, one which the Institute has also embraced notably through quality control and the promotion of standards. However such actions by the profession did not prevent the extension of compulsory competitive tendering to housing management. The full impact of tendering on housing management has not yet been seen and is being incorporated into its performance based replacement 'best value' which was promoted from within the profession and by housing organisations as an alternative mechanism.

However these questions were not asked by government alone. The profession initiated a review of housing work in 1985 (Davies and Niner 1987), one of the first pieces of substantive work undertaken by the Institute. During this period the Institute was also able to establish degree courses within the higher education sector, both the Department of the Environment and the Scottish and Welsh Office supported postgraduate training and education to further enhance knowledge based learning within the sector as against the traditional approach of skills training. The majority of training and education within the sector is on a part-time basis, however, and is thus supported by organisations within the profession rather than by the state. Of the 6,400 students registered on housing qualification courses in 1991, less than a thousand of these were full-time students and the majority were at undergraduate level (DoE 1994). Government provision of full-time postgraduate bursaries was initially seen as a significant support for the profession. However this provision has subsequently meant the profession losing control of postgraduate education as these bursaries have been subsequently transferred to the ESRC whose rationale for academic excellence has resulted in the number of bursaries falling by over fifty per cent in England. This fall has forced a restructuring of courses, raising questions about housing knowledge and threatening graduate education within the sector (though bursaries still continue in Scotland and Wales).

During this period the dominant organisational form remained the bureaucratic. Internal decentralisation raised itself as an issue, but unevenly across the sector (Hoggett 1991). Issues of deprived housing estates where addressed from the late 1970s onwards through the development of the government's own Priority Estates Project (PEP) to bring more intensive forms of housing management. Operating at a very local level the PEP brought housing management closer to the customer and also attempted to devolve resources and to involve tenants in decisions. In the longer term this has provided a role model and dissemination mechanism upon which other organisations can build. Limited decentralisation was seen elsewhere within local authority housing as a leftist response to defend local services (Walsall) or to devolve resources (Glasgow and Rochdale). Moves towards decentralisation begin to signal the importance of consumers within the sector and to give them a voice and choice in deciding on what services they want.

Rationalisation and efficiency drives still have resonance in the late 1990s and have led to increased government control over the stock and management of housing organisations and the services they deliver to tenants. It was during this period that the housing profession asserted its authority as a profession for the first time. The Institute gained its charter, a professional qualification was introduced, the expectation that housing officers should be members of the Institute spread, the Institute became a powerful voice in questioning and influencing housing policy and promoted policy initiatives which have became part of government legislation.

Markets and networks - the extension of new forms of control and behaviour?

Beyond questions asked about the nature of social housing organisations, limited examples of internal decentralisation and the reduction in the size of local authority housing the fundamental forms of organisation and control within the sector had not substantially altered during the early to mid 1980s.

Moves to post-bureaucratic forms of organisation imply a move towards a new managerial paradigm resulting from socio-economic restructuring and turbulence, technological advancement and bureaucratic dysfunctionalism (Heckscher 1994). Hoggett (1991) argues that bureaucratic dysfunctionalism stems from inherent contractions in bureaucratic forms of organisation and control. Firstly problems of ordered centralisation and the need for functional specialism have, in the case of local government, led to the dominance of departments and their associated professions. This organisational segmentation created not monolithic bureaucratic structures but rather large bureaucratic organisations more akin to 'pluraliths' with problems of departmentalism and factionalism, for example reflected in housing's struggle to create comprehensive housing departments. Secondly the formalisation of control through regulation to define, specify and regiment aspects of social life produces rule bending behaviour. Furthermore bureaucratic forms of organisation and control are unresponsive in times of rapid change as compared to organic forms of organisation, which are team-based, flexible and outcome-based (Burns and Stalker 1961).

117

The Conservative government of the late 1980s responded to these problems, and the associated criticisms from public choice theorists and new institutional economics, by introducing a range of market-led reforms. These reforms have located housing management and social housing organisations within a much changed housing system. The key changes were contained in the Housing Act 1988 and the associated changes brought through the NHS and Community Care Act, which extended markets to social housing provision and created a need for local level inter-organisational networks to ensure local policy implementation. The central tenet of the legislation was to enhance the strategic function of local authorities, the new enabling authorities would coordinate the local housing market. Housing associations were promoted as the providers of new homes and local authorities' power to intervene through new building was further reduced by the Housing and Local Government Act 1989. This Act also placed controls on local authorities' housing revenue accounts, creating a devolved trading account within local government which had to balance if not be in surplus each year, and extending long sought for government controls over local authority rent setting policies and finance.

Market mechanisms were also brought into subsidy systems with the aim of moving towards market rents, providing a further stick to encourage tenants into home ownership and to subsidise demand rather than supply. For housing associations producer subsidies were reduced and private finance became a central funding element. The balance of subsidy between bricks and mortar and personal subsides were shifted to the latter, leading to substantial rent increases in the socially rented sectors further exacerbating residualisation trends and creating a range of affordability and welfare dependency problems (Clapham et al. 1995). The impact of these rent rises on local authority tenants, more so than housing association tenants, has been to charge tenants a higher rent for a decreasing product and to increase pressures on housing managers caught between their employers and tenants' demands.

Housing organisations have responded to these reforms in a variety of ways. Key in this has been the decentralisation of activities, services, resources and managerial control to create non-hierarchical forms of production and control based around a differing set of norms, behaviours and values, new employment contracts, partnerships and working across boundaries, alteration in communications through information technology and new managerial roles. Hoggett (1991) identifies these new norms through three processes. Firstly the enhancement of strategy and centralised control through the decentralisation of operational activities. Secondly control by contract though the management of either internally or externally decentralised operations. Thirdly a reduction in formalised procedure and inputs and more emphasis on results, outputs and outcomes. Together these factors, it is argued, work to produce a system which regulates autonomy within boundaries set down through contract. Thus the range of organisational and control mechanism are broadened.

For social housing organisations the process of internal decentralisation started in the 1950s but was given a new lease of life by PEP. Decentralisation has now become a relatively common form of management, though unevenly applied, with the aim of getting closer to the customer, devolving decision-making and finance to increase service responsiveness and the effective use of resources and is promoted as best practice. In addition to the internal decentralisation of services, external decentralisation has taken place through the establishment of compulsory competitive tendering contracts with private sector organisations, the development of housing associations as providers of social housing and local authority opt out stock transfers in a variety of forms. It is important to stress that the nature of decentralisation, internal or external, may or may not produce different forms of organisational control. For example the external decentralisation brought about by housing management compulsory competitive tendering is more concerned with cost control than with improved service quality, though government rhetoric has been about increasing the quality of services (Kirkpatrick and Martinez Lucio 1995). If contracts are tightly specified contract managers may gain increased control over budgetary operation but are limited in the extent to which they can develop policy and implement new procedures. Furthermore the contract is managed through a process of hierarchical control through client officers to the more senior echelons of the organisation. Franklin and Clapham (1997) also argue that competitive tendering by specifying the nature of housing management reasserts definitional problems about the nature and boundaries of housing management which could threaten the professional body, housing organisation and staff freedoms to determine its nature by codifying professional practice.

This diversity of organisational form and control has been given additional complexity through the creation of networks. These have developed as local authorities have become enablers and the strategic housing agency for their areas. Local authorities have traditionally worked through hierarchies and market mechanisms to provide social housing and regulate the private sector through housing grants and the enforcement activities of environmental health officers. However over recent years networks have become more complex and a more 'normal' way of working embracing the financing of social housing, renewal and rehabilitation, community care, consumer involvement and joint approaches to service delivery (Reid 1995). The promotion and redefinition of local housing departments as the strategic housing authority is a key example. Authorities have to work with housing associations to ensure that sufficient low cost rented housing exists within their area for a variety of groups of people who might have special needs or want to access home ownership. In order to be able to establish needs within their areas they have had to undertake increasingly sophisticated housing needs surveys and to develop an understanding of the local housing market rather than just of their own stock and tenants' needs. In relation to the allocation of dwellings housing departments also now work more closely with social services departments to assess the needs of people being rehoused through the community care route or under the requirements of the Children's Act and who might be housed by the authority, an association or a voluntary group. These changes have led to the expansion of the number of actors involved in the local housing market to meet social needs or market demands.

These changes have taken place whilst the vast majority of social housing remains provided predominantly by relatively large hierarchically functioning and controlled organisations - local authorities and housing associations. Historically government has directly intervened in housing provision through New Towns, agencies such as the North Eastern Housing Association, now Home Housing Association, and continues to do so through its agencies such as Scottish Homes which still has a property portfolio. It also exerts hierarchical control over resource allocation to both local authorities and housing associations and is heavily involved in opt outs such as Housing Action Trusts (HATs).

The extension of housing organisations involved in the provision and management of social housing and the concurrent growth of the profession can be seen in both the overall increase in the number of housing staff with membership of the Institute but also through the growth in the range of organisations with professionally qualified staff (table 1). Most notable here is the seven fold increase in commercial organisations and the substantial growth in housing associations as this sector has been brought back into the professional core. However local authority membership is substantially higher than that of housing associations and other organisations, reflecting the dominance of this tenure and the development of housing management as an occupation role within this sector.

Table 1
Housing organisations with Chartered Institute of Housing members

	1985	1995
Local authorities		
England	341	354
Scotland	49	52
Wales	35	34
Housing associations	292	508
Non-registered housing associations	n/a	27
Public authorities	31	89
Voluntary and representative organisations	17	137
Commercial	34	246
Total	799	1447

Source: CIH Yearbooks 1985 and 1995

Table 1 also indicates that membership is not universal in all organisations, for example there were 37 local housing authorities in Wales in 1985 and 1995 whilst there are over 3,000 registered housing associations.

Housing associations

For housing associations the Housing Act 1988 brought competition over the development and management of homes and simultaneously passed the risk to associations, while requiring them to raise a proportion of development costs from

120

the private sector. Historically housing associations were protected from risk by the Housing Association Grant system established in 1974. Government subsidy cushioned risk, if costs overran in the development process a larger subsidy cheque would be issued and if an association ran its management services at a deficit that too would be written off, though surpluses were 'clawed' back. In moving to a system of fixed production grants associations had to bear the risk if problems arose while also having to generate surpluses to cover longer term maintenance costs. The new financial regime fundamentally altered housing associations and the ways in which they operate. They now needed to develop new negotiation and bargaining skills and demonstrate management competence to raise private finance. Financial management has come to dominate the strategic and day to day functions as associations have had to ensure that sophisticated treasury management strategies are in place and to translate this strategic emphasis to housing officers, who are under greater pressure from private finance institutions to collect the rent and allocate homes rapidly to prove financial management competence. This new emphasis has resulted in changed power relations within associations. Historically the finance department undertook administrative tasks associated with claiming grant and associated subsidies. Now the finance section is a full department with a number of staff who look to ensure financial viability, and who are typically increasingly drawn from outside the 'traditional' housing profession - accountants for finance or built environment professions for development and maintenance. Thus the sector is in a process of moving towards business-like management and an associated ethos, suggesting cultural change (Smith and Walker 1997).

This emphasis on economy and efficiency is still strongly witnessed within the housing sector (Walker, forthcoming) and has been a driving force in reform and change during the Conservative administrations regime during the 1980s and 1990s. However in relation to housing Walker (forthcoming) has argued that broader restructuring processes have been witnessed in relation to housing associations. Some housing associations have responded to this through decentralisation and downsizing which has also been driven by technological change.

Associations are moving to core-periphery organisational structures where the core plans strategy and provides a range of centralised services including human resources, training and development functions. The peripheries are then given operational freedom to develop policy and practice to suit local circumstances and locally held skills. These processes have been aided by technological change which allows local performance and financial activity to be monitored through information technology links, a key element for internal decentralisation. In the case of some associations the role of information technology has been taken further to restructure the nature of housing management services. Call centres are being established taking the lead from the current private sector financial services model. This model allows tenants to contact the organisation by freephone to gain access to the waiting list for new applicants or access the range of usual housing management services. Technological change also allows associations to 'outsource' aspects of their services. An experimental demonstration project at

Riverside Housing Association extended freephone systems to the Association's repairs contractor who took repair requests and undertook work without reference back to the Association within certain constraints. Through information technology monitoring this created a virtual housing organisation where tenants believed that they were contracting the repairs section of the association. Research evidence also suggests that tenants are happy to use such services seeing them as more responsive, while associations save money by reducing relatively expensive face to face contact (Walker, forthcoming).

Housing officers' views of these typically top-down change programmes are mixed. In some instances it means reduced contact with tenants particularly in relation to notions of helping people, often the prime motivation for people to take up careers in housing. Job roles are also redefined. The operation of a call centre implies a deskilling of front line staff with an increasing emphasis on genericism, or a reduction in professionalism. For more senior staff within the organisation it frees up their time to concentrate on core business and to resolve more complex issues.

Pressures for organisational change have also come from the regulators - the Housing Corporation in England, Scottish Homes and Housing for Wales. These regulators have interpreted and implemented policy differently. In England the Housing Corporation has developed an internally, highly competitive system for bidding for producer subsidies which has led to many associations under cutting each other. Housing for Wales, adopting a more interventionist approach, has reduced the level of competition by zoning associations to work in particular local authority areas. Interest in the effectiveness of associations as developers grew in the early 1990s and the sector was slightly restructured following a series of consultations with associations (Smith and Walker 1997). Competition was introduced for associations for the first time in during 1995/96 through rent bidding with regulator concerns about affordability, variations in rent levels in areas of similar development costs and the questions asked about the reserves associations had developed. Rent bidding forced associations to predict future rents on new build homes: if their bid was ten per cent higher than the lowest bid for their area they lost the development programme. Rent bidding can also be seen as an attempt to measure the outputs, here rent levels, from the highly complex range of services provided by associations. This has been extended from 1997/98 to a form of rent control through rent benchmarking where the uncertainty of the rent bidding system has been removed with the publication of threshold rents for all associations rents if they wish to develop (Smith and Walker, 1997). These policy initiatives indicate the extent to which the regulator is able to influence organisations and their financial management but that associations have also sought to develop new organisational forms and ways of working.

Opting out

The Housing Act 1988 produced a range of interesting and unanticipated organisational responses. The promotion of Tenants' Choice and HATs galvanised many authorities into a consumerist mode of action. Authorities developed a range of mechanisms to increase their responsiveness to tenants to ensure that they did not move to an alternative landlord. This has in part led to the development of private sector management practices such as customer care, market based research through tenant satisfaction survey and notions of excellence. However tenants themselves were by and large hostile to this legislation which attacked local democracy. They campaigned vigorously to ensure that they were not subjected to a HAT (Woodward 1991) and sufficient pressure was brought to bear during the legislative process to ensure that a vote took place (Karn 1993). The Conservative government was also seen to misunderstand tenant perceptions - a perceived desire that tenants wanted to leave the sector - through the Tenants' Choice proposals. Here only half a dozen stock transfers took place. Only two of them were of any major significance. In the case of one, Glyn Taff Farm in South Wales, tenants did not wish to leave the local authority sector but could only access the resources to improve their homes through a stock transfer which triggered a stock valuation process which negatively valued their homes thus ensuring that resources had to be forthcoming. The government's attempt to create and force through with little consultation 'opted' out housing organisations led by tenants - Tenants' Choice - or by government together with local authorities - HATs - were both unsuccessful and have been discontinued. Nonetheless these opt out processes represent a move away from bureaucratic forms of organisation as tenants, the private sector, local authorities and housing associations are represented in the process of establishing HATs and Tenants' Choice organisations, a process which involves complex inter-organisational networks. The now defunct Estates Action programme in England, which was drawn into the single regeneration budget leading to the loss of housing resources, and the on-going Estates Partnership scheme in Wales, also involve these complex networks for the improvement of local authority housing estates.

The Tenants' Choice legislation can also be linked to the enhanced role given to tenant participation in a variety of forms and supported by government. Housing co-operatives have a long history in the housing associations sector and represent locally determined solutions to housing problems and local control. The introduction of the Right to Manage now allows for a variety of organisational forms whereby a local authority can subcontract specific aspects of its housing management services to tenants, ranging from the entire management of the local authority service as in the case of Kensington and Chelsea LBC through to estate agreements, estate management boards and tenant management co-operatives. These changes are creating new forms of organisational working and practice and a reliance on inter-organisational networks.

The Local Government and Housing Act 1989 created a more stringent financial regime for local authority housing departments. A direct and innovative response of now some fifty local authorities has been to transfer their stock into the housing association sector thus privatising the stock, in line with the former Conservative government's policy, but retaining the social function of the stock, excluding the right to buy and allowing new homes to be built (Reid 1995). Such transfers have typically taken place in the more affluent southern England where property prices have been high and housing debt low. The ability of large scale voluntary transfer (LSVT) landlords and local authorities to extract relatively large profits from such transfers, whilst increasing Treasury costs though the need to increase housing benefit payments (as there is no longer any cross subsidisation of tenants rents between earning and benefit dependent tenants) led government to impose new regulations to limit the size of single parcels of stock transferred (attempting to diversity the socially rented market) and introduce a tax on the costs of transfer to offset increased personal subsidy payments.

For the local authorities concerned these transfers mean that they no longer have any direct input to or control of social housing within their boundaries, having through their own volition externally decentralised many of their responsibilities. Where local authority influence has continued it has been through networks via local authority member representation on the board of the new association, and through management by implicit contract to provide and maintain social housing and through inter-organisational working on waiting lists, nominations and housing homeless households. However the loss of direct hierarchical control over associations has led in some instances to a breakdown of communications between the two organisations and differing priorities - in Tunbridge Wells local members were elected off the board of the LSVT association. These transfers, together with the promotion of Local Housing Companies (LHC), are changing the face of British social housing. Transfer associations now hold twenty-five per cent of the total stock holdings in the housing association sector and have led to the sector being redesignated the registered social landlord sector.

As reductions in resources have impacted on the housing sector so innovative responses have been developed by housing organisations. The LSVT model is only applicable where stock has a positive valuation. In cases where stock is negatively valued the Chartered Institute of Housing together with others have developed and promoted Local Housing Companies. These have been primarily promoted to overcome fiscal policy regulations, notably the continuation of counting local authority expenditure against the public sector borrowing requirement, meaning that local authorities unlike housing associations were unable to borrow on the capital markets, and because of the former Conservative government's dislike of local authority housing and monetary policy views on the inflationary impacts of releasing the receipts of Right to Buy sales. What has been notable in the move towards LHC has been the professional bodies' role in wholeheartedly embracing the concept and helping to sell it to government as the 'only' mechanism by which resources can be brought into the sector to undertake the necessary improvements and address rationalisation processes. This attitude has produced conflict between the CIH and authorities who see the LHC model, and its various constitutional permutations to maintain some form of accountability, as undermining the democratic role of local authorities further in their provision of social housing. The process of opting out has changed the face of the sector and led to the formation of new organisations that are increasingly regulated by the Housing Corporation, Scottish Homes or Housing for Wales.

Conclusions

The overall impact of the rationalisation process has been to assert the supremacy of the market in co-ordinating public policy, reducing the interventionist powers and service delivery role of local authorities, and privatising provision leading to substantial local-central government conflict. However the extent to which this represents a move away from bureaucratic forms of organisation and control is uncertain - a new ex-local authority housing department becomes a housing purpose only body rather than one in which housing is one of a number of functions and is still hierarchically organised and controlled. This in some senses is not surprising as it took bureaucratic forms of organisation many years to develop. Bureaucracy developed in limited ways in the mid 1850s and was not widely applicable until 1920s and not fully worked out until the 1950s (Heckscher 1994). It is thus not surprising to see this form of organisation still dominant within housing where forms of bureaucratic organisation have traditionally been prevalent and where the profession does not seek closure but better services and standards for tenants.

What is indubitable is that the sector has become more complex, fragmented and changed through the introduction of market mechanisms and the ways in which housing organisations have responded to this notably through the development of networks to ensure local policy implementation predominantly in relation to the provision of new homes, refurbishment and to support the growing number of organisations opting out of direct local authority control. What stands out within the social housing sector has been the growth of central government control of social housing organisations and the belated attempts of the profession and organisations to search for alternative solutions and a new agenda.

In addition to increased government control the processes of rationalisation, restructuring and the emergence of new forms of organisation and organisational control, predominately driven by government reform, have created new boundary dispute problems within the occupational area of housing management (Franklin and Clapham 1997). As social housing has become increasingly residualised a gap has opened up between the traditional property based approach to housing management and social work which leaves tenants-led demand for care, support and physical help unaddressed. This vacuum raises important issues: 'once housing managers have started to provide some elements of a social and welfare service the question has to be asked, where do they stop, and are they stepping into territory rightfully belonging to other welfare agencies?'(Franklin and Clapham 1997, p.15).

This returns us full circle to the questions concerning the nature of housing management. It can be argued that uncertainty about its boundaries, knowledge and core competencies have left housing in a weak position which has allowed government to impose change and fragment social housing provision, giving responsibilities to a wide variety of independent organisations who need to work in collaboration and co-operation to secure housing services. However as the profession has grown and strengthened it has been able to develop a range of new organisational forms and responses and promote the privatisation of the profession into the regulated semi-accountable world of housing associations, again returning full circle to its origins. These processes leave the housing profession in a curious position. Professional practitioners themselves are concentrated in the local authority sector, where there is the most stock, yet these professionals increasingly focus on service delivery issues, all be it through complex networks. However the continuing promotion of local housing companies, together with austerity cuts in the housing association sector, are bringing the two sectors closer together to find joint solutions and so potentially moving housing management beyond being simply a service delivery profession.

The range of areas where housing managers are now expected to intervene at the local level - care and support, community development, local economic development, urban regeneration - also suggests the further fragmentation of knowledge beyond approaches to housing management into a range of complex areas where their claims to expertise are precarious. The creation and formation of networks may offer housing managers hope as they work with other agencies to meet local needs. Housing managers' claims to knowledge and skills have been sustained and extended through the redefinition of local authorities as strategic housing organisations with responsibility for planning, managing and regulating the local housing market, yet these functions remain only a small part of the totality of the social housing profession. Thus the new language of social housing emphasises issues of organisation and management in practice, policy and the training and education of housing officers. This language not only harks back to the Cullingworth Report (CHAC 1969), but also reflects the emergence of new public management and the need to manage increased complexity. Such changes support the view that housing management is management with specialist skills and knowledge rather than a profession (Stewart 1988), yet has to be promoted as a profession as an emphasis on generic management would undermine its status (Clapham 1997). Yet the tension still remains between the property based housing management approach, which typified the profession for most of the twentieth century, and the social housing approach, a tension likely to intensify as housing management is increasingly pushed towards the use of surveillance strategies to police poverty, crime and anti-social behaviour. The Blair Labour administration's promised expansion of local authority housing, and thus social housing, will further intensify this tension and perhaps shift the balance between bureaucracy and new organisation forms and so present new challenges to the housing profession in how housing services are delivered.

References

Ackroyd, S. (1996), 'Organisation Contra Organisations: Professions and Organisational Change in the United Kingdom', *Organizational Studies*, Vol. 17, No. 4, pp. 599-621.

Audit Commission (1986), *Managing the Crisis in Council Housing*, HMSO: London.

Bines, W., Kemp. P., Pleace, N. and Radley, C. (1993), *Managing Social Housing*, HMSO: London.

Burns, T. and Stalker, G. (1961), *The Management of Innovation*, Oxford University Press: Oxford.

Central Housing Advisory Committee (1938), *Management of Municipal Housing Estates*, HMSO: London.

Central Housing Advisory Committee (1959), *Councils and the Houses*, HMSO: London.

Central Housing Advisory Committee (1969), *Council Housing: Purposes, Procedures and Priorities*, HMSO: London.

Clapham, D. (1989), *Goodbye Council Housing*, The Fabian Series, Unwin: London.

Clapham, D. (1992), 'A Women of Her Time', in Grant, C. (ed.), *Built to Last? Reflections on British Housing Policy*, Roof Magazine: London.

Clapham, D. (1997) 'The Social Construction of Housing Management Research', *Urban Studies*, Vol. 34, Nos. 5-6.

Clapham, D., Walker, R., Meen, G., Thake, S. and Wilcox, S. (1995) *Building Homes, Building Jobs: Housing and Economic Renewal*, National Housing Forum: London.

Coleman, A. (1985), *Utopia on Trial*, Hillary Shipman: London.

Davies, M. and Niner, P. (1987), *Housing Work, Housing Workers and Education and Training for the Housing Service*, Institute of Housing: London.

Department of the Environment (1994), *Education and Training for Housing Management*, HMSO: London.

Forrest, R. and Murie, A. (1991), *Selling the Welfare State*, Routledge: London.

Franklin, B. (forthcoming), 'Constructing a Service: Context and Discourse in Housing Management', *Housing Studies*.

Franklin, B. and Clapham, D. (1997) 'The Social Construction of Housing Management', *Housing Studies*, Vol. 12, No.1, pp. 7-26.

Heckscher, C. (1994), 'Defining the Post-Bureaucratic Type', in Heckscher, C. and Donnellen, A. (ed.), *The Post-Bureaucratic Organisation: New Perspectives on Organisational Change*, Sage: London.

Hoggett, P. (1991), 'A New Management in the Public Sector?', *Policy and Politics*, Vol. 19, No 4., pp. 243-56.

Karn, V. (1993), 'Remodelling a HAT: the Implementation of the Housing Action Trust Legislation 1987-92', in Malpass, P. and Means, R. (eds.), *Implementing Housing Policy*, Open University Press: Buckingham.

Kirkpatrick, I. and Martinez Lucio, M. (1995) (eds.), *The Politics of Quality in the Public Sector*, Routledge: London

Laffin, M. (1986), *Professionalism and Policy*, Aldershot: Avebury.

Maclennan, D., Clapham, D., Goodlad, R., Kemp. P., Malcom, J., Satsangi, M., Stanforth, J. and Whitefield, L. (1989), *The Nature and Effectiveness of Housing Management in England and Wales*, HMSO: London.

Malpass, P. and Murie, A. (1994), *Housing Policy and Practice*, Macmillan: London.

Power, A. (1987), *Property before People,* Unwin Hyman: London.

Proven, B. and Williams, P. (1991), 'Joining the Professionals? The Future of Housing Staff and Housing Work', in Donnison, D. and Maclennan, D. (eds.), *The Housing Service of the Future,* Institute of Housing/Longman: Coventry/London.

Reid, B. (1995), 'Inter-organisational Networks and the Delivery of Local Housing Services', *Housing Studies*, Vol. 10, No. 2, pp. 133-150.

Smith, R. and Walker, R. (1997), 'Regulatory and Organisational Responses to Restructured Housing Association Finance in England and Wales', Paper presented at the ENHR/NETHER Conference *Social Housing Finance in the EU* Nunspeet, The Netherlands.

Stewart, J. (1988), *A New Management for Housing Departments*, Luton: Local Government Management Board.

Walker, R. (1994), 'Putting Performance Measurement into Context: Classifying Social Housing Organisations', *Policy and Politics,* Vol. 22, pp. 191-202.

Walker, R. (forthcoming), 'New Public Management and Housing Associations: from Comfort to Competition', *Policy and Politics.*

Walker, R. and Symon, P. (1995), 'A Consumer Perspective on Performance Indicators: the Local Authority Reports to Tenants Regimes in England and Wales', *Environment and Planning C: Government and Politics*, Vol. 13, pp. 195-216.

Walker, R. and Williams, P. (1995), 'Implementing Local Government Reorganisation in the Housing Service: The Case of Wales', *Local Government Studies*, Vol. 21, No. 3, pp. 483-508.

Williams, P. (1997), 'Getting the Foundations Right: Housing Organisations and Structures', in Williams, P. (ed.), *Directions in Housing Policy: Towards Sustainable Housing Policies for the UK*, Paul Chapman: London.

Woodward, R. (1991), 'Mobilising Opposition: The Campaign against Housing Action Trusts in Tower Hamlets', *Housing Studies*, Vol. 6, No 1, pp. 44-56.

8 Environmental health

Paul Thomas

The history of the environmental health service in the UK can be traced to the origins of British local government. Some of the earliest local authority functions concerned the provision of water supplies and sewerage systems, and the control of overcrowded and insanitary housing conditions. Several Acts of Parliament in the 19th century provided for the appointment of 'inspectors of nuisances' and, later, sanitary inspectors, subsequently known as public health inspectors working under the 'general direction' of the local authority's medical officer of health (Local Government Act 1933 and the Public Health Officers Regulations 1959).

In the local government reorganisation of 1974 the role of environmental health officers (EHOs), which became the new name for public health inspectors, was given increased recognition with the publication of the Bains Report (Department of the Environment 1972) whose recommended structures were implemented by most of the new local authorities. Bains recommended that each district council should appoint a Chief EHO as one of its chief officers. At the same time medical officers of health disappeared from the managerial structures of local authorities, to re-emerge as community physicians appointed by Health Authorities within the reformed National Health Service in 1974. EHOs thus emerged with greater professional status and autonomy than they had enjoyed previously.

The EH function is a wide ranging one, covering aspects of housing, food control, air pollution, noise control, health and safety at work, waste disposal and pest control. The vast majority of EHOs were, and still are, employed within local government, with a small minority being self-employed as consultants, or employed by food wholesalers, retailers or central government departments. By the 1970s graduate entry to the profession had become the norm.

The work of EHOs is broadly of two main kinds. Firstly the enforcement of legislation relating to environmental health, for example in the fields of food hygiene, housing conditions, health and safety at work and air pollution. Secondly EHOs have an advisory function whereby they are asked to comment and advise on noise problems, land use planning proposals and food hygiene. Generally EHOs work within a local government context and they need a thorough grasp of the administrative, managerial, political and legal processes which operate at the level of the local state. The routine work of EHOs is based on the standard operating procedures of local authority work generally. It involves hierarchical relationships at officer level and committee and sub-committee work at member level. EH Departments both plan and provide the necessary services to control a wide range of local environmental hazards.

The 1980s onward

The Local Government, Planning and Land Act in 1980 heralded a new approach to management practices in local government. The Act required local authorities to go through a tendering process in respect of their construction and maintenance work. Authorities' direct labour organisations (DLOs) could therefore no longer safely assume that they would continue executing the work which they had traditionally undertaken. DLOs were now going to have to demonstrate that they were providing 'value for money' in an increasingly competitive context. During the 1980s the range of services for which competitive tendering was compulsory was widened to include refuse collection, the cleaning of buildings, street cleansing, catering (for example in schools), ground maintenance and the repair and maintenance of council vehicles.

The imposition of compulsory competitive tendering (CCT) required new working practices, including the writing of work specifications, advertising for, and evaluating, tenders, awarding work to successful contractors (either in-house or not as the case may be) and monitoring the subsequent work. The change also led to the separation of each local authority into client functions (those which specify the work to be done and who monitor and control the work in progress) and contracting functions (those, either in-house or external companies, which bid for contracts and who provide the service in question); and corporate and support services (the group of officers who provide advice to members and those who provide 'central services', such as salaries, personnel services and IT services). CCT also increased cost consciousness within local government in order to compete effectively with 'outside' contractors, and to some extent the emergence of an 'if it's not in the contract, we won't do it' ethos.

At first CCT was only applied to blue collar work. Some local authority EH departments had few, if any, such staff. But in other authorities the expanded empire of the EHO included the work of refuse collection and street cleaning. Environmental health departments were therefore having increasingly to enter the new world of competition and markets.

In 1991 the government published its white paper *Competing for Quality: Buying Better Public Services* which announced its intention of extending CCT to cover a range of white collar jobs in local government (HM Treasury 1991). In due course the Local Government Act of 1992, taking further the provisions of the 1988 Act, arrived requiring local authorities to subject some aspects of white collar work to CCT. These provisions may be seen as a part of the shift towards seeing local authorities and other government agencies as 'enablers' as opposed to exclusive 'providers' of services, a shift both described and prescribed by Osborne and Gaebler (1992). The 1991 white paper also made reference to the enabling role of local authorities:

> For local services, the Government's model of an enabling authority will promote more effective, business-like management, which pays more attention to customer requirements and value for money. The separation of service delivery from strategic responsibilities enables authorities to concentrate on the core responsibilities of setting priorities and standards and finding the best way of meeting them. (HM Treasury 1991, p. 2)

To what extent has this new model affected the work of EHOs? A substantial part of EH work comprises enforcement of legislation in a wide range of domestic, commercial and industrial premises. Such legislation includes provisions relating to food hygiene, health and safety at work and housing improvements. The enforcement role of EHOs has been largely untouched by CCT provisions. But this is not to say that EH generally has been unaffected. Much depends on what is regarded as a part of EH work, and this varies considerably between different local authorities. A narrow view of the EH function would entail the traditional EH activities of food hygiene, health and safety at work, housing improvements, pollution control and pest control. However in some cases local authority EH departments have taken on a wide range of other functions including the work of public analysts, trading standards officers, building control and cleansing and refuse collection services. In some of these areas CCT has been in operation for some years, for example in relation to refuse collection.

In addition the development of CCT into white collar work is also leading to the emergence of client-contractor splits in other activities, particularly personnel, legal, IT and financial services. The work of staff, in any local authority department as well as EH departments, who spend more than specified proportions of their time dealing with these matters has to be put out to tender. There is reason to wonder about the degree of clarity in the split between client and contractor within a local authority. For example might it be possible for a group of managers to see themselves as clients on some days of the year and, having won the contracts, as contractors for the other days of the year? Government policy would seem to discourage such arrangements. The preference is to have, where possible, clients and contractors clearly separate from each other. This means that even if very few EH functions are directly affected by CCT initiatives on the contractor side, EHOs may nevertheless be involved in client-side roles.

The development of contractual arrangements, and the intra-organisational equivalents of service level agreements, has led to an increase in the extent to which expectations and commitments are specified in writing. Many EH services are no exception to the generalisation that 'the balance has shifted towards public organisation being contract based' (Deakin and Walsh 1994, p. 5). However it is hazardous to extrapolate these developments too far, especially in relation to professional services. As Deakin and Walsh argue: 'It is easier to operate market based contracting approaches for simple repetitive services than for complex professionally based activities' (1994, p. 6).

CCT is generally thought to have been introduced in order to secure improvements in efficiency, but it is still unclear whether such improvements have been achieved. When the costs of preparing and monitoring contracts are properly taken into account the efficiency gains might well be considerably less than expected. Deakin and Walsh (1994) have pointed out that 'there is relatively little evidence on the transaction costs of operating market based systems (Audit Commission 1993, Walsh and Davis 1993)'. More importantly is whether the introduction of CCT has contributed to the creation of a post-bureaucratic form of organisation. To some extent hierarchical relationships are being replaced by contractual relationships, but in other senses (for example, the use of rules and regulations) one could argue that the use of CCT increases the bureaucratic form rather than changes it to a new 'post-bureaucratic' form. In this vein Deakin and Walsh argue:

> The introduction of markets creates increased organisational formality. Services are more strictly specified. Payment systems are precisely defined, involving orders and invoices. Record systems are central to the management of contracts.... . There need to be mechanisms for the resolution of differences between clients and contractors, for example methods of arbitration. (1994, p. 9)

The use of Service Level Agreements and management approaches such as ISO 9000 and the Investors in People (IIP) standards, increasingly influential within EH services, are likely to have the same effect, increasing rather than reducing the bureaucratisation of EH services.

On the other hand CCT also seems to drive EH services in a post-bureaucratic direction. For example CCT processes imply an enabling rather than a direct service delivery role, and relationships come to depend on contracts as well as hierarchies. And in place of monolithic hierarchical structures we begin to see the emergence and development of more complex network arrangements. However these arrangements have not so far emerged in most EH services. Rather an increased culture of cost consciousness has developed within local government generally. This culture also reflects the 'value for money' emphasis in local government pioneered by the Audit Commission since the early 1980s.

Blurring the boundaries

Some anecdotal evidence suggests that the boundaries between officials and politicians in the EH services have become more blurred. Senior officials are increasingly expected to have some sympathy with council members' policy objectives. In addition, in cases where a local authority is controlled by a different political party from that in government, councillors have been known to expect officials to find 'ways around' a piece of legislation or circular. Such 'loophole seeking' is thought by some to be on the increase, though there is little systematic evidence about this.

As in other services the elected members are more likely than in the past to have a greater presence in EH Departments. This might involve an office being available within the department for the chair of the relevant committee, or an increasing tendency for members to 'drop in' or otherwise contact the relevant case officer. This contrasts quite sharply with common practice, say, twenty years ago when member-officer contact was much more likely to be almost exclusively at chief officer level.

Boundaries are also more blurred in the sense that EH Departments are increasingly and regularly involved in a wider network of organisations than hitherto. Partnership arrangements are not uncommon, for example with private firms of architects, consultants and builders, housing associations, and Training and Enterprise Councils (in relation to job creation in the construction industry for young people). Furthermore intra-organisational and inter-professional boundaries are more blurred: there are increasing linkages between traditional EH work and related functions such as trading standards and the work of public analysts.

A further development has been the removal of some functions from EH Departments and the creation or strengthening of other agencies. One important example is the Meat Hygiene Service created in 1995 as a 'Next Steps' Executive Agency of the Ministry of Agriculture, Fisheries and Food. This agency is now responsible for enforcing hygiene inspection and animal welfare regulations in licensed fresh meat plants throughout Great Britain, a role traditionally fulfilled by EHOs and 'authorised meat inspectors' (AMIs) within local government. It is the AMIs who now largely do the meat inspection work under the umbrella of the Meat Hygiene Service. The creation of the Meat Hygiene Service was, at least partly, the result of pressures from the food trade concerned over allegedly uneven enforcement practices among local authorities and European Union pressures arising from the difficulties of recognising the wide ranging qualifications of British EHOs who do not have any European equivalents.

Another example of agency reform is the creation of the Environment Agency which took over the functions of Her Majesty's Pollution Inspectorate, for example the licensing of waste disposal, the passage of waste and the control of industrial air pollution, and of the previous National Rivers Authority. However few EHOs work in the Environment Agency.

Some blurring of the private and public sectors has also taken place in the increasing use by local authorities of consultants to carry out some EH work. Examples include house condition survey work and the provision of a 24 hour noise control service. This work is commonly still done by EHOs but it is sometimes now carried out by those EHOs working outside the public EH service. This trend towards using 'private sector' EHOs has not yet progressed very far, but it does seem to be gradually increasing.

Traditionally only 'qualified EHOs' would be seriously considered for 'EH jobs'. Until the 1970s EHOs or their predecessors, public health inspectors, were statutory officers whose tenure and qualifications were specified in law. More recently people from a wider range of backgrounds have been employed within EH Departments. Furthermore the increase in networking, the blurring of boundaries and greater organisational pluralism seem to indicate a shift in a post-bureaucratic direction.

Controls, constraints and professional autonomy

As has been noted, some functions have been removed from local government EH Departments, for example meat inspection and the control of some categories of waste. But even for those responsibilities remaining the range of controls over how the work is carried out have increased and EHOs' discretion correspondingly reduced. For example food hygiene work (including the inspection of food shops, restaurants, cafes, hotels, pubs, food factories and food stalls) used to be undertaken on the basis of the local EHOs knowing their districts and deciding on the appropriate frequencies of inspection for the various categories of food premises. The system has changed in recent years, and now the frequencies of inspection are more likely to be prescribed centrally, with local authorities producing information for the EHOs on the expected frequencies based on the degree of risk in terms of the kind of food premises and the perceived quality of its management systems. The numbers of inspections carried out can then be monitored as a part of performance measurement within the authority. In addition the qualifications of the inspectors permitted to undertake inspections are now more tightly controlled than previously, especially in cases of premises which require a licence to export food to members of the European Union. These trends amount to a noticeable reduction in the professional discretion or autonomy of EHOs including a reduction in the Chief EHO's decision-making power in the allocation of EH staff.

In the future the food control function could be removed from local authority control altogether and a national food hygiene service created to parallel the meat hygiene service. Such a national service could help to overcome the problem of inconsistent standards and requirements of nation-wide supermarkets: after all, it is difficult to justify requiring one set of standards in a supermarket in one part of the country and a different set in a supermarket belonging to the same chain elsewhere. This issue raises the question of whether consistency of standards or responsiveness to local circumstances and local democratic accountability are the more important criteria in EH policy.

Another aspect of changing control structures in EH work is the increased use of performance monitoring. Some aspects of EH related work are relatively easy to measure in a way that is useful for effective management. For example the collection of refuse and the cleaning of streets are, in principle at least, simple and repetitive tasks which are amenable to relatively easy measurement. However measuring work related to food hygiene is more problematic. If 'number of inspections' is used, should the inspection of a corner shop and that of a large supermarket both be measured as 'one premise inspected'? And in any case measuring the numbers of inspections only gives an indication of activity, it offers little useful information on what is being achieved by the inspections. Any measurement of the extent to which inspections help to raise food hygiene standards, leading to a measurable reduction in the incidence of food poisoning, must be inherently problematic.

The autonomy of EHOs has also been challenged in relation to health and safety work. The Health and Safety Executive advises that inspections of premises classified as 'high risk' should not be undertaken by 'newly qualified' EHOs.

However some trends do seem to be increasing the autonomy of EHOs. For example elected members in committee are increasingly delegating decisions to officers with reports going to committee 'for information only', despite moves in some areas to move towards the notion of a 'member led' authority. This trend is likely to continue more in relation to EH work than with (say) social services where lay councillors believe that they are more likely to understand the 'technical' aspect of the work because it is about 'people' as opposed to technical issues such as pollution levels. A councillor is more likely to have an opinion about whether a child should be taken into care than about how to measure the ground level concentration of a particular air pollutant. To some extent the apparent greater technical features of EH work serves to insulate EHOs from undue 'interference' from elected members, an insulation that many EHOs value.

External orientations

For many years local authorities have been urged to be more responsive to the wishes and needs of their communities. A number of commentators espoused such an approach prior to, during and after the 1974 local government reorganisation. In the years that followed there were few signs that EH Departments were changing their processes in the ways prescribed. But environmental issues, including food safety, have entered the public's consciousness in significant ways in recent years. There have been oil spills, food scares, including Salmonella, Listeria, BSE and E-Coli, and a variety of other environmental and green issues have been covered substantially by the mass media. Councillors have been increasingly keen to demonstrate their responsiveness to community concerns and EHOs have increasingly been expected to answer to a better educated, articulate and assertive public.

These trends have been further boosted by the increased emphasis in consumerism in public organisation, for example the increasing use of published performance indicators, league tables and the Citizen's Charter. The combination of increased interest in environmental issues and consumerism has given EH work a greater profile than it had in the past. EHOs face the music in the mass media with increasing frequency and some members of the profession feel that this increase in public accountability has reduced their professional autonomy and discretion. EHOs are increasingly likely to have to answer to a potentially hostile public and press for their actions and inactions. On the other hand, under some circumstances, increased public interest and involvement could assist the EH profession as EHOs can more readily point to the public and political importance of environmental issues when arguing for more resources. Public interest is thus a double edged sword - both a potential challenge and potential aid. Public support (or lack of it) has been seen less ambiguously by some other public sector professions: social workers and teachers have been consistently under attack in recent years while the police force has enjoyed considerable public support.

At the national level the recognition by government and political parties of EHOs and their work is increasing. Recent examples include the representation by the EH profession on the Pennington Committee (1997) on Scotland's E-Coli food poisoning epidemic and requests from the Labour Party, prior to the 1997 election, for help in developing housing policies.

The present Labour government seems to be making more positive moves towards integration with Europe than the previous government. Most member states of the EU do not have 'EHOs' as such and a danger for the profession lies in the difficulties of achieving and maintaining Europe-wide recognition for such a relatively unfamiliar profession. However the EU has been very influential in recent years in relation to legislation relating to food control, pollution and health and safety, and in the UK at least, EHOs have been at the forefront in the task of operationalising many of these laws.

Accountability, control and power

Accountability is a particularly important issue in public sector management as accountability is the link between bureaucracy and democracy. The traditional hierarchical structure within bureaucracies actually makes explicit some of the lines of accountability - with authority flowing downwards and accountability or responsibility flowing upwards. Changing patterns of accountability can therefore be a useful guide to the extent to which public service are still being run by bureaucracies or whether we have moved on to some new (post-bureaucratic?) form of organisational arrangements.

Recent work by Ferlie et al. (1996) emphasises an emerging 'accountability deficit' within today's public sector organisations. They point out that many of these organisation 'have adopted some of the characteristics and culture or private sector firms and may be directed by senior personnel with a private sector background' (1996, p. 196). Ferlie and his colleagues go on to argue: 'The rhetoric is often one of unleashing entrepreneurial potential, getting away from the Weberian bureaucratic vices (or indeed virtues) of due process and standard treatment ... . In this model, improved performance is seen as getting in the way of results' (1996, p. 196). They also highlight increasing concerns over the loss of 'traditional standards of probity' in both public and private sectors (1996, p. 197).

How have the dimensions of accountability changed, if at all, in recent years within the EH services? As far as the location of accountability is concerned it could be argued that EHOs are more likely to be held accountable for their activities than they used to be. They are more visible to the general public than they have ever been and individual EHOs are more likely to be contacted by council members than in the past when it was usual for only the local authority's Chief EHO who dealt with the elected members. In addition performance standards are increasingly likely to be made explicit for individual EHOs who are then expected to account for the achievement, or not as the case may be, of agreed targets.

What about the direction of accountability? The head of the department (for example the Chief EHO or Director of EH) will at different times be answerable to a range of people and agencies - taxpayers, the local electorate, the community at large, central government departments, the courts, the users of specific services, the local ombudsman and the press. For most operational level EHOs, however, the line of accountability will be the same as it has been traditionally - to the head of department.

The content of accountability has changed somewhat. Traditionally EHOs were expected to keep their noses clean and to complete a diary of daily inspections carried out in their respective districts. There were few (if any) specified standards, although most EH managers had a crude idea of what constituted a 'fair day's work' in terms of numbers of inspections carried out. In more recent times it is more likely that there is a system of performance monitoring in terms of the number of prescribed inspections determined on the basis of some system of risk assessment. Such systems are designed in an attempt to concentrate scarce resources on the high priority areas or kinds of premises. The content of accountability is thus becoming increasingly defined in terms of expected standards and frequencies of inspection.

What of the mechanisms of control? To some extent and for most EHOs for most of the time, little has changed. Individual EHOs are still held to account through the operation of 'position power' (Handy 1993) within their departments. However in recent years there has been an increasing tendency to contract out some services. For example a relatively well defined task such as the carrying out of house condition survey can be put out to tender with the local authority EH department 'steering rather than rowing' (Osborne and Gaebler 1992). The mechanism of control in these circumstances will therefore have more to do with the monitoring and enforcement of contracts than with traditional hierarchical controls. In this sense it is possible to see a shift towards a 'post-bureaucratic' form of operation.

In judging whether there has been any significant change in accountability patterns within the EH service, it is useful to fall back on the distinction made by Day and Klein (1987) between political and managerial accountability. The former entails the ability of the public to make judgements (in the context of contestable criteria) about whether decision-makers have acted honestly and wisely. The latter is about making those with delegated authority accountable for carrying out agreed tasks according to agreed criteria.

It can be argued that because the EH service is still largely planned and delivered by directly elected local authorities (as opposed, say, to the bodies running NHS Trusts, Training and Enterprise Councils and Urban Development Corporations in all of which Stewart's (1992) 'new magistracy' of non-elected nominees has emerged), there has been little change in political accountability. However it may be that managerial accountability has increased for EHOs in recent years because of the increasing emphasis on managerial mechanisms such as performance monitoring, explicit target setting and a general increase in 'managerialism' within the service.

Issues of accountability, power and control tend to be more complex in the case of professionals than in the case of other occupational groups because of the 'professional power' which some high status occupations traditionally enjoy. This professional power tends to be based on the attributes which professions are commonly thought to possess, namely autonomy, acknowledged expertise, legally enforceable rights, code of ethics, a professional association which regulates members' behaviour, control over entry, control over training, claim to be serving society at large and status (Greenwood 1957, Friedson 1970).

Most of the professional attributes which EHOs have acquired have come about largely because of what happens at national level and EHOs are not unusual in this. However it can be argued that at organisational and practice levels, the status of EHOs is under attack. At organisational and practice levels the autonomy, acknowledged expertise and status of EHOs are under attack from increasing interventions by politicians, an increasingly assertive public and the relentless energy of mass media. While the technical expertise, and therefore status and autonomy, of EHOs comes under increasing scrutiny, especially when EH problems take on a high profile as in a number of food safety issues in recent years, EH managers can use their more broadly based managerial skills to take on wider responsibilities as local government managers of not only traditional EH services but also a number of related functions such as trading standards, housing and technical services.

This reflects a long standing debate within the EH profession between those who see the preferred future - or even salvation - of the profession as lying in claims to possess a strong technical basis and those who stress a wider managerial role for practitioners. The technical emphasis tends to circumscribe the role of the profession whereas the latter gives it a wider role and enables practitioners to make claims to head up more broadly defined departments.

To the extent that EH managers increasingly see themselves allied to senior management roles within local authorities, there is the potential for conflict between this elite and what some might perceive as an increasingly proletarianised (or at least routinised) group of professionals at the street-level. It is possible that this conflict will become more acute over time with the increasing emphasis on CCT (even if the compulsory element is reduced) and the possibility that a growing number of EH functions will be put out to tender. There is already some evidence of this happening in recent years, for example in relation to house condition surveys (in addition to refuse collection and street cleaning services which have already gone through early rounds of private contracting).

Chief EHOs have to spend an increasing proportion of their time dealing with issues of financial and strategic management (a trend in public sector professions generally and not unique to EHOs) and to some extent may develop a greater orientation to their senior local government management colleagues rather than their more junior EHO colleagues. This might indicate a move for the Chief EHO away from being a 'leading professional' to being a 'hybrid professional/manager' (Ferlie et al. 1996).

Ham and Hill have argued (1993) that organisations which make extensive use of professionals are those in which there is high expertise in the lower ranks, a complex task to perform, difficulties in developing effective patterns of supervision and a need for flexibility and openness to change. Of these four conditions, as far as EH is concerned the third is the only one in doubt. Although top-down notions of management rarely operate as effectively as most managers would like, recent trends suggest that the role of supervision is facilitated by many of the managerialist changes imposed on local authorities, including the increasing use of the specification of standards (as a part of accreditation processes like ISO 9000 or of CCT processes), the monitoring of work loads, and variants of 'management by objectives' (including staff appraisal systems). Such managerial and supervisory practices make it difficult for EHOs to achieve and maintain as high levels of professional autonomy and discretion as many of them would like. However it is possible that the relative dearth of discretion is, to some extent, compensated for by the fact that most EHOs are street-level bureaucrats (Lipsky 1980).

EHOs as street-level bureaucrats, and the claim to a territory

Lipsky (1980) casts doubt on traditional models of policy-making and implementation which assume that policy, once made by politicians, is automatically and faithfully implemented via a hierarchy of officials and offices each in 'perfect obedience' to an acknowledged superior organisational level. He also recognised that the reality is a little different from this deceptively simple hierarchical top down model. Policy is commonly mediated, and possibly modified (intentionally or otherwise) through a range of institutions and individuals operating at the interface between organisation and the public. Lipsky referred to some of these mediators as 'street-level bureaucrats' - those public service workers 'who interact directly with the public in the course of their job and who have substantial discretion in the execution of their work' (Lipsky 1980). Examples include nurses, doctors, social workers policemen, teachers, housing officers and EHOs.

The argument is that as street-level bureaucrats (SLBs) carry out their day-to-day work they inevitably have to exercise discretion in the way in which they approach and undertake their duties. Examples of the use of discretion might include (Ham and Hill 1993): categorising, initiating, investigating, prosecuting, negotiating, advising, threatening, publicising, concealing, planning, recommending and prioritising.

The use of discretion is what gives SLBs more influence in the policy implementation arena than they would otherwise have. This is especially so in the case of workers who are both SLBs and professionals. As the proportion of a SLB

EHOs work that is codified increases, so the EHO's discretion and autonomy is likely to be reduced. In this way the codification of work is likely to be inimical to the autonomy of most SLBs and professionals. Codifications relevant to EHOs might include predetermined targets for number and frequency of inspections, accreditation systems such as ISO 9000 and inspection checklists relating to how to undertake inspections and the action to be taken in cases of non-compliance with statutory requirements.

Such codifications have the potential to reduce the mystery of the EHO's craft and make it easier for other occupational groups to lay claim to the territory, for example trading standards officers, housing officers, engineers, building surveyors, micro-biologists and chemists. One of the features of the training and work of EHOs arguably makes this a bigger danger for EHOs than for other professions. The domain of EH work is extremely wide ranging, drawing as it does on both the natural sciences and social sciences. It could be argued that there is no single part of the work of an EHO which could not be carried out competently by a member of another profession.

However what is unique about the training of EHOs is that they are equipped to deal with the whole range of environmental hazards - from air pollution to pest control, and from food safety to unhealthy workplaces and dwellings. It is this wide range that is the claimed exclusive cognitive jurisdiction of the EHO. However at a time when administrative and managerial arrangements are becoming increasingly fragmented it is difficult for EHOs to sustain an argument that there is any specific territory which is exclusively theirs. This affects the extent to which others - including other professions, the laity and local politicians - are dependent on EHOs to achieve improvements in environmental conditions. One should not overstate this. EHOs can legitimately argue that it is only they who have a training which looks at the full range of environmental hazards and at the administrative and legal mechanisms available to tackle such problems. The difficulty that they face is that government agencies seem unconcerned over the possible fragmentation of their expertise. Why bother to have all the expertise wrapped up together in one professional?

The counter argument might be that in the real world aspects of EH are inextricably linked in practice; for example, the washing of flue gases in order to reduce sulphur dioxide air pollution can lead to another problem, namely the need to dispose safely of the resulting waste. Professionals who can take the overview of EH problems are therefore necessary. The government's response might be that the Environment Agency which it has created provides such an overview. So the argument goes on. It leaves EHOs unsure whether their continued existence as a professional group is valued sufficiently highly by policy makers, especially as the profession is not a well established one in most member states of the EU.

If the trend towards contracting out an increasing range of local government work continues, the continued perceived need for reducing public expenditure is likely to threaten EHOs as the only providers of environmental health work. Others will claim to be able to provide the same (or even 'better') services at a lower cost. In these circumstances SLB EHOs are likely to be the losers and the elite EHO managers on the client side (for example the senior EHOs within the local government management structure) will be the relative gainers. The process may be seen as a potentially irreversible deprofessionalisation or 'proletarianisation' (Scarborough and Burrell 1994) of the rank and file EHO.

Future strategic options

In 1997 the report of the Commission on Environmental Health was published by the Chartered Institute of EH (CEH 1997). The Commission had been set up by the CIEH in 1996 'to analyse the present state of environmental health and make recommendations for the future' (CEH 1997 p. 4) and to undertake 'a general review of the scope of environmental health and the function of environmental health professionals and organisation' (1997, p. 6). The report overviews the EH service in the UK and identifies the strategic choices facing the profession. The report argues for a more integrated approach to policy formulation, recognising the complex interactions between the physical, social and economic environment, human behaviour patterns and health. Such interactions, it is argued, mean that EH professionals 'need to forge links with other professionals and other sectors - teachers, engineers, planners, industrialists - to provide a source of multiple expertise' (1997, p. 2). There is a recognition here that the effective provision of EH services requires an approach that is cross-functional, cutting across professional and organisational boundaries.

The report emphasises the importance of sustainable development, of interdependence between key stakeholders and of collaboration and partnerships between public and private sectors: 'No longer should professionals be able to hide behind the structural barriers of their employing agency. The major problems in environmental health cannot be solved by individuals or organisation acting alone. They require collective action and the active co-operation of many parties.' (1997, p. 9). An idea of the Commission's broad view EH can be gleaned from the following statement:

> Environment can no longer be pursued as a self-contained policy. It must be integrated with other policies - for transport, agriculture, energy and so on. The sustainability agenda was amplified with great force throughout the world at the United Nations Conference on the Environment and Development in Rio in 1992. One of the results of the Earth Summit was Agenda 21, a comprehensive strategy for advancing sustainable development internationally. (1997, p. 35)

This big picture approach may be appropriate to the complex interactions involved in the creation and maintenance of healthy environments, but the challenge is how to operationalise such strategic thinking at the local level. Any response requires not only technical expertise but also a high degree of interagency collaborative capability. The need will be for flexibility and multidisciplinary skills, and the ability and willingness to work effectively with an increasingly wide range of private sector and voluntary bodies, including pressure groups, community representatives and other non-statutory groups. In these senses managerial, political and participatory competences and sensitivities are likely to become increasingly important within the EH profession. Indeed the key to most of the Commission's recommendations lies in the integration of roles and responsibilities at local, national and international levels: 'Some of the proposals will require legislation and reorganisation of existing structures. Some will require rethinking of professional tasks and boundary lines'. And: 'All will require new ways for public bodies and professions to relate to their local communities and to the private sector' (1997, p. 83).

The EH profession has the opportunity to become a leader in the emerging governance of health related services. Indeed EH, in common with town planning, is one of the few local government professions to have strengthened its position in recent years. As a largely regulatory service the profession could be well placed to lay claim to a place within the core of local authorities - planning and monitoring the service delivery of others at the periphery. The alternative scenario would be if local authorities came to see regulation itself as a peripheral function. The EH Commission's report provides argumentative ammunition intended to equip EHOs to lay claim to a policy role in local government. Such a claim could be underpinned by the increasingly valued skills of EHOs in relation to risk assessment, environmental impact assessments, regulation and enforcement. However the claims are likely to be contested as other professions compete for the centre ground.

Conclusion

To sum up, how is EH work changing and in what direction? At least some EH work is moving from being exclusively service and regulatory based towards taking on more managerial and co-ordinating tasks, but it would be easy to overstate the shift. The EH service has become focussed more on strategy and enabling roles, with major contributions from other agencies both in the public sector (for example, the Environment Agency) and the private sector (for example, cleaning and refuse collection contractors and ex-local government EHOs who are now working as private consultants). Yet most of the work traditionally done by local government EHOs is still located within local authority EH departments which remain largely monopolistic bureaucracies. A shift from unified bureaucracy to organisational pluralism is recognisable but is so far muted.

A move away from control by hierarchy to a greater diversity of control mechanisms has taken place, especially in those EH departments which have taken over services like refuse collection and street cleaning where the operational work is often done by private contractors. However as most EH work is of a white collar kind, the moves towards contracting out such work have so far been marginal. Furthermore it is still unclear what the new Labour government's 'best value' approach will entail for future trends in contracting and quasi-contracting in EH work.

There has been some blurring between public and private sector and between politicians and officers. Some EH work is now being performed by the private sector, for example house condition surveys and some noise control work. Furthermore, there is some evidence that even within the public sector EH department (in fact in most local authority departments), 'private sector' managerial practices are becoming more common, including increasing use of fixed term contracts for staff, and the use of a wide range of 'managerial practices' including staff appraisal, strategic management and performance indicators and measurement. Nevertheless considerable concern remains over how important public sector values can and should be maintained within local government departments, including for accountability, probity and equity.

In terms of member-officer relationships some authorities, especially in large urban areas, have seen a move towards 'member led' departments, with councillors taking an unprecedented (at least in recent times) interest in the implementation of EH policies. In other areas, councillors are 'backing away' from detailed implementation and are happy to delegate to the 'technical experts'. In these cases councillor involvement becomes likely only when members of a local community are vociferously complaining about what is happening in their back yard.

The work of EHOs entails networking with an increasing range of agencies outside the employing local authority. An example is the way in which social housing now tends to be provided by the voluntary housing sector as opposed to local authority housing departments. At an earlier time, if a council house tenant felt unable to get the authority to carry out a needed repair, an option was for the complainant to contact the local EHO (who worked for the same authority). Either formally or informally the EHO could then bring pressure to bear on the housing department to get on with the repair as soon as possible. The same pattern of activity is still possible, but now it is more likely than in the past that the EHO would be pressuring a different organisation (for example a housing association). The EHOs' ability to pressurise this new landlord may be less than in the past (when the employer of the housing officers and EHOs was the same organisation), and the mode of operation is one of networking between different organisation.

Other agencies which require EHOs to be increasingly involved in inter-organisational collaboration include the Environment Agency, the Health and Safety Executive, The Meat Hygiene Service, TECs, Community Health NHS Trusts, various waste disposal organisation and a number of competing professional groups. As Rhodes (1996) has argued, such institutional complexity increases the degree of uncertainty and potential confusion within which professionals have to operate. Such confusion can mean that what were relatively simple patterns of accountability may now be blurred as networks lack a single hierarchy to ensure accountability at least in the traditional sense. In the post-bureaucratic polycentric system the watchwords become diplomacy, interdependency, trust and negotiation based on exchanges of money, information and expertise.

The governance of networks is an alternative or supplement to bureaucracies and markets. In the context of the EH Commission's ambitious report (1997) the ability of the profession to thrive into the millennium will depend, to a large extent, on the ability and willingness of EHOs to understand, and appropriately manage, the governance of networks.

References

Audit Commission (1993), *Realising the Benefits of Competition: the Client Role for Contracted Services*, HMSO: London.

Blau, P. M. and Scott, W. R. (1966), *Formal Organisation*, Routledge and Kegan Paul: London.

Brown, R. and Steel, D. (1979), *The Administrative Process in Britain*, Methuen: London.

Commission on Environmental Health (1997), *Report*, CIEH: London.

Cabinet Office (1991), *The Citizen's Charter*, Cmnd. 1599, HMSO: London.

Day, P. and Klein, R. (1987), *Accountabilities: Five Public Services*, Tavistock: London.

Deakin, N. and Walsh, K. (1994), 'The Enabling State: The Role of Markets and Contracts', Paper presented to the Employment Research Unit Annual Conference, Cardiff Business School.

Department of the Environment (1972), *The New Local Authorities: Management and Structure*, HMSO: London.

Ferlie, E., Ashburner, L., Fitzgerald, L. and Pettigrew, A. (1996), *The New Public Management in Action*, Oxford University Press: London.

Friedson, E. (1970), *Professional Dominance*, Atherton: London.

Greenwood, E. (1957), 'Attributes of a Profession', *Social Work*, Vol. 2, pp. 45-55.

Ham, C. & Hill, M. (1993), *The Policy Process in the Modern Capitalist State*, Wheatsheaf: London.

Handy, C. (1993), *Understanding Organisations*, Penguin: London.

HM Treasury (1991), *Competing for Quality: Buying Better Public Services*, Cmnd. 1730, HMSO: London.

Lipsky, M. (1980), *Street-Level Bureaucracy: Dilemmas of the Individual in the Public Services*, Russell Sage: New York.

Mullins, L. (1996), *Management and Organisational Behaviour*, Pitman: London.

Osborne, D. & Gaebler, T. (1992), *Reinventing Government*, Addison-Wesley: Reading, Mass.

Rhodes, R. (1996), 'The New Governance: Governing without Government' *Political Studies*, Vol. XLIV, pp. 652-67.

Ridley, N. (1988), *The Local Right*, Centre for Policy Studies: London.

Scarborough, H. and Burrell, G. (1994), 'From Downsizing to Demanaging? the Prospects for Radical Change in Middle Management Roles', British Academy of Management Conference, Lancaster University.

Stewart, J. (1992), 'The Rebuilding of Public Accountability' in Stewart, J., Lewis, N. and Longley, D. (eds.), *Accountability to the Public*, London: European Policy Forum.

Walsh, K. and Davis, H. (1993), *Competition and Service: The Impact of the Local Government Act 1988*, HMSO: London.

Acknowledgements

The author would like to thank Graham Jukes and Bryn Jones for their comments on earlier drafts of this chapter.

9 School teaching

Eric Hoyle and Peter D. John

It is conventional when writing about an emerging phenomenon to consider the pre-history of its emergence in order to identify its antecedents. This paper takes this familiar approach and in fact begins with a consideration of the period immediately after the Second World War. At first glance it may seem odd given the relatively recent emergence of the phenomenon of post-bureaucracy to go back fifty years. However it is part of our argument that the potential for post-bureaucracy in education is to be found in the period 1960-1975 and that this was mapped out by a shift in the political climate from the mid 1970s onwards. At this point the earlier consensual educational settlement gave way via the critical moment of the 'Great Debate' and the following Conservative educational offensive, to a major restructuring of the education system from the mid 1980s onwards.

The purpose of this chapter is to provide an analytical overview of these changes and to evaluate their effects on the nature of teacher professionalism. The chapter, therefore, is structured according to four post-war periods: 1945-1960; 1960-1975; 1975-1979; 1979-1997. Each of the subsections is structured as follows: (a) a brief comment on the socio-political context; (b) the structure of education at the national and institutional levels; (c) school governance and management; and (d) implications for teachers and other educationalists as professionals. We will work with no fixed definition of either bureaucracy or of profession though it is the bureaucracy-control-autonomy-profession nexus which provides the focus. One important reason for avoiding fixed definitions is that a semantic shift has been occurring, especially in relation to the concept of professional, which itself is to be treated as a key change.

1945-60 Post-war welfarism

The period from 1945-1975 has often been described as one of political consensus. This has been justified in relation to social policy where there was for three decades an all party commitment to the principles of a mixed economy, the maintenance of full employment and a belief in universal welfare provision. Despite the defeats of the Labour Party in 1951, 1955 and 1959 it was these social democratic ideals which underpinned the bi-partisan political support for the welfare state.

In the educational sphere many of the deep continuities of the pre-war system remained intact. One in particular was to prove particularly potent for teachers, was that they were relatively independent of the state and professionally autonomous since throughout England and Wales the Local Education Authorities (LEAs) as locally elected bodies were responsible for the running of the education system. That is not to say that there was not oversight from central government in the shape of the Ministry of Education and later the Department of Education, but the traditional landscape of a national system locally administered, remained valid for years to come.

For a useful metaphor for understanding school governance during this period we are indebted to Carlson (1964) who distinguished between domesticated and wild organisations. British schools were fed and watered by public funds and their governance was unproblematic, that is they were domesticated and not wild organisations in having to forage for survival in a competitive environment. Their governing bodies had a somewhat vacuous role and made very little contribution to the management of the school. Interestingly in this period the term 'management' was rarely used in relation to the day to day running of the school.

However some of the formal characteristics of Weber's model were present. There was a staff hierarchy, limited before the Burnham Agreement of 1954, more extended following it but the authority relationship was still between the head and the teacher, particularly in the primary school, rather than through intermediary position of deputy heads and heads of department etc. This dimension of bureaucracy increased somewhat during the period as large comprehensives were established. Bureaucracy in the sense of detailed rules and procedures was, where it occurred, a function of managerial style rather than any structural imperative. Schools were in Weick's (1970) later term 'loosely coupled'. Heads attended to policy and administrative matters, handled external issues and they interfered little with curricular matters or with pedagogy. For their part teachers enjoyed their relative autonomy and showed little desire to involve themselves in policy matters. Hanson (1979) was later to describe heads and teachers as having interacting spheres, largely independent of each other but in the overlapping zones both sides seeking an accommodation, though in Britain, very much more through implicit negotiation.

The head's role was less bureaucratic than in Weber's terminology traditional. The British headteacher had been very much the leading professional rather than the chief executive (Hughes 1973). The authority and influence of the head, though legally sanctioned, implicitly flowed from tradition which stretched back far beyond universal state provision of education. It was a central mission of teacher unions during the period to defend teacher autonomy, for instance their resistance to Eccles' attempt to enter 'the secret garden of the curriculum' which ended in the creation of a non-prescriptive Schools Council for Curriculum and Examinations on the sub-committees of which teachers were in a numerical majority (Manzer 1970).

Teacher accountability in this period could therefore could be described as 'default professional'. Although there was, of course, legal accountability there was minimal political and minimal bureaucratic and no market accountability in the public sector. Professional accountability held sway by default rather than by positive bestowal: governors were usually in fief of the 'professional' head, HMI were professionals relatively independent of the civil service, and LEA inspectors had a variety of functions few of which could be said to entail ensuring teacher accountability. Parents were rare visitors indeed to schools.

1960-1974 The high point of professionalism

The period up to the end of the decade marked the zenith of popular belief in state education. Paradoxically it was also the period during which serious misgivings were expressed about its efficiency and effectiveness. The Crowther Report (DES) and the Newsom Report (DES) on the education of children of average or below average ability began the erosion on the bipartite policy which followed the 1944 Act (although they were working from a consensual position). These and other academic findings confirmed misgivings about the efficiency of a system which allocated different types of school to children on the basis of an examination at eleven years of age. Because of these objections many LEAs had already begun to introduce comprehensive schooling by the time of Labour's election triumph of 1964.

A year later Tony Crosland, the then Labour Secretary of State for Education, in Circular 10/65 asked LEAs to submit plans for the reorganisation of secondary education in their areas along comprehensive lines. These deliberately egalitarian measures were continued by the incoming Heath administration in 1970. Admittedly the attack on grammar schools was scaled down with the publication of Circular 10/70. However by then the LEA juggernaut was too difficult to stop and comprehensive reform went on apace even under Margaret Thatcher's period as Secretary of State.

On the back of this major reorganisation came a welter of curricular changes and the rise of para-curricular organisations such as the Schools Curriculum and Assessment Council which spawned a number of reforms and innovations in the curriculum sphere. Furthermore, although the 'gold standard' of 'O' and 'A' levels remained, the Certificate of Secondary Education (CSE) was introduced in 1965 for the majority who lay outside the academic remit. In the primary sector the publication the Plowden Report stimulated the shift to what became termed 'child centred learning' and British schools became models for such innovations.

Nonetheless many of the changes were introduced piecemeal and had attendant problems. The new comprehensive schools, regardless of their broad social and educational aims, were trapped by changing priorities, mainly a lack of overall support from within and outside the profession and by the emergence of a small but vociferous band of critics exemplified by the authors of the Black Papers of 1969. This critical perspective continued throughout the 1970s and beyond creating what might be termed a 'perception of failure' which formed the basis to a radical right critique in the early 1980s.

Part of the problem appeared to stem form the fact that in terms of the curriculum, Crosland and his successors confirmed that government influence over the content of education would be limited to some inspection and LEA guidelines and as a result the curriculum still remained within the control of the professionals. Other of the characteristics of schooling during the period were as follows:

1 *Independent units*. Although schools were administered by the LEAs they remained somewhat loosely coupled. Although some could be said to have developed a LEA culture often defined by an influential Chief Inspector or powerful Chief Education Officer, such as Alec Clegg in the West Riding, there was little which could be called, in later terminology, a corporate plan. Heads were powerful and the bureaucratic network was supportive rather than intrusive. LEA inspectors were renamed advisors and adapted their functions accordingly and HMI whilst retaining the title re-defined its role accordingly. Thus schools enjoyed a high degree of independence.

2 *Constructionism*. This term is used to convey the fact that individual schools were in a position to construct themselves in terms of pedagogy, assessment and curriculum etc. There was little constraint on primary schools in areas, increasingly during the period where the 11 plus had been abandoned. At the secondary level the main constraint was constituted by the public examinations set for the more able pupils. One should not, however, overemphasise the degree to which schools constructed radical forms of schooling especially at secondary level. R. A. Butler told new secondary modern schools that 'your future is your own to make' and a variety of patterns emerged but ultimately the majority opted for external examinations for their upper streams which tended to shape the culture of the curriculum for all. Nevertheless much radical innovation occurred and is still the subject of obloquy by conservative politicians.

3 *Boundary erosion*. The main innovations of the period included: interdisciplinary curriculum, discovery learning, resource based project work, flexible timetabling, mixed ability grouping, multiple modes of assessment, collaborative teaching, and open plan architecture.

A characteristic common to these changes is the erosion of other boundaries - between subjects, between teachers and learners, between the structural components of the timetable, between modes of assessment (such as the inequalities of the exam or test replaced by continuous assessment, and profiling and modularized assignments), between teachers (at the level of policy, planning and pedagogy e.g. team teaching), between the physical boundaries of the school and between school and community. The ideal pattern was a group of teachers working with groups of pupils of varying size and abilities in resource based contexts and constructing curriculum, content, pedagogy and assessment. This mode of schooling with its flexible, negotiated and protean nature was assumed to fit pupils for a world where rapid change was endemic or 'beyond the stable state', culturally relative, and economically driven by rapidly developing technology. A society which needed its future citizens to be adaptive to have learnt how to learn, to be creative, to make choices between an increasing number of competing alternatives and committed to life long learning.

There was also the potential for and the beginnings of change in school management. Two trends were at work here: one was the growing emphasis in socio-political culture on participation - the belief that those affected by decisions should participate in making them; the other was the fact that constructionism in relation to the curriculum etc. was predicated on the notion of teacher collaboration. This was a challenge to heads who exercised rational or bureaucratic leadership which they handled with varying degrees of success (Hughes 1973).

This period marked the apotheosis of teaching as profession in terms of the conventional criteria. Some of the salient features of this process were as follows:

1 The minimum period of teacher education was extended from two to three years and then four years, and with the introduction of the BEd degree, a move to an all graduate profession with a strong theoretical basis to the training.

2 The organised teaching profession, mainly the teacher unions, was involved in what Manzer (1970) termed the 'sub-government of education' which entailed governments ensuring that they consulted the teacher unions on major policy matters.

3 The relatively high degree of autonomy of the school and of the teachers within them continued but with increasing opportunities for collaboration.

However although there was during this period the potential for a fundamental transformation of schools as organisations and teaching as profession, ultimately the elements failed to come together and by the mid 1970s the innovations were running into the sand. The loss of many of the previous certainties in education without a corresponding shift in other social institutions, compare this to Bernstein's (1969) question: 'Open schools, open society?' led to problems which are still being cited by politicians and commentators as the source of the perceived failures of schooling at the present time. A full historical analysis of why the movement failed is beyond the scope of this chapter and still lacks its historian. However the following elements can be identified:

1 An increasing economic stringency which led to a consequent reappraisal of the role of education and welfare generally. Linked to this was the emergence of the questioning of the costs and the powers of professions.

2 An increased questioning of the curriculum and teaching methods by parents and others, who by and large, did not understand the innovations which were taking

place because they had neither been consulted nor had them explained, and by politicians who picked up on parental concerns. The problems were highlighted by a number of educational scandals of which the case of William Tyndale School in Islington was the most famous (Auld 1970, Getton and Jackson 1976).

3 The fact that teachers had not been prepared to cope with innovation in curriculum and methods and hence many were floundering and suffering from innovation fatigue.

4 Likewise headteachers had not been prepared for the changes in school organisation and management on which curricular innovation had been predicated. Many found difficulty in coping with greater teacher involvement in decision making whilst retaining legal responsibilities for the internal activities of the school.

Overall the fact remains that, according to Chitty (1988), the concerted effort to displace teachers as the guardians of curriculum and pedagogy did not develop until the mid 1970s. The event which is usually taken as marking the end of this particular state is Jim Callaghan's Ruskin Speech of 1976 and the 'Great Debate' to which it gave rise.

1975-1979 The hiatus

As has been shown, the 1944 Act allowed central government to maintain its residual power to control and direct but left operational decisions within the hands of LEAs and the profession. However when such a decentralized policy was seen to be failing, the clamour for more centralization was unstoppable. Of crucial importance in this emerging critique were the changing fortunes of the British economy. An unstable minority Labour government although in power found it increasingly difficult to govern. The period therefore can be seen as one in which the increasingly strong manifestations of Britain's economic problems - inflation and unemployment - together with the falling value of the pound and increasing industrial conflict, forced a re-appraisal of the spending programmes of the state.

In education Labour's five years in power saw three secretaries of state come and go. The 1976 Education Act also saw the government legislate to enforce the continuation of its comprehensivization policy. The other major event was Callaghan's Ruskin College speech which heralded a shift in emphasis away from equality to one of raising standards and the need for schools to be more sensitive to the needs of industry and commerce. Arising out of the speech the Department of Education launched a series of conferences and published a document on the need for a core curriculum. These shifts in rhetoric presaged many of the reforms of the 1980s. It was somewhat ironic that the party of the comprehensive school produced a policy that was to be the foundation for the ideological blizzard which hit the education system little over a decade later.

1979-1997 Centralised bureaucracy and institutional autonomy

It is impossible to begin any discussion of the period without first making reference to the phenomenon which shaped it. Thatcherism, however, cannot be reduced to simple economic liberalism. Gamble's (1988) book *The Free Economy and the Strong State* perhaps best captures the essence of the notion. The strong state has been marked out because of its interventionist elements and in terms of social policy, far from being the opponents of social engineering, modern conservative ideologues have relished the opportunity to use policy to change behaviour. The laissez-faire principles enshrined in the notion of a free economy have also had a widespread impact. In its most active form this has been transformed into various types of privatisation sometimes operating within internal markets. Such an ideology has led to new relationships within the public sector and has recast the long standing relationship between central and local government.

Using this definition as a starting point it is easy to see how a sense of a progressive past moving ineluctably towards even greater social and educational improvement would have been dealt a severe and perhaps permanent blow during the 1980s - although as we have shown the seeds of that decline can be traced back into the previous decade. In this decade the recent past, rather than being seen as an engine of progress came to be viewed as the problem.

The prevailing undercurrent of concern and dissatisfaction which stemmed from the so-called 'progressive revolution' of the 1960s continued unabated. The decentralised governance of the education system and the freedom of the professionals to control the curriculum and pedagogy had all been enshrined as part of the British way of education. These verities came under attack in the 1980s as Britain's record of industrial decline cast doubt on such received wisdoms. Various international comparisons also appeared to show Britain lagging behind their European and World counterparts in literacy and numeracy. Studies by Sig Prias at the National Institute for Economic and Social Research, for instance, reached disturbing conclusions about the mathematical ability of British children compared to those in West German schools; while other studies showed British children being consistently outperformed by their peers in the Pacific Rim.

This 'perception of failure' had by the mid 1980s become widespread. The protracted 1985-6 dispute between teachers and their employers the LEAs highlighted the sense of a system in chaos. The Conservative government egged on by an increasingly influential right wing began to construct wholesale plans for dismantling the system based on the 1944 Act. However, this assault was built on shaky empirical foundations. Throughout the 1980s and beyond there is clear evidence of improved examination results; year by year statistics indicate a gradual rise in achievement at both GCSE and 'A' level. On the other hand there is a body of evidence showing a long tail of under achievement particularly for those the bottom 40 per cent of the ability range. This led Michael Barber to comment that improbable though it may seem, it appears that we have rising standards and falling standards at the same time'.

The perception was made more potent because the analysis upon which it was based was fundamentally populist in origin and intent. The radical Conservative government targeted the liberal educational establishment and teacher autonomy as fundamental causes. In the same firing line came the education departments at the universities and staff in the colleges of education who had propagated such trendy pedagogical strategies as well as highlighting social excuses for poor performance.

Furthermore this critique was underpinned by a private past that was elevated and eventually incorporated into educational policy (McCulloch 1996). Most notably Mrs. Thatcher referred to her own experience in emphasising the importance of direct grant and grammar schools and the decline attendant upon their demise: 'It is my passionate belief that since the war we have... strangled the middle way. Direct grant schools an grammar schools provided the means for people like me to get on equal terms with those who came from well off backgrounds.' (1995, p. 378). While Kenneth Baker, the architect of the 1988 Act, in his autobiography talked about his own experiences of the 1960s and highlights his hostility to comprehensive schooling and his distrust of the educational establishment: 'I had been amazed that Britain had decided to abandon the structure of its education system in this way, and as each year passed it became clearer that the high hopes of the comprehensive movement had not been fulfilled.' (1993, p.165). Such thoughts and beliefs acted as counterweights to current trends and were used as ways of creating and enacting a new educational agenda.

The primary focus of this new agenda was the raising of standards through organisational change. However the early 1980s saw this radical vision muted with the abandonment of the educational vouchers scheme and the withdrawal of the attempt to end the public funding of higher education. Other reforms also marked a shift in emphasis rather than a sharp break with the past. Parental power became a rubric for a series of changes relating to the extension of choice. The lifting of the statutory order to close grammar schools (imposed in 1976) was withdrawn and assisted places for children of poor families to be educated in Independent schools were to be financed. The statutory provision to provide more information about individual schools culminating years later in league tables of examination results was seen as a major step forward. Furthermore the demand that parents have a greater representation on governing bodies combined with pressure on LEAs to grant parents a place for their child in the school of their choice represented a genuine shift in emphasis.

In mid decade teachers also won a significant victory in their battle to create a unified examination at 16 with the joining up of the Certificate of Secondary Education (CSE) and the General Certificate of Education (GCE) in to the General Certificate Secondary Education (GCSE). However by the mid-1980s a full frontal assault was looming and the two year long industrial action by the teachers in 1985 proved to be the catalyst. The ending of the strike saw teachers deprived of their right to national pay bargaining (a right enshrined in the 1944 Act) and more dramatically saw the beginnings of more draconian measures which ended a century of tradition by bringing the United Kingdom in line with other European countries with the imposition of a National Curriculum.

The 1988 Act effectively replaced the 1944 version as the defining piece of legislation of the era. The new Act required that a National Curriculum be established with core and foundation subjects and that children be tested at the ages of 7, 11, 14 and 16 years. The Act also enabled the governors of state schools with the support of parents to apply to the Secretary of State to be funded by central government grant rather than by LEA devolved funding. The latter being based on a formula and centrally determined.

The Act then represented a significant departure from the philosophy of the 1944 Act which left most education under local authority control and left issues about the organisation and determination of the curriculum largely in the hands of teachers. In effect the Act not only enhanced central control over the structure and content of education but also put semi-autonomous schools into a situation whereby they were in direct competition with each other.

In some respects the 1990s have seen a slow down in the pace of change. The Dearing Review of the curriculum and its assessment introduced by the then Secretary of State John Patten, marked a period of consolidation and review and a time of claw back for teachers as their traditional relationship with the curriculum was in part restored. The Review also acknowledged a limited role for teachers in determining the content of the curriculum within the overall framework of the national guidelines. This slimming down process was created in order to 'allow scope for professional judgment' (Dearing 1993, p. 20) but only within the confines of a 'matched accountability to parents and society including that from simple tests in the core subjects.' (Dearing 1993, p. 25). Barber (1994) has suggested that these revisions have created a new relationship based on new forms of public accountability and partnership. Whether this is the case remains to be seen. However in Teacher Training the reform process has been speeding up. The creation of the Teacher Training Agency to oversee the training and professional career structure of teachers has seen the traditional independence of University Departments and Colleges of Education further eroded.

Teacher autonomy was not the only form of independence to suffer under the new legislative framework, local authorities were also victims. Throughout the early 1980s their financial independence had been slowly eroded by the increased rights of parents as well as a number of administrative and financial changes. The Act moved things at an even greater pace. Devolved budgeting in the form of Local Management of Schools, the radical attempt to permit schools to opt out of LEA control through Grant Maintained status and the drive to set up new City Technology Colleges were all moves which weakened the transitional role of local government. In one sense the reforms had a logic whereby local government was being asked to exchange its executive role for a more strategic one. However this role was often clouded by the lack of clear planning, and an almost ceaseless flow of amendments, curtailments and regulations. In addition the theory that parents would make clear choices of good schools using test results was not fully thought out. Good schools would be encouraged to expand and thereby get a larger resource slice but how exactly they should expand given the range of complex issues associated with capital costs was not clear. Neither was it clear what should happen to the declining schools. As a result the theory of inter-school competition acting as the progenitor of rising standards was not easily translated into practice.

The most significant implication for schools during this period was the spread of managerialism. With the shift in funding from LEAs to schools and with some schools opting for Grant Maintained status, schools became much more self managing particularly in relation to their budgets. However although they became less tightly coupled to their LEAs, they became more tightly coupled to their governing bodies in relation to finance and policy and to central government in terms of the delivery of the National Curriculum, national tests and a variety of other policies such as OFSTED (Office for Standards in Education) inspections. Thus it became possible for a school like a business to fail and hence they became more managerially focused on meeting external forms of accountability.

Inspection was thus seen then as a central plank in the recasting of teacher professionalism. The original HMI of 480 elite inspectors was felt to be insufficient in number to carry out detail inspections of all the nation's schools. In addition many politicians were suspicious of the HMI and felt that too often they had 'gone native' supporting and indeed espousing the causes so despised by the radical right. Apart from the political correctness of the Inspectorate, there were also the logistics of inspection. If all schools were to come under the remit of the Inspectors then a massive expansion would have to take place. The setting up of OFSTED in 1992 with a remit to concentrate on the task of inspecting all schools within four years also had a significant impact on teacher autonomy and professionalism. There is no doubt that OFSTED reports add considerably to the information available about schools and teachers. However the grading of lessons and the narrowing of effect such judgments on the process of teaching has had an impact on the professional independence of teachers.

Broadly these changes have led to a much tighter coupling between various components of the school than had ever been the case formerly. This tighter coupling was exemplified through the need to formulate mission statements, produce development plans and install a variety of monitoring procedures. The self managing school became one in which curriculum development, organisational development and staff development were integrated (at least at the level of intention). Thus schools gained a greater degree of autonomy in some areas, but teachers lost much of the autonomy which they had previously enjoyed. Ironically teachers actually became more collaborative than in the 1960s and 1970s and such terms as 'collegiality' and 'empowerment' have became common slogans. There is some evidence that teachers welcomed increased opportunities for greater collaboration but also that they have experienced a loss of autonomy (Hoyle and John 1995).

It would seem that whilst schools have to a degree lost the shackles, real or imaginary, of the LEA, teachers themselves have not enjoyed increased autonomy. In fact the structural looseness of schools has been replaced by a neo-bureaucracy legitimised by the concept of empowerment. The organisational form of neo-bureaucracy entails sub-committees, working parties, problem solving teams, task-forces and the like. These groups develop mission statements, policy documents, appraisal schemes and so forth. These activities are variously described as 'participative', 'collaborative' or 'collegial'.

There are indications that teachers appreciate these forms of greater collaboration (Pollard et al. 1994), though ironically one of the reasons given is mutual support in the relief of stress. Thus one of the central issues arising out of the neo-bureaucracy is whether empowerment is giving teachers more 'real' power that is authority, or simply influence, or whether it is means of control - what has been referred to as 'enforced collegiality' (Smyth 1991) and 'contrived collegiality' (Hargreaves 1994). Nonetheless despite the widespread rhetoric of empowerment there is still not enough empirical evidence upon which to come to any firm conclusions.

These changes have had considerable implications for teaching as a profession. This process has been given various labels: 'proletarianisation', 'deprofessionalisation' and the 'new professionalism'. We find 'proletarianisation' unhelpful and see the debate as turning on whether teaching is experiencing a period of deprofessionalisation entailing a loss of autonomy, deskilling, work intensification, less influence on policy at the national level or whether a new concept of professional is emerging which might be described as: 'To be a professional is to have acquired a set of skills through competency-based training which enables one to deliver efficiently according to contract a customer-led service in compliance with accountability procedures collaboratively implemented and managerially assured.' (Hoyle 1995, p.78).

If such a trend continues the familiar distinction between the principles of bureaucracy, which emphasises rules and procedures, and professionalism, which emphasises knowledge and judgment, will become less clear.

The process of tightening control on the training of teachers has also continued. In between the introduction of CATE in 1984 which accredited courses and the creation of the TTA a decade later, initial training has gradually come under the control of central government and its agencies. Often seen as 'the enemy within', education departments during the 1990s, were singled out for specific criticism and reform. The result has been the creation of an internal market within the sector and the rise of school based training overseen by the new Teacher Training Agency. This attempt to break the monopoly of the supplier has had wide reaching implications. This new body has already assumed control over the curriculum and assessment of teacher training and is likely to further strengthen its bureaucratic hold through the establishment of standards of competency and expert teacher status. It also has the power to control the number of entrants into the profession (although fluctuations in the economic cycle appears to a better indicator) as well as pronounce on the standards of their base line qualifications

The relationship between the LEAs and schools has also changed. Devolved funding via LEAs has meant that many of the services previously received as a matter of course now have to be bought back. Schools are now in the driving seat vis-à-vis the LEAs but the authorities have retained some vestiges of monitorial responsibility, for instance problems experienced at school level, whether pedagogical, curricular or managerial, still have to be solved by the LEA. However in most areas the governing bodies have effectively taken over the managerial responsibilities that once fell to the local authority and now oversee the appointment and contracts of teachers. Furthermore it is these bodies' responsibility to see that the Curriculum and other statutory regulations are being adhered to within their schools.

A number of researchers have given empirical nuances to the effects of these changes on teachers as professionals. Many claim that the reforms have resulted in a complex, sometimes contradictory and often confusing response from teachers. Some studies have shown teachers as interacting with, confirming as well as subverting, particular policies. Others have highlighted the emergence of a new professionalism whereby some teachers comply with the reforms as a remedy to both perceived weaknesses in the old system and as a way of helping them develop their careers (Troman 1995). Mac an Ghaill terms these 'the new entrepreneurs,' and describes them as:

> members of a teacher association emphasising the professional status of a career, opposed to trade unions and industrial action, in favour of a non-strike contract agreement and supportive of increased management responsibilities and classroom teachers' accountability and appraisal while having a strong commitment to the promotion of new courses, supportive of an enterprise culture, overtly ambitious with a strong commitment to career advancement and with a projected high profile within the school. (1995, p.180)

Still others have seen the potential in the reforms for the emergence of new collaborative practices (Hymans 1995) while Osborne et al. (1996) speak of a shift from isolation to collaboration driven by a substantial minority who saw a range of opportunities within the reforms for innovation and creative new ways of regaining their lost independence. The research data also point to the effect that different career histories as well as differing subject and pedagogical beliefs have on the variety of responses given by teachers.

Whether these new professionals are suffering from a 'false consciousness' (Hargreaves 1994) is a matter for conjecture. However these 'mediators', as Osborne et al. (1996) have termed them, have become more focused and were coping and indeed developing their professionality within the confines of the National Curriculum.[1] Interestingly the same researchers found significant differences in the views expressed by those teachers in inner-city schools compared to their colleagues in more affluent suburbs. The former saw the National Curriculum as taking no account of classroom realities and that the framework was not suited to children with special needs, while the latter saw the National Curriculum as providing more continuity as well as enhancing their teaching skills.

Taken as a whole then, the research evidence reveals a varied and uneven post-reform landscape. However what we can say with some certainty is that teachers are becoming composite professionals in their responses to the changing conditions and roles they are expected to fulfill. And here the tactic of resistance within a general strategy of accommodation appears to be the most favoured option. The extent to which this will remain given the continued reform of initial teacher education and the likely tightening of the OFSTED model of inspection we can only estimate, although there is some evidence, both anecdotal and empirical, of teachers managing the OFSTED visit with considerable ingenuity and control. Such findings again give credence to the powerful role that human agency continues to exert in the shaping of teachers' professionalism.

Conclusion: 1997 and beyond

Many of the changes that have affected society over the past two decades have been given various labels with 'post-modern' perhaps the most favoured. The break up of the old certainties often characterized in industrial terms by post-fordism, in the cultural sphere by relativism and in commercial terms by consumerism have had a profound influence on the educational landscape. The championing of choice and diversity in terms of schooling and the rise of the self managing school have all become beacons to a so-called fragmented system of education. And yet there is a curious paradox here: despite relativist chants, many of the current and future reforms have been and will continue to be underpinned by the language and practice of what Habermas has termed instrumental rationality, a belief in the power of management principles typified by technical and scientific power. These tendencies can be seen in any number of OFSTED's checklist or in the TTAs pronouncements on teacher training and the future of the profession. Even the National Curriculum in its slimmed down, user-friendly, post-Dearing prescription, still has the vestiges of this language locked into its structures.

So what effect are these 'mixed messages' (Hartley 1994) likely to have in the future? Firstly in terms of schooling the concept of the self-managing school is destined to stay. However there are a number of directions in which such schools may choose to move. The demise of the LEAs, perhaps one of the most lasting signs of post-bureaucracy, have opened up both problems and possibilities. Given that most schools still operate under LMS rather than GMS, a patchwork of local networks made up of various types of stakeholder (parents, students, business, community leaders etc.) is likely to evolve. These schools will then enter into various forms of partnership, sponsorship and consortia in order to secure their future.

These arrangements could take a number of forms: in the first instance, as Caldwell and Spinks (1992) have suggested, they may coalesce under a charter model whereby a formal agreement among schools, central and local government will be entered into. Funding would be guaranteed provided that the policies of these superordinate levels are met. A second type, according to Caldwell and Spinks (1992), might be based on a local support model which sees central government as having a strategic core with clusters of schools being formed to manage their resources more effectively. These schools would be managed within a centrally determined framework. The third model would see schools grouped within a re-centralised structure whereby a national system would operate which would be closely monitored with tiers of support at state and regional levels.

Running through each of these types is the seemingly contradictory rhetoric of central control with local management and choice. Whatever route is chosen it is likely that there will be an increasing isomorphism (Hartley 1995) in the management of control and that choice will be limited. Parents will be able to choose but only within the limits of the curriculum. Teachers will be able to choose appropriate pedagogy but only within set guidelines and the constraints of the curriculum, testing and inspection. Central strategic control will therefore be maintained over an increasingly diverse and heterogeneous education system. It is also likely that the previous Conservative government's attack on comprehensive education will continue since the Labour Party has shown no particular sign of preserving comprehensive education in its earlier guise. Labour, like the Conservatives, is committed to choice, diversity and quality albeit within the general rubric of social justice.

Lastly in terms of teachers as professionals the 'official teacher' (Barton et al. 1994) line taken by various Secretaries of State in the early 1990s is showing signs of being superseded by a more limited version of 'licensed autonomy' (Grace 1989). As a result, in the shorter term at the very least, there is likely to be a reaffirmation of educational leadership and teacher autonomy albeit in a new form. This will not lead, however, to a return to default professional accountability but to the development of new quasi-professional forms perhaps given shape by a General Teaching Council. For such a body is unlikely to resemble the General Medical Council since the weakening of boundaries between professionals and clients means that a GTC, in whatever form, will only have limited operational power.

Note

1   There are perhaps three levels of professionality referred to here. At the practical level, professionality entails a body of skill and knowledge which teachers must have if they are to be effective classroom practitioners. The second level of professionality lies in the capacity for exercising sound judgment. The third level entails the effort made by teachers to equip themselves with the competences required to make effective judgments. Three aspects of this third level have can be discerned, they are: professional development, reflectiveness and ethics. For a full discussion see Hoyle and John (1995).

References

Auld, R. (1976), *Report of the Public Enquiry into the William Tyndale Junior and Infant School*, Inner London Education Authority: London.

Baker, K. (1993), *The Turbulent Years: My Life in Politics*, Faber and Faber: London.

Barber, M. (1994), 'Unions' Testing Boycott Threatens to Raise Standards', *Sunday Times*, 22 May.

Barton, L., Barrett, E., Whitty, G., Miles, S. & Furlong, J. (1994), 'Teacher Education and Teacher Professionalism in England', *British Journal of Sociology of Education*, Vol. 15, No. 4, pp. 529-542.

Bernstein, B. (1967), 'Open School, Open Society', *New Society,* 14 September, pp. 351-53.

Boyle, M. L. (1995), 'The Corporate Head: Coping with Changes in a Primary Headteacher's Role', paper delivered at the British Educational Research Association conference, University of Bath, September.

Caldwell, B. J. & Spinks, J. M. (1992), *Leading the Self Managing School*, Falmer: London.

Carlson, D. (1964), 'Environmental Constraints and Educational Consequences' in Griffiths, D. (ed.), *Behavioural Science and Educational Administration*, University of Chicago Press: Chicago.

Chitty, C. (1988), 'Central Control of the School 1944-1987', *History of Education,* Vol. 17, pp. 321-34.

Dearing, R. (1993), *The National Curriculum and its Assessment: Final Report*, Schools curriculum and Assessment Authority: London.

Gamble, A. (1983), *The Free Economy and the Strong State*, Macmillan: Basingstoke.

Grace, G. (1987), 'Teachers and the State in Britain: a Changing Relationship' in Lawn, M. and Grace, G. (eds.), *Teachers: The Culture and Politics of Work*, Falmer: London.

Gretton, J & Jackson, M. (1976), *William Tyndale: Collapse of a School or a System?* Allen & Unwin: London.

Hanson (1979), *Education Administration and Organisational Behaviour*, Allyn & Bacon: Boston.

Hargreaves, A. (1994), *Changing Teachers, Changing Times: Teachers' Work and Culture in the Post-Modern Age*, Cassell: London.

Hartley, D. (1994), 'Mixed Messages in Education Policy: Signs of the Times', *British Journal of Educational Studies*, Vol. 42, No. 3, pp. 230-43.

Hoyle, E. (1995), 'Changing Conceptions of a Profession', in Busher, H. and Saran, R. (eds.), *Managing Teachers as Professionals in Schools*, Kogan Page: London.

Hoyle, E. (1994), 'Education in the Next Hundred Years', in Turner, J. D. (ed.), *One Hundred Years Not Out: Education in the 1990s and Beyond*, University of Manchester Press: Manchester.

Hoyle, E. & John, P. D. (1995), *Professional Knowledge and Professional Practice*, Cassell: London.

Hughes, M. (1973), 'The Professional Administrator: the Case of the Secondary School Head', *Educational Administration Bulletin*, Vol. 2, No. 1.

Lowe, R. (1994), *The Welfare State in Britain since 1945*, Macmillan: London.

Mac an Ghail (1992), 'Teachers' Work: Curriculum Re-structuring, Culture, Power and Comprehensive Schooling', *British Journal of Sociology of Education*, Vol.13. No. 2, pp. 177-97.

Manzer, R. A. (1970), *Teachers and Politics*, University of Manchester Press: Manchester.

McCulloch, G. (1997), 'Privatising the Past? History and Education Policy in the 1990s', *British Journal of Educational Studies*, Vol. 45, No.1, pp. 69-82.

Osborne, M. and Black, E. (1996), 'Working Together in Primary Schools: Changing Relationships at Key Stage 2', in R. Chawla-Duggan and C. Pole (eds.), *Reshaping Education in the 1990s: Perspectives on Primary Schooling*, Falmer: London.

Perkin, H. (1989), *The Rise of Professional Society*, Routledge: London.

Pollard, A. (1994), *Changing English Primary Schools: The Impact of the Educational Reform Act at Key Stage 1*, Cassell: London.

Simon, B. (1985), 'The Tory Government and Education: 1951-1960', *History of Education*, Vol. 14, pp. 283-96.

Smyth, J. (1991), 'International Perspectives on Teacher Collegiality', *British Journal of Sociology of Education*, Vol.12, No. 3.

Thatcher, M. (1995), *The Path to Power*, Harper-Collins: London.

Troman. G. (1996), 'The Rise of the New Professional', *British Journal of Sociology of Education*, Vol. 16, No. 4, pp. 626-41.

Weick, K. (1970), 'Educational Organisations as Loosely Coupled Systems', *Administrative Science Quarterly*, Vol. 21.

10 Higher education

Mary Henkel

The social, political and economic salience of higher education increased across the world during the 1980s and 1990s. Governments have come to see the expansion of higher education as the key to improved economic performance. Yet current economic performance remained inadequate to fund expansion at existing rates of investment, thus units of resource were set to decline. In Britain higher education had been an elite sector of society, concerned substantially with the production and sustainment of other elites. Yet by the 1990s higher education participation rates had risen enormously and the number of institutions with university status had proliferated.

The movements affecting the academic profession are similar to those affecting other parts of the public sector, notably the advance of the cultures and mechanisms of management and the market. But partly because of the elite nature of higher education, the academic profession has traditionally been weakly organised and highly fragmented: 'British university teaching was strongly contained within the gentlemanly tradition' (Halsey 1992). The profession took its power and status for granted and therefore has in some respects been unprepared to face new challenges.

Higher education has other features which makes any discussion of it in the context of the politics of public management particularly interesting. Firstly the organisation and management of higher education are integrally linked with ideas about the nature of advanced knowledge and its modes of production. Organisational changes may thus influence or reflect changes at the heart of higher education. Secondly the former Conservative government allowed and later took credit for the massive growth of the sector. That government unified higher education, giving the former polytechnics university status, and bound it more strongly into the state yet also pressurised universities to embrace the market.

The organisational forms and the mechanisms of control developed and used in this process are comparable with those introduced elsewhere in the public sector despite the latter's distinctive features - the relatively low level of bureaucratisation, tendencies towards horizontal rather than vertical relationships and the central role played by one professional group. These forms and mechanisms have been labelled 'new public management' and can be identified as follows: capping budgets and making resource allocation more transparent; disaggregating traditional bureaucratic organisations into separate agencies; decentralising management authority within public agencies; separating the purchaser and provider functions in public services; introducing market and quasi-market mechanisms; requiring staff to work to output and performance targets; shifting the basis of public employment from permanency and standard national pay and conditions to fixed term contracts and local determination of pay and conditions; increasing emphasis on quality and customer responsiveness (Pollitt 1995).

Have these changes set in motion a coherent dynamic? If so is this dynamic strengthening managerial control and vertical accountability, albeit in a complex and unstable context? Is the underlying purpose to enable managers to manage by increasing managerial autonomy and accountability but within a fundamentally vertical conception of the organisation? Yet such a top-down, hierarchical approach is likely to be weakened by the incorporation of market mechanisms and the deliberate blurring of the boundaries between the public and the private. Markets introduce other influences to which organisations must respond and, if introduced at all levels, encourage alternative locations of power to emerge, foster horizontal relationships and blur the boundaries of the organisation. Such market effects encourage the discretion of multiple actors to engage in diverse activities in pursuit of the overall values of the institution, reminiscent of the language of Peters and Waterman (1982).

Is then the fundamental question about whether new managerial mechanisms in higher education have been directed towards accountability and conformity? or is the question about how far higher education has moved towards a mixed economy in which there are multiple stakeholders with implications for the balance between internal and external, and provider and purchaser or user influences? What have been the consequences, in either case, for the academic profession and its influence? Has the profession been signficantly weakened?

Even so how fruitful is it to think in terms of alternatives at all? On line of argument is that the language of paradox and ambiguity and the management of contradiction, characteristic of writing about post Fordist models of management in the private sector, is more appropriate: 'freedom within boundaries', 'formalized freedoms', 'centralized decentralization', the managerialization of professionals (Hoggett 1991).

The academic profession: political strengths, weaknesses and uncertainties

Perhaps the most distinctive characteristic of British higher education has been its long resistance to changes that were more than evolutionary. As late as 1984 it was still an elite system in Trow's classification of elite, mass and universal systems higher educational systems (Trow 1970). Elite systems recruit less than fifteen per cent of the traditionally eligible population of school leavers, mass systems between fifteen and forty per cent. Those recruiting forty per cent or more are defined as universal.

This resistance to change was underpinned by the interplay between political and social forces and a continued belief in what Kogan has termed 'higher education essentialism'. This term refers to how higher education entails a particular and intrinsically exclusive conception of knowledge, mediated by strong internal control and adherence to epistemic rules of inquiry and testing, logic, use of evidence, norms of conceptual and theoretical rigour and creativity, and the disinterested pursuit of truth. This view of knowledge was supported in Britain for most of this century by a particular political arrangement, in which universities were the beneficiaries of a 'handsome corporatist bargain' (Kogan 1988) struck with the state at the formation of the University Grants Committee (UGC) in 1919. A bargain between elites, based on mutual trust, self regulating universities were assumed to be the best way of providing the advanced forms of knowledge and elite education required to sustain national elite values: military power, reputation in science, key institutions and culture. Despite their growing financial dependence on the state, universities' sense of exceptionalism and autonomy remained secure: they were chartered institutions and their members controlled the key public resource allocation systems.

By the time of the 1963 Robbins Report only twenty-four universities existed, with a further six planned. In none did the student population exceed 10,000, in more than half it was less than 3,000 (Halsey 1992). In the 1960s the growth of higher education was achieved largely through the creation of a second and unequivocally public sector of higher education. This second sector filled a different role in advanced technological and vocational education and could be more firmly planned in terms of the public interest. However the concept of higher education that developed within that sector was ambiguous. Polytechnics were from the beginning subject to validation by a national body, the CNAA, that demanded conformity to the academic standards set by the universities. They would come to be seen not as 'equal but different', as their creator Tony Crosland envisaged, but rather as potential or alternatively second class universities.

Polytechnics were also essentially urban institutions under local authority control and, whilst their national profile was growing, they recruited strongly from their local populations. They were relatively open systems and responsive to new demands (Scott 1995); and thus set in motion a dynamic of growth. Despite continuing to recruit within the fifteen per cent figure, the traditional age group of higher education students, they became increasingly explicitly committed to a philosophy of wider access (Becher and Kogan 1992). For some in the 1980s they were seen as having the potential to become a popular model of higher education, contrasting but complementary to the elite model (Ball 1988).

So from the 1960s a dual and asymmetric system of higher education existed. Universities and polytechnics were rooted in different structures and cultures. Universities retained the forms and the ideal (or perhaps the rhetoric) of collegial governance and assumptions of individual as well as institutional autonomy and academic equality. They had not wholly emerged from a pre-bureaucratic age. The dominant norms were those of individual or professional responsibility rather than public accountability. In contrast the polytechnics were explicitly dependent institutions, subject to external academic regulation and local authority governance. Their organisation was one of professional bureaucracy and their culture informed by norms of public accountability and public service, as well as academic values.

When central government wanted change in higher education, it was to some extent able to exploit the different interests of the two sectors, and the universities found that the power they had taken for granted was not so secure. For example the UGC decided to deal with the 1981 cuts to higher education by maintaining the unit of resource and reducing student numbers. The polytechnics adopted the opposite strategy. Throughout the decade the universities' responses to government pressures for change were a combination of resistance, reluctant concession and preemption. They saw most policies as threats to the autonomy that they had sustained as a fundamental principle. The polytechnics showed themselves to be more ready to deliver what government wanted. The political demand for growth was almost certainly a part product of their access policies. They gained in political influence during this period and polytechnic directors became an interest group of growing importance.

When the binary divide ended in 1992 the Committee of Directors of Polytechnics (CDP) was absorbed into the Committee of Vice Chancellors and Principals (CVCP). Never a strong political force, the CVCP now embraced even more diverse interests, which made it harder to act effectively within the policy process.

The academic profession had other long standing sources of weakness. Despite the affiliation of the Association of University Teachers (AUT) to the TUC in 1971, the profession retained many guild characteristics, for example in the relatively low internal salary differentials and in assumptions about integrated patterns of work incorporating research, teaching and administration (Halsey 1992). Indeed in some ways the profession would be better described as a series of interlocking guilds, organised around disciplines, fields of knowledge and individual institutions. The most powerful norms into which academics are socialised are not those of collective action but those of academic autonomy, self motivation within self regulating communities, and the need to establish a distinctive academic identity and competitiveness.

The profession lacks a professional association, although the AUT has recently been seeking to shift its function in that direction. As the political nature of the environment has become more evident, divisions within the profession have become increasingly obvious for example, between scientists, social scientists and the humanities. The scientists have stronger structures for the pursuit of their interests and more institutionalised connections with government, though even many of these are sectional and in competition with each other for scarce resources.

Factors affecting policy change

The impetus for change came from government, changed economic circumstances and the increasingly contested nature of knowledge in contemporary society. From the early 1980s to the publication of the White Paper on science policy in 1993 government ministers were the main drivers of change in higher education.[1] At first government policy for higher education was similar to that in other policy sectors: tighter control of public expenditure; increased accountability, in particular for the economic and efficient management of scarce resources; and better performance against output criteria, notably the production of students with skills and competencies relevant to employment.

By 1987 higher education policy became more complex and difficult policy tensions emerged. The policy aim of rapid growth to create not just a mass but a universal system of higher education by the end of the century appeared to conflict with concerns that higher education should preserve the functions of reproducing science, business and governing elites. More specific aims stressed the need for institutional accountability for quality as well as efficiency; to maintain science and technology at the leading edge to provide the foundations of long term economic competitiveness and (sotto voce) quality of life; to build strong links between higher education, industry and employers of all kinds; and for new curricula designed to promote neo liberal values of enterprise and a skilled, flexible workforce. All of these aims were to be achieved in the context of a declining unit of resource.

The economy was a critical factor in higher education policy change. The economic turbulence of the early 1980s, high unemployment, the steep decline of manufacturing industries and the restructuring of the economy towards service industries affected demand for higher education and perceptions of its economic contribution. The 1985 Green Paper highlighted the issue of competitiveness and Britain's lack of success in producing qualified scientists, engineers and technologists compared to other countries. The paper stressed positive attitudes to business, entrepreneurialism and vocationalism in higher education, alongside a more general focus in government policies on the acquisition of competencies, skills and relevant and applicable knowledge (DES 1985, Silver and Brennan 1988, Barnett 1994).

But other, more profound changes in the international economy began to shape higher education: the impacts of the new technologies on modes of production and consumption and on the international nature of businesses and products themselves (Harvey 1989, Scott 1995). These changes provoked the development of new programmes, primarily but not exclusively, in the polytechnics such as business and management studies, communication studies and computer studies. Growth in higher education was stimulated by the interplay between the demands of changing industries, changes in the population of aspiring students, increased insecurities of employment and educational provision. The language of policy shifted towards a 'new vocationalism', in which representatives of industry, careers services and educational studies combined to advocate personal transferable skills, student centred learning, learning to learn and lifelong learning.

The economy was not the only factor in changing perceptions of higher education, its organisation and its boundaries and relationships with other sectors of society. Formerly uncontested beliefs in the intrinsically exclusive nature of advanced knowledge and its acquisition, in the logical connection between the attainment of truth and academic autonomy and in the essential unpredictability of the implications of advances in science have all been challenged. Sociologists of knowledge have been in the vanguard of challenge. There is now some consensus among them that knowledge is neither wholly internally nor wholly externally driven. The issue is rather 'the extent to which social and cognitive factors interpenetrate' and the different types and degrees of interpenetration in different areas of research and under different conditions (Elzinga 1994).

But the idea that knowledge must be advanced and taught without reference or accountability to the public domain has become unsustainable. The notion articulated by Trist (1972) in the context of social science that new knowledge needs to be developed through new forms of collaboration between academics, policy makers and practitioners has gained new support. Gibbons et al. (1994) argue for the advance of a 'Mode 2' production of knowledge, alongside the 'Mode 1' that is discipline based. Mode 2 knowledge is generated in the context of application but often when there is no existing knowledge to apply; it is heterogeneous knowledge produced in networks constituted by all sorts of organisations and individuals at all sorts of sites; and it is accountable to society and against new definitions of quality (Scott 1997). Knowledge thus becomes, in Mode 1 terms, subject to 'epistemic drift', to external influence on its organisation, rules and evaluative criteria (Elzinga 1985).

But perhaps the most fundamental challenges from sociology, philosophy and from postmodernism in all its forms are to the concept of truth and of knowledge as discovery. Scientists and scholars are seen as engaged in the 'production of knowledge', in 'cognitive practices', in various incommensurate and irreconcilable 'discourses'; as competing to determine what is orthodoxy in their field or what power their 'discourse' will have to shape social beliefs and practices. Postmodernism would make obsolete the idea of hierarchies of knowledge and adherence to knowledge rules.

This confusion and paradox in changes in knowledge and theories of knowledge has affected higher education. The growth of knowledge and its influence on societies has been massive and the speed of its development continues to accelerate, with major implications for patterns of learning and application. But the forms of knowledge have also multiplied, from ever greater scientific and technological specialisation to the codification and certification of ordinary, experiential, occupational and procedural knowledge. The idea that modern societies are knowledge societies has become a cliché to a point where the authority of knowledge, perhaps even its meaning, has been rendered uncertain. The demand for certified forms of knowledge has greatly increased and universities have become more central institutions in such societies. But their monopoly over advanced forms of knowledge has gone and they find themselves in an increasingly competitive arena.

These substantive changes have made higher education vulnerable to the new public management. They are opening up traditional boundaries to the acquisition and production of knowledge which make those process more difficult to manage. They also undermine the claims of higher education to exceptionalism. Instead public interest demands for greater accountability in higher education and strengthened mechanisms for accountability have become more difficult for academics to challenge.

Policy change and a new public management: the national level

Mechanisms of control

Early in the 1980s the tightening grip on resources brought shifts towards stronger central planning in the public sector through the establishment in 1982 of the National Advisory Body (NAB) and in the university sector when by 1985 the UGC had become 'a full blooded planning organisation which required universities to respond in the same mode' (Becher and Kogan 1992). The Education Reform Act 1988 abolished both the NAB and the UGC and made the polytechnics and universities subject to parallel funding councils: the Universities Funding Council (UFC) and the Polytechnics and Colleges Funding Council (PCFC), so significantly reducing the asymmetry between the sectors. Polytechnics gained corporate status and were freed from local authority control. The ending of the binary line in 1992 brought this move to its logical conclusion with the UFC and the PCFC replaced by Higher Education Funding Councils for England, Wales and Scotland.

The mechanisms of control established after the 1988 Act were a mix of evolution and more radical change. The most explicit mechanisms were those of resource allocation and evaluation, which in some cases were combined, and contracts. One consequence of the absence of a professional body for academics is that no national framework exists for calling them to account across the range of their responsibilities. Instead academic accountability is to a variety of bodies, including funding councils, research councils, other research sponsors and professional organisations. Beyond these they have responsibilities, but no formal accountability, to the users of their services, most notably students and employers. Changes in the funding framework for higher education following the 1997 Dearing Report, under which students will be charged tuition fees for the first time, will not alter this, although it will give students more power in their relationships with universities.

Both predecessor bodies of the national funding councils aimed to set in place transparent and output related resource allocation. This was explicitly and radically expressed in their introduction of contract funding in 1988. Institutions were to make contractual undertakings about their academic outputs with the councils in exchange for the resources allocated to them and their performance would be monitored accordingly. Performance indicators were to be developed to facilitate this (DES 1987, Morris Report 1990).

Undoubtedly the most powerful mechanism had its origins in the UGC which put in place the first research selectivity exercise in 1985, foreshadowed by the selective cuts made in 1981. The protagonist in this development was the chief executive, an academic scientist concerned that scarce resources should be allocated to support the best scientists. It has grown into the quadrennial Research Assessment Exercise (RAE), in which all universities wishing to receive resources for research from the funding councils under the dual support system must participate. The exercise is subject based and evaluation is by peer review. Subjects are graded, now on a seven point scale, and approximately ninety-five per cent of the HEFC research funding is allocated on the basis of the grades. For the first time government had instituted evaluations of the substantive core of academic work.

Despite the fact that under the binary system polytechnics received almost no funding for research and therefore were greatly handicapped in the research stakes, most new universities entered at least some subjects in the 1992 exercise and all did in 1996. It has had a huge impact on the strategies and behaviour of higher education institutions. The effect has been to reinforce a highly stratified system within an evaluative framework over which academics have retained firm control. Some institutions have successfully moved themselves up what was previously an implicit pecking order but there have been no real concessions to diversity or pluralism in the exercise.

Assessment of the quality of education provided by higher education institutions was built into the functions of the funding councils under the 1992 Act, with a view to linking this as well with resource allocation. The CVCP had hoped vainly to prevent such external assessment and to secure the principle that the quality of education was best assured by institutional quality assurance systems regulated by the academic community itself. This was to be achieved initially by the Academic Audit Unit set up by the CVCP in 1990, and then its successor body, the Higher Education Quality Council established following the 1992 Act (in 1997 the audit and the assessment of the quality of education were combined into the Quality Assurance Agency, whose membership suggests a further loss by institutions of control of their quality assurance systems).

Meanwhile each of the Funding Councils set up their own subject based system, with evaluation by peer review. Resource allocation is still only minimally linked with assessment. But teaching quality assessments have made a significant impact on institutional and departmental behaviour, again in the direction of conformity rather than diversity.

These developments have to be put in the context of overarching policy objectives: to reduce institutions' financial dependence on the state and to promote a market culture and market mechanisms in higher education. In particular the generation of alternative resources to those from the funding councils is now seen as an institutional imperative. Universities are being forced into local, national and international markets. The proportion of research resources that come from the funding councils is diminishing, partly because some of those monies have been transferred to the research councils. They are thus allocated in the form of competitive grants for specific and time limited purposes for which grant holders will be held to account. Some monies from research councils are now conditional on institutions' success in obtaining matching funding from industry. In addition government has developed a range of policies to encourage partnerships between universities and the private sector in research, development, technology transfer and also in education and training.

The government stopped state funded growth in student numbers in terms of undergraduate admissions in 1995. Universities now have to look for alternative growth points such as postgraduate courses, teaching companies, distance learning developments or the franchising of courses. Masters' degrees, self funding or supported by research councils, are increasingly seen as new markets and sources of additional income and growth in student numbers.

For all these developments success in research and teaching quality assessments (TQA) and placement in the media league tables based upon them are seen as important. The assessments are instruments of selective resource allocation and accountability. But equally they are reputational systems that impact directly on institutions' capacity to succeed in the market place. The RAE is the more powerful, primarily because of its link with significant resources but also because it reinforces the values long embedded in academic reward systems.

In combination these mechanisms provide a substantial countervailing force to the potentially independent influence that customers or users of higher education might have on their priorities. The workings of the market are, in other words, strongly structured by the state: the RAE and TQA, instruments of accountability and convergence, could be seen as shaping and perhaps constraining the entrepreneurialism and diversification that might be expected from the pressures towards market behaviour. Despite academic perceptions that TQA is imposing new criteria on them, patterns of institutional success in them follow closely those of success in the RAE (HEFCE 1995). It could be argued that the funding councils have been a strong and unifying influence, sustaining rather than challenging academic values and conceptions of knowledge.

However there are other sides to the argument. The effects, particularly of the RAE, might not be stable. The more selective the RAE becomes, the more targeted institutions will have to be in the investments they make in it and the more attention they will need to pay to other markets such as particular student populations, local industries and voluntary or private services. Also the funding councils are said to be sensitive to criticisms of the weighting given to research as against teaching in their current policy mechanisms. One proposal from the Dearing committee offers them a solution: that the next RAE should be amended to provide an incentive for departments without a strong research record to strengthen the research and scholarship base of their teaching rather than build up research in a way that might militate against the development of teaching (Dearing 1997).

Funding councils claim that they have established a framework more conducive to institutional autonomy than the more planning oriented UGC and NAB. They point to the growing proportion of universities' research funding that comes from other sources. Other factors too may be creating differences in the structured context of higher education institutions. Both the funding councils and the research councils have seen major change since the beginning of the 1980s in their membership and, more particularly, their leadership. Academics have lost rights to control academic funding bodies that they had previously taken for granted. Since the establishment of the UFC and the PCFC, funding councils have been chaired by industrialists. Research councils' chairs are selected from industry and commerce, though they may also be scientists, and their agendas are increasingly set by collaborative planning between academics, industry and government.

Organisational structures: central government frameworks

The 1980s and 1990s have also seen attempts by the politicians to change the central government framework for higher education, and with it the values that permeate the system. Most striking have been the attempts to strengthen the influence of the Departments of Employment, and Trade and Industry on higher education and research. The government initiative that sought to make an unprecedented intervention into the higher education curriculum in the name of entrepreneurial values, the Enterprise in Higher Education Initiative, was launched from the Department of Employment.

The subsequent merging of the Department of Employment and Education was at one level an embodiment of a far-reaching rhetoric, the logic of which is to dismantle the idea that education and work are separate spheres of action. Strictly speaking there are several rhetorics: those of the knowledge society, work based learning and the accreditation of prior learning, personal transferable skills and of life long learning, the interplay between which suggest a world in which education can be reconceptualised in terms of work and vice versa.

The subsuming of the Office of Science and Technology under the DTI is a more direct representation of arguments about the commodification of knowledge. Lyotard (1984) warns that 'the relationship of the suppliers and users of knowledge to that knowledge will increasingly be similar to the relationship of commodity producers and consumers to the commodities they produce and consume: it will take the form of exchange value', Knowledge will cease to be valued for its own sake.

Conclusions: national level

Policy developments in higher education at the national level in the 1980s and 1990s reflect quite radical attempts by government to change the relationship between higher education and the state. At one level it has sought to bind into the state a newly enlarged and unified system and to do so through new mediating bodies with more powerful mechanisms of control than those possessed by their predecessors. However these mechanisms do not necessarily imply any immediate or radical redirection or reordering of values and purposes. At the same time both Conservative and Labour governments have attempted to incorporate higher education into a new ideology of the market, which has its own mechanisms of control and, perhaps also, its own conception of knowledge and education as commodities, distanced from rather than an integral part of those who develop and use them. The redrawing of departmental boundaries can be seen as symbolising the dissolution of boundaries long taken for granted, between higher education and work and higher education and the economy. It also institutionalises value conflict rather than coherence at the top of the higher education system.

Policy change and a new public management: the institutional level[2]

In their study of the higher education system Becher and Kogan (1980 and 1992) raised the question, though answering it in the affirmative, 'Is the institution a viable level?' They asked whether the institution 'has a substantive and distinct purpose or how far it is, in effect, a holding company, a legal and organisational formula designed to authorise and control the activities extrinsic to itself?' (Becher and Kogan 1980, p. 63). To raise such a question now would be almost unthinkable. That represents a major change.

The same study demonstrates the abiding complexities of academic institutions. They combine the authority relationships of collegium and hierarchy, which in turn give rise to both committee and executive roles and structures. Hierarchy and executive systems and roles were more dominant features of the then polytechnics than universities. Although polytechnics had been increasingly successful in practice at freeing themselves from local authority control before they acquired corporate status, they had developed in a system of regulation and bureaucracy.

However all the institutions were characterised by ambiguities about authority relationships and problems in resolving the overlaps and inconsistencies of decision making structures. In most substantial authority resided in the basic units. Institutions often had little power to affect professorial heads of department who had achieved their career ambitions and whose authority in their disciplines, the invisible colleges that controlled the key academic reward systems, was substantial (Becher and Kogan 1980). The numbers and size of the basic units varied markedly, particularly in old universities, where there could be large numbers of departments, some of which were very small. Academic heterogeneity was greater, however, in the post 1992 universities which had grown partly through responsiveness to the educational needs and opportunities of new employment trends and a changing society.

By the early 1980s, political and economic pressures were exerting an increasingly explicit and powerful influence on academic institutions, constituting an important counter force to that of the academic world. Government's wish to install a new culture of management in higher education became clear. The CVCP, recognising this, secured the agreement of the Secretary of State in 1984 that the efficiency study of the universities which he wanted should be undertaken under their aegis (Cave et al. 1997). The result was the Jarratt report (1985), which made few concessions to traditional conceptions of academic organisations.

The report argued that 'universities are first and foremost corporate enterprises to which subsidiary units and individual academics are responsible and accountable' (1985, para. 3.4.1.). They require strong management and strategic planning structures and mechanisms which can and should be combined with devolved responsibility to units. The vice chancellor should be both academic leader and chief executive; devolution must be to budget centres large enough to ensure flexibility and redeployment of resources. Senior and middle management needed to be developed. Heads of department should also be both academic leaders and managers, but managerial capacity is the essential qualification as aspects of academic leadership can, if necessary, be devolved to others.

All of these themes inform the institutional life of contemporary higher education. Critical factors have been the rapid changes in institutional size and the complexities and urgency of the challenge generated by the new policies. Total student numbers in higher education increased by seventy-two per cent in the decade from 1986 and within this overall rise there have been major increases in part time and postgraduate students, as well as full time first degree students (Smithers and Robinson 1996). Out of hundred universities twenty now have over 15,000 full time equivalent students and thirty-one between 10,000 and 15,000 (Brennan and Ramsden 1996). It is a more varied population: for example, twenty per cent of full time first degree students are over twenty-one (Smithers and Robinson 1996). The gender balance overall is now about even and ethnic minority students make up twelve per cent of the student population.

Increasingly universities see themselves as under pressure to develop multiple and not easily reconcilable objectives: rapid and extensive growth; respond to new educational demands; greater research productivity against more rigorous criteria and intensified competition; new educational and research partnerships with external organisations; more comprehensive systems of quality assurance. To structure and put into effect feasible futures universities must become multi-functional, multi-professional organisations, geared to the management of complexity.

Universities have embraced the idea of strong management. Vice chancellors and principals are now clearly regarded as chief executives as well as academic leaders. They have senior academic management teams to support them. New roles have been created at the centre, with increasingly well-defined responsibilities, beginning with the pro vice-chancellors, although they are still often fixed term positions (see also Scott 1995). Attempts are being made to streamline committee structures, to clarify their relationship with management structures and to establish a management structure down through the university. Budgets are being devolved and details of income and expenditure becoming more transparent, although the extent of devolution and the determination and clarity with which it is implemented are often contested by departments. At present centralisation is experienced as a stronger force than decentralisation in universities.

One mark of the new public management is the substitution of strategies for rules and procedures (Bleiklie 1996). British universities are developing institutional strategies but simultaneously with expanding regulation and documentation, in particular in consequence of quality assurance policies and almost universal moves to modularise curricula. Mission statements show reluctance to close off options and make clear decisions about institutional identity. Strategies are strongly shaped by dominant national policies. So the logic of the RAE, together with student numbers, has brought some up against hard choices: to abolish departments and to make resource transfers between departments in the name of optimal institutional performance. In some cases universities have been reluctant to make such decisive moves, despite growing anxieties about resources. But in a study carried out for the HEFCE McNay reports that seventy-five per cent of the respondents to his questionnaire confirmed that there had been strong vertical integration in institutional research policy and planning (McNay 1996).

Staffing strategies have been changing during the last decade. There has been a shift towards the differentiation of staff contracts, in terms of salary, definition of work and security. Key criteria have been research outputs. Traditionally academic staff have combined research, teaching and administration in their roles. One strategy used by institutions to improve their research performance, particularly in targeted areas, has been the creation of research only contracts or contracts in which teaching and administration have been significantly reduced. Conversely the RAE requires staff to be categorised as research active or non-active. Those categorised as research non-active are unlikely to be able to shift that label. They will effectively become teaching only staff.

Universities are moving towards becoming organisations with a core of highly rewarded staff on permanent contracts and a large periphery on fixed term or part time contracts. Graduate teaching assistants have become a feature of social science and humanities departments. Criteria for security and high reward have moved even more strongly towards research, despite institutions' claims that they wish to give better rewards for teaching.

New co-ordinative, planning, administrative and management responsibilities are falling to heads of departments, as well as to deans of faculties, although these appointments are often time limited. Those in our study tended to describe their role as that of a manager (Bauer and Henkel 1997). But they were moving cautiously and often uncertainly towards determining what that might mean. As one said: 'We are working without a script.' Most had highly restricted powers over resource allocation. None saw themselves as having managerial authority and the fact that many of them were heads only for a fixed term made them even more reluctant to impose decisions on their colleagues. A number saw departmental culture as a significant part of their responsibilities. The development of a more actively collective culture was often mentioned, although in some institutions it was felt that this was precisely what was being threatened by the more differentiated, performance related policies.

Different forms of matrix structures have been developed, as well as the stronger line relationships from the centre to the faculties and departments. Strategy groups are one example. Also cross-institutional, service units have proliferated, some for the pursuit of new institutional tasks, marketing, public relations, international relations. Many are for academic support - quality assurance, teaching and learning, staff development, information technology, for example. Personnel are often drawn primarily from administrators and occupational groups other than academics, even if they are academically-led.

In many cases the units' role is described as to support departments. But they also generate policies for the university and some are active in promoting change in departments, extending in the strongest cases to the redefining of departmental research agendas, so shifting the locus of initiative for development from departments to the centre (Bauer and Henkel 1997).

External pressures, particularly for more competitive research capacity and for the capture of new student markets, have in some institutions brought the development of more interdisciplinary organisational structures. The interfaces between these and the existing structures in terms of lines of authority and communication or procedural rules are not always clearly defined.

External quality assessments of research and teaching are frequently strongly managed by the centre of the university, whose own quality assurance systems are also influenced by them. An ex pro-vice-chancellor commented that perhaps the first thing that struck academics about the audit and assessment policies was that now the institution was supposed to set corporate standards, which it probably never had before. Both audit and assessments give priority to aspects of administration which might previously have been neglected or given a low profile: comprehensive documentation of course aims, objectives and structures, for example, and university-wide rules for assessment.

Accordingly some administrators have found their roles evolving and impinging more on the primary functions of institutions. They might work together with senior academics and with internal audit committees to implement quality policies. A senior administrator spoke of external audit giving him the authority to 'open the black box' of academic decision making, to ensure that academics could justify the procedures that they had. He and most career administrators continued to see their role as supportive, providing policy options and strengthening the infrastructure, rather than giving them direct power over the academics. But the increase in the range of institutional functions has also widened the range of their tasks (Kogan, forthcoming).

Conclusions: institutional level

What conclusions might be drawn from these developments about the organisational forms of higher education institutions, the ways in which they control their members, the texture and shape of their boundaries and the balance of external and internal influences on them?

The individual institution has become significantly more important. The institution is a key mediator of national policies and the main arena in which academic accountabilities are played out. Institutions structure academics' working lives and although academic identities are still shaped by their disciplines, the influence upon them of the institution has substantially increased. Institutions are also the site of ambiguity and tension. They are becoming more like corporate enterprises, while the range of functions and occupational groups encompassed in them has substantially widened. Institutions now rely on a number of professions in addition to academics. They have stronger and more centralised management and almost all now have frameworks for institution wide standards and curriculum provision. Deans of faculties and heads of departments are avowedly part of a management structure but their experience is also one of increased bureaucratisation. Centralisation is generally more evident than decentralisation and devolved budgets give limited room for manoeuvre. Nevertheless deans and heads are explicitly formulating aims, plans, structures that will enable them better to manage their futures.

Control mechanisms can be perceived as conducive to convergence and constraint and also to diversity. They are explicit but do not directly impinge on the traditional norms of professional relationship that deny command or control: modular curriculum frameworks, quality assessments and quality audits, employment contracts and output criteria. In some respects core academic staff are more tightly bound into their institutions in the same way as higher education is into the state under the 1992 Act. However some of these mechanisms, such as differential contracts linked with the competition for high performing researchers, have also encouraged greater inter-institutional mobility and less institutional loyalty.

The implications of the greater variety of organisational forms in institutions are as yet uncertain. Some are set up to change department behaviour: enterprise units and teaching and learning units, for example, bring perspectives other than those of academic disciplines to bear on core work. Their influence is uneven, to some extent they must create their own momentum but then they are dependent on changes of perception in departments. Other entities, research institutes, science parks and entrepreneurial centres, are set up to facilitate academic outreach from the institution to new forms of partnership, new forms of service or new markets, or new internal connections leading to new configurations of research, activities that might be inhibited by conventional departmental boundaries. They constitute potential but not easily predictable sources of development.

Higher education institutions are shifting towards a more mixed economy. They are more dependent on funding sources other than the state. Individual academics based in institutions can establish private companies or consultancies for part of their work or indeed these might become their primary base from which they contract to do some work for the university. Institutional structures, mechanisms and expertise have been developed in universities to facilitate research partnerships with commercial bodies and the patenting of new developments. Intellectual property law has become highly significant for universities.

Academic institutions are increasingly competing not only with each other but with commercial organisations, some of which are even establishing their own degree programmes. Management consultants compete with academics for research grants. Academic knowledge is no longer universally regarded as superior or unique.

Whereas cosmopolitanism, external connections and collaboration have always been important for individual academics and research groups, particularly the most successful, these have been primarily academic and based on the discipline. More recently they have become institutionalised and linked with the pursuit of markets. Therefore institutional boundaries as well as the definitions of public and private have become more complex and fluid.

Policy changes and their implications for the academic profession

Academic autonomy has been at the heart of academic professional culture and is probably still its most highly prized value. A key question for this chapter is whether the developments outlined so far, in particular the new significance of the institution and new mechanisms of control within the framework of new public management and the market have impinged on individual autonomy. Broad trends are in that direction, although the impacts on individuals vary substantially, depending on the institutions to which they belong.

Individual lives have become structured and controlled by multiple mechanisms, mediated largely through the institution. External output oriented assessments impose time structures and targets for production (of publications) that get incorporated into internal institutional systems (RAE deadlines, research degree review periods, research funding bodies' deadlines for grant applications). Time has to be strictly rationed and directed towards specific activities and outputs. Modularisation and semesterisation have meant the packaging of teaching and assessments into tightly defined time slots.

Applications for research grants must increasingly be framed within externally formulated agendas. The combination of increased workloads and defined time frames makes it more likely that individual initiatives towards new teaching programmes or research partnerships will be responses to external stimuli rather than being self starting. The pressures of multiple demands may compel individuals to make clearer divisions between research and teaching activities, periodically if not permanently, so changing deeply held assumptions about the nature of academic work, in which research and teaching have been intricately connected.

Institutional moves towards differential and fixed term contracts for teachers and researchers now have a significant impact. An increasing proportion of academics can predict their employment over strictly limited periods. This, on top of the loss of tenure in 1988, is one way in which academics' sense of their own exceptionalism has been undermined, alongside the major relative decline in their salary levels. They are deeply involved in the changing structures of the labour market, which pose harder options: gearing performance more strongly to others' demands and criteria; taking the risk of working to personal goals and patterns; or in a world where the boundaries of higher education institutions and other organisations are becoming blurred taking the structuring of one's career more into one's own hands.

Institutional leaders are aware that ultimately the strength of the institution lies in its basic units, the energy, discipline and innovative power of individuals and groups of academics. However there has been a shift to collectivist values and practices. Academics are now under no illusion about the mutual dependence of individuals, departments and institutions for survival in the developing markets of higher education. The productivity and quality of academic work are profoundly important to the institution and the department. And degrees of academic freedom to pursue specialist interests are to a considerable extent a function of their departments' and institutions' competitive success (Henkel 1997).

Academic control of the educational process has also come under challenge from several directions: changes in curriculum structures, in student populations, in funding arrangements, together with alternative, administrative, market, and democratic ideologies of quality (Bauer and Henkel 1997, Harvey 1995).

Modularisation is widely experienced by academics as imposing restrictions, bureaucratisation and fragmentation on curriculum development. But it has also provided opportunities for them to review their programmes, to make new connections and applications and to give entry to new ideas about teaching and learning. Perhaps more significantly it has given more power over the curriculum to students: they have more choice and the assessment requirements are more comprehensible and manageable. Academics for the most part resist notions of students as customers and are sceptical about the value of the student evaluations of courses that are increasingly part of quality assurance systems. But as funding arrangements move further towards transactions between the individual and the institution, and as student populations are older, better qualified and clearer about what they expect in the context of life long learning, it will be more difficult for academics to assume that they have a monopoly over conceptions of quality.

Already they have had to extend their thinking beyond their technical or specialist, discipline based ideas to more generic, systemic (Joss and Kogan 1995) or holistic concepts of educational environment and student welfare and support services (Dill 1995). Force of numbers exert their own momentum towards administrative conceptions of quality: predictability, formality, documentation and bureaucratisation of processes and structures, even without external pressures.

Despite these developments academics, academic values and conceptions of knowledge, teaching and research are proving robust across the spectrum of universities. Staff, and perhaps particularly young staff, are absorbing heavier demands within their own frameworks of belief and they are using structures to sharpen the way in which they work, to become more professional. They are helped by the fact that the most powerful mechanisms of control are still in the hands of academics. However many have not grasped the nettle of mass education and are still struggling to sustain the values and modes of working characteristic of an elite system.

Conclusions

During the last two decades higher education has been politicised in an unprecedented way: growth and political, social and economic salience have enabled government to bring institutions, some of which were highly autonomous, others of which were emancipating themselves from the diminishing influence of a QUANGO and local government, into a unified. As yet uncertainty remains over the balance between unity and diversity.

Individual institutions have assumed increasing significance, both as mediators of government policies, and as providing the structures and strategies that strongly shape academic careers. They have become more corporate enterprises and adopted some principles and structures of the new public management.

The major changes were the outcome of strong, if unsystematic ministerial actions. While polytechnics' leaders were able to exert some influence in the process, the government largely imposed the new policies on the universities. Attempts at pre-emptive action had limited success. In the process of creating change government has reached deeply into the core work of higher education and attempted to shift its values and the key structures.

Some of the mechanisms of change may be well entrenched: performance related resource allocation and reward systems, and fixed term contracts. However the dynamic that has been set in motion is not straightforward. There is a deep contradiction at the heart of new public management between the drive towards powerful vertical and bounded systems of public accountability and that towards the more diffuse, horizontal influences of multiple markets.

One clear outcome is the reinforcement of a highly stratified university system, in which command over resources, public and private, is increasingly concentrated in a limited number of institutions. The boundaries and arenas in which these institutions work may change but academic authority is likely to remain strong here, as it has done in the key resource allocation systems. Academic socialisation processes and academic values are powerful and they do not conform to vertical accountability systems. More significantly their hold over knowledge at the leading edge is still firm.

Further away from these elite institutions, the picture becomes less clear and the possible futures more diversified. New organisations, new structures and new patterns of the production of knowledge and of the teaching and learning process may well emerge as forms of knowledge multiply and technologies for their communication advance. They will need management but it is not clear that understanding of the form that might take is well developed in higher education.

Wide differences of power and status among members of the academic profession are certainly not new. But some have become more explicit and institutionalised during the last two decades. Formal inequalities in the profession are likely to increase. The power of institutional leaders has substantially increased and far more academics are now participating in management at all levels in institutions, even if academic management is still not widely acknowledged as a valued career path in the profession.

Degrees of academic freedom and the power to absorb new restrictions within individual working patterns and aspirations vary widely between academics. But as yet most feel that they retain at least the minimal level of autonomy they perceive as essential to their professional identity. Professional flight from conventional academic institutions is not as yet a significant phenomenon. But alternative forms of knowledge-based organisation are multiplying, at the same time as the overall rewards and status of the academic profession in society have significantly declined.

Notes

1   These issues are being explored empirically in the English component of a three country study of higher education reforms from 1975 to the present being carried out by teams from the universities of Bergen, Brunel and Gothenburg.

2   The empirical data in this section is drawn primarily from the three country study mentioned earlier. The study entailed documentary analysis and interviews at the national, institutional and practice levels in eleven universities.

References

Ball, C. (1988), 'Keynote Speech' in Eggins, H. (ed.), *Restructuring Higher Education*, SRHE and Open University Press: Buckingham, pp. 3-12.

Barnett, R. (1994), *The Limits of Competence*: *Knowledge, Higher Education and Society*, SRHE and Open University Press: Buckingham.

Bauer, M. and Henkel, M. (1997, forthcoming), 'Responses of Academe to Quality Reforms in Higher Education - A Comparative Study of England and Sweden', *Tertiary Education and Management*.

Becher, T. and Kogan, M. (1980 and 1992) *Process and Structure in Higher Education*, 1st and 2nd ed., Heinemann Educational Books: London.

Bleiklie, I. (1996), 'Rendering unto Caesar ... . On Implementation Strategies in Academia', Paper presented at the annual CHER conference, Turku.

Brennan, J. and Ramsden, B. (1996) 'Diversity in UK Higher Education: a Statistical View', *UK Higher Education in the 1990s*, Quality Support Centre, London.

Cave, M., Hanney, S., Henkel, M. and Kogan, M. (1997), *The Use of Performance Indicators in Higher Education*: *The Challenge of the Quality Movement*, 3rd ed., Jessica Kingsley Publishers: London.

Department of Education and Science (1985), *The Development of Higher Education into the 1990s* (Green Paper), HMSO: London.

Department of Education and Science (1987), *Higher Education: Meeting the Challenge*, (Cmnd. 114), HMSO: London.

Dill, D. (1995), 'Through Deming's Eyes: a Cross National Analysis of Quality Assurance Policies in Higher Education', *Quality in Higher Education*, Vol.1, No. 2.

Elzinga, A. (1985), 'Research, Bureaucracy and the Drift of Epistemic Criteria' in Wittrock, B. and Elzinga, A., *The University Research System. The Public Policies of the Home of Scientists*, Almqvist and Wicksell International.

Elzinga, A. (1994), 'Disciplinary Development and Institutional Change'. Paper given at a research seminar, Higher Education Policy and the Organisation of Knowledge Production, LOS, University of Bergen.

Gibbons, M., Limoges, C., Nowotny, H, Schwartzman, S., Scott, P. and Trow, M. (1994), *The New Production of Knowledge: The Dynamics of Science and Research in Contemporary Societies*, Sage: London.

Halsey, A. (1992), *The Decline of Donnish Dominion*, Oxford University Press: Oxford.

Harvey, D. (1989), *The Condition of Postmodernity: An Enquiry into Cultural Change*, Blackwell: Oxford.

Harvey, L. (1995), 'The Key Issues: the Quality Agenda', *Quality in Higher Education*, Vol. 1, No.1.

Henkel, M. (1997), 'Academic Values and the University as Corporate Enterprise', *Higher Education Quarterly*, Vol. 51, No. 2.

Higher Education Funding Council for England (1995), *Report on Quality Assessment 1992-1995*, HEFCE: Bristol.

Hoggett, P. (1991),'A New Management in the Public Sector?', *Policy and Politics*, Vol. 19, No. 4, pp. 243-256.

Jarratt Report (1985), *Report of the Steering Committee for Efficiency Studies in Universities*, Committee of Vice Chancellors and Principals: London.

Joss, R. and Kogan, M. (1995), *Advancing Quality: Total Quality Management in the National Health Service*, Open University Press: Buckingham.

Kogan, M. (1988), 'The Case of Education', paper given at ESRC Workshop on Corporatism and Accountability, 7 January.

Kogan, M. (forthcoming), 'Academics and Administrators in Higher Education', *Higher Education Management*.

Lyotard, J. (1984), *The Postmodern Condition: a Report on Knowledge*, University of Manchester: Manchester.

McNay, I. (1997), *The Impact of the 1992 Research Assessment Exercise on Individual and Institutional Behaviour in English Higher Education*. Summary Report and Commentary, Centre for Higher Education Management, Anglia Polytechnic University.

Morris Report (1990), *Performance Indicators: Report of a Committee of Enquiry Chaired by Mr Alfred Morris*, Polytechnics and Colleges Funding Council: London.

Office of Science and Technology (1993), *Realising Our Potential: A Strategy for Science, Engineering and Technology*, (Cmnd 2250) HMSO: London.

Peters, T. and Waterman, R. (1982), *In Search of Excellence*, Harper and Row: New York.

Pollitt, C. (1995), 'Justification by Works or by Faith? Evaluating the New Public Management', *Evaluation*, Vol.1, No.2 (October), pp.133-154.

Scott, P. (1995), *The Meanings of Mass Higher Education*, SRHE and Open University Press: Buckingham.

Scott, P. (1997), 'The Changing Role of the University in the Production of New Knowledge', *Tertiary Education and Management*, Vol. 3, No. 1, pp 5-14.

Silver, H. and Brennan, J. (1988), *A Liberal Vocationalism*, Methuen: London and New York.

Smithers, A. and Robinson, P. (1996), *Trends in Higher Education*, Council for Industry and Higher Education, London.

Summa, H. and Virtanen, T. (1995), 'New Public Management in the Context of Academic Freedom: Evaluating the Success of Result-Oriented Management Reform in Finnish universities', paper presented at the Annual Conference of European Group of Public Administration, Erasmus University, Rotterdam.

Trist, E. (1972), 'Types of Output Mix of Research Organisations and their Complementarity' in Cherns, A. et al. (ed.), *Social Science and Government*, Tavistock: London.

Trow, M. (1970), 'Reflections on the Transition from Mass to Universal Education', *Daedalus*, Vol. 99.

11 The police service

Barry Loveday

The emphasis on management has been a relatively recent development for the police. For a variety of reasons criminal justice agencies were the last to succumb to new public management measures, introduced much earlier in other public services. In the 1980s demands for greater economy, efficiency and effectiveness (the three Es) within the police service were overshadowed by the government's challenge to the authority of organised labour. The 1984-5 miner's strike placed unprecedented strain on those police forces involved and also on the concept of locally accountable policing. An earlier government commitment to economy was forgotten as the strike progressed. It was not until the strike that the government felt able to assess the level of service provided by the police and draw some radical conclusions. Despite, therefore, the publication of a circular as early as 1983 on police manpower, efficiency and effectiveness in the police service (Circular 114), reform of the police remained at best piecemeal. It was not until 1993 when the Major government initiated significant changes in the Police Service in the White Paper on Police Reform.

Police reform

The case for the reform of police structures was and remains overwhelming. As successive Audit Commission reports on the police have argued (particularly Audit Commission 1991), the managerial overheads sustained by police forces were of such a magnitude that they significantly impeded the provision of front line police service to the public. Management overheads have been traditionally significant in an organisation strongly committed to strict hierarchical chains of command. This organisational characteristic of the police was reinforced by chief officers who believed that effective supervision required extended chains of command. This view was further reinforced following the 1970s amalgamation of many police forces which created a small number of big police bureaucracies. The trend towards further police force amalgamations was again sped up in 1993 when the then Home

183

Secretary, Kenneth Clarke, outlined his plans to reduce the remaining forty three forces to around twenty, despite the fact that it was not proven that better service had resulted from the creation of larger units of policing. By the early 1970s as a result of amalgamations, it was no longer possible to talk in many areas of local police forces. Large regional police forces dominated the Metropolitan areas, while outside of these, police forces areas often combined two or three counties. The pressure towards the creation of ever larger police forces went largely unquestioned both in the Home Office and among many chief officers. Yet the impact of such change was to be significant. As the size of police forces grew, so their ability to provide front line uniformed patrol actually declined (Loveday 1990). If there were efficiency gains through amalgamation, these gains appeared to be achieved at the cost of reduced effectiveness in terms of service provision. Larger police forces meant larger bureaucracies which could always be expected to grow at the expense of uniformed patrol officers (Jones 1980).

The bureaucratic expansion of police forces was not seriously questioned within government circles for some time. This may have been a consequence of the successful ability of police forces to evade effective external review. Local police authorities, which ostensibly had a responsibility under the Police Act 1964 for police efficiency were rarely, if ever, willing to question bureaucratic growth in police forces. Internal organisation was, anyway, a responsibility of the chief officer and one protected by the convention of police independence (Marshall 1975). As a consequence of managerial inertia such internal change as was achieved did little to challenge the crisis of increasing managerial oncosts. Chief officers appeared to merely rearrange the deck chairs on their individual Titanics. These developments were probably only encouraged by a commitment to incremental growth sustained by a funding system which emphasised inputs (establishment increases) rather than outputs as a measure of effectiveness. Annual bids to the Home Office for manpower often demonstrated neither logic or clear need only exacerbated the problem, while successful manpower bids enabled chief officers to avoid asking awkward questions concerning what the police force did with its existing workforce.

Bureaucratic growth

As many studies of American police forces have demonstrated, the problem of overgrown bureaucracy is not unique to Britain. One interesting study of police forces from the late 19th to the early 20th century found that as police departments grew, the patrol function declined (Monkennen 1981). Moreover police expansion was not necessarily based on need, but rather the existence of more senior police officers who had the time to lobby successfully for further increases in police establishments. Similarly a longitudinal analysis of the growth of American police departments between 1948 and 1984 concluded that where police growth occurred it was unrelated to external demand and did not provide either greater levels of police service or increase the police response to victims of crime (Nalla 1992, p. 52). In England and Wales a similar situation appears to have occurred as police forces grew in size. One analysis of the impact of specialisation on police forces and 'manning up' policies showed that where vacancies for divisional specialisms and supervisory ranks occurred, they were filled by staff posts drawn from the uniform patrol strength (Jones 1981, p. 41). As Jones observes these organisational policies severely limited the ability of the uniform patrol branch to provide a 'satisfactory patrol service'. This problem became critical as opinion surveys consistently demonstrated that the public placed a very high premium on visible patrol presence particularly in high victimisation areas. The 1990 Police Operational Review (OPR) demonstrated that this demand for visible patrol presence crossed geographic and class boundaries, notably poor inner city residents were found to place particularly high priority on visible patrol. Yet the ability of the police to provide such service appeared to be increasingly unrealisable despite, or perhaps because of, incremental growth throughout the post war period. Even following the influx of substantial numbers of civilian personnel employed to release police officers for operational duties, the ability of the police to provide the most basic function, that of uniform patrol, has continued to decline (Loveday 1990).

Professional policing

The expansion of police forces has been matched over time by the creation of numerous specialist units. The police have expanded from general patrol work police, via Criminal Investigation Departments (CID) and Traffic Departments, into a myriad of specialist activities and squads, each of which is sustained by a recruitment from the uniformed branch. This stress placed on specialist activity by the 'professional police model', where organisational emphasis is placed on ever increasing specialisation at a functional level, was probably best reflected in the rise of the CID. Those able to join the CID enjoyed higher status and usually better working conditions than their uniformed colleagues, as well as greater promotion opportunities. As Reiner (1991) argues, given that many chief constables had themselves belonged to the CID they tended to promote those from a career background similar to their own. Higher status and promotional opportunities explain why as early as 1969 Martin and Wilson commented that manpower shortages in the police appeared to be confined to certain specific functions while not arising in others at all. They found that while manpower shortages for uniformed patrol appeared to be constant, the specialist departments such as CID and Traffic never suffered from labour shortages (Martin and Wilson 1969). Nor was this feature of the professional police model a new phenomenon in the 1960s. In 1957 Harold Scott, a former commissioner of the Metropolitan Police, argued in relation to the then staffing crisis in patrol work that the 'steady increase in specialised duty' meant that the situation had worsened by the early 1950s 'in a way that can only be described as disastrous'. As he noted, while in 1932 eighty-eight per cent of the men required for beat and patrol duty were available, by 1952 only forty-four per cent were available (Scott 1957, p. 51).

In an increasingly complex and technological society, some specialisation of police activity was inevitable. Yet the absence of any internal police evaluation of specialist units meant that no one could be sure that the scarce resources now being directed to at least some specialisms were being used effectively. As the trajectory of growth achieved by the CID demonstrated, very large investments can be made in specialist duties which have only a limited value in terms of crime fighting. The absence of any independent or critical evaluation of the CID function meant not just the diversion of scarce resources, but also a decline in the provision of a visible patrol presence, often in areas of greatest need. As American research found, successful crime clearance depended more on the ability of the victim or witness to identify the offender, than on professional detective skills (Greenwood et al. 1977). Similarly research conducted by Reiss confirmed the importance of uniformed patrol officers whom, he found, could expect to be involved in at least fifty per cent of arrests for serious offences (Reiss 1972). It was perhaps for this reason that Reiss was to highlight the centrality of the police patrol function, a function which the professional police model was at this time already leaving behind.

The continuing commitment to the professional police model based on specialisation and hierarchy has been most recently highlighted by a police federation report on police patrolling. (Police Federation 1996). This report stressed the low esteem accorded uniformed patrol, widespread managerial indifference to the status of patrol officers and a clear perception among patrol officers themselves that specialist roles were better rewarded than their own. Not surprisingly most probationers, who make up the bulk of patrol officers, were anxious to move from patrol and hoped to be performing a specialist role within the next two years (Police Federation 1996, para. 2.2). Yet despite the low status accorded to patrol work, the same report found that two out of every five patrol officers who responded to the survey had made an arrest during their most recent patrol period (Police Federation 1996, para. 24), thus further confirming the importance of patrol work in fighting crime.

Government intervention

The Conservative government's commitment to law and order and to the police force was most visibly demonstrated by the consistent increase in real spending on the police service during the 1980s. As the government argued in the *Protecting the Public* White Paper, which outlined its strategy on crime in England and Wales, the police service had received a large increase in resources between 1978/9 and 1996 (HMSO 1996). The government claimed that spending on the police had increased by ninety-eight per cent in real terms, including provision for over 1,500 more police officers and 17,000 more civilian staff (Protecting the Public 1996, para.

3.5). However the government had also become increasingly concerned that this increased spending on the police had not led to any significant falls in the crime rate. Indeed the recorded crime rate had actually risen faster during the late 1980s than at any time since records began. Not surprisingly Kenneth Baker, when Home Secretary, reported widespread disillusionment with the police among his senior Cabinet colleagues. Many senior minister had concluded that despite their large investment in the police service, the police themselves had failed the government on crime (Baker 1992).

The 1992 general election victory allowed the Major Government to implement the most radical intervention by government into policing since its inception in 1829. Led by Kenneth Clarke, the Home Office initiated a set of proposals which, had they been all implemented, would have significantly changed both the government of the police and its management. The proposals contained in the 1993 White Paper on Police Reform proposed that the Home Secretary should directly nominate chairs to smaller streamlined police authorities. The intention was to break the link between the police and locally elected authorities. Additionally the police were to be encouraged to pursue their primary task of crime fighting by shedding non-crime related duties. The 1992 Posen Review on Core and Ancillary Tasks was required to identify those functions peripheral to 'real police work' and which could be directed to other agencies, or privatised. The White Paper also stated that it was appropriate for the government to give the police service a 'clear steer' to ensure that it focused on the 'right objectives'. Overall the aim of the government was to refocus policing priorities 'in line with the government's key objectives for policing' (Police Reform 1993, para. 7.5). As has been detailed by Jenkins, the thrust of the reform of the police service under Kenneth Clarke was not dissimilar to his reforms of other public services. It was essentially predicated upon significant centralisation of control. In the White Paper the Conservative government made clear that it intended to exercise direct control over the selection of chairman and independent members of each of the local police authorities. In addition the identification of National Objectives, along with contract arrangements and the introduction of personal performance measurement were planned to give central government startlingly wide powers and influence in determining local police arrangements. If the proposals put forward in the White Paper had been implemented, these would have effectively nationalised the police service.

However the government's proposals were successfully challenged in the House of Lords. A series of amendments to the Police and Magistrates Bill rejected the wider powers proposed for the Home Secretary. Instead elected members would constitute a simple majority on the new reformed police authorities. The police authorities, not the Home Secretary, would selected their chairs. Only five rather than eight independent members would be recruited to the new authorities and these would only be 'indirectly scrutinised' rather than directly selected by the Home Secretary.

Nor in the event were the Sheehy proposals for police management implemented in anything like their full measure. Michael Howard, who succeeded Clarke as

Home Secretary, rejected the proposals to place all ranks on initial ten year contracts and subject them to performance pay. Similarly he also turned down local pay bargaining which one member of the Sheehy Enquiry, Eric Caines, argued would undermine the power position of the Police Federation. Additionally structural severance which would have allowed chief officers to remove police officers who under performed, or whose duties were no longer required by the service, was also abandoned.

National level: ACPO

Both the Posen Review and the Sheehy Enquiry highlighted the substantial influence of the Association of Chief Police Officers. The increasing role of ACPO, which consists of all police officers of Assistant Chief Officer and above, has been documented elsewhere (Cope et al. 1997). In what proved to be an interesting demonstration of its ability to influence policy making at central government level, ACPO argued for the creation of an advisory panel consisting of ACPO members to monitor the core and ancillary review process. ACPO's involvement effectively ensured that the final recommendations did not challenge the public monopoly enjoyed by the police, and that the final recommendations would be relatively minor and easily accommodated by the police service. Thus the Posen Review, which originally had been expected to remove a substantial amount of non-crime police work to alternative providers, ended by merely questioning the need for the police to escort wide loads on motorways. The ACPO advisory panel had been instrumental in limiting the potential damage the police service would have experienced, if the social market principles which guided the original review been given free rein (personal communication to author from ACPO member).

ACPO also proved to be influential in challenging the worst features, from the ACPO viewpoint, of the 1993 Sheehy Enquiry. The Sheehy Report recommended fixed contracts for all officers, structural severance, performance related pay and local wage bargaining. Collectively and individually, chief officers rejected most of the Report's proposals. Unusually for a public service, chief officers also rejected the large performance bonus payments offered to them as an inducement to accept the Enquiry's proposals. The Metropolitan Commissioner of Police declared publicly that if the Sheehy proposals were introduced, particularly those relating to performance pay, he would resign. Other chief officers were also prepared to resign, rather than accept the Sheehy plan. These officers argued that performance pay would be particularly divisive in police forces which depended on mutual support and teamwork in often critical situations. This open and very public rejection of Sheehy by senior members of the police service indubitably largely contributed to ensuring that much of the Sheehy report became no more than an historical curiosity.

ACPO demonstrated a very similar key influence during the Police and Magistrates' Courts Bill 1993 passage through the House of Lords. ACPO recognised that the planned legislation challenged not just local policing but also the highly prized independence of the chief constable. It was indeed an irony that a Conservative government, which in the 1980s had done so much to protect the independence of the police, should by the 1990s promote the biggest challenge to the convention of constabulary independence in recent history. Yet the original plan to place all chief officers on short contracts and to give a police authority chair, appointed by the Home Secretary, direct responsibility for monitoring their performance clearly threatened the operational independence traditionally exercised by chief officers.

ACPO built a close alliance with the local authority associations and promoted a powerful public campaign against the bill. In a co-ordinated move police forces publicised the value of traditional and locally-based policing. This organised opposition had a big impact on debates over the bill in the House of Lords. No less than four former Home Secretaries from both major political parties challenged the need and purpose of such legislation, and proposed amendments which dramatically altered both the shape of the Bill and the powers proposed for the Home Secretary over the police service in England and Wales. As I noted earlier these amendments took the power of appointment of chairs away from the Home Secretary and increased the number of elected members. This revised legislation was enacted by Parliament in 1994.

The Association has also been influential in counteracting the then Conservative government's plans to enhance significantly the role and influence of Her Majesty's Inspectorate of Constabulary (HMIC). Despite publishing lengthy and frequent reports on individual police forces, HMIC have not been able to exercise the degree of influence over police performance which had been originally planned for them by Kenneth Clarke.

As these cases demonstrate ACPO has been able to exert considerable influence in determining the final outcomes of policy proposals initiated by government. If, when Home Secretary, Douglas Hurd had in 1989 argued the case for the need to strengthen the collective voice of the police service, this appeared to have been achieved in the 1990s. Other than seeking to influence policy outcomes, ACPO has also been increasingly involved in seeking to define the overall role, purpose and goals of the police service in contemporary England and Wales. Following the publication of the Operational Policing Review in 1990, ACPO was to publish its own statement of Common Purpose in relation to policing. Interestingly this highlighted the significant re-orientation among professionals away from crime fighting as a primary police objective to more community orientated and public reassurance roles. Areas identified by ACPO included community relations, public re-assurance and order, calls for assistance and 'crime prevention and detection'. These priorities contrasted remarkably with those identified by the Conservative government in the 1993 White Paper on Police Reform which gave as priorities for the police: fighting crime, upholding the law, bringing to justice those who broke the law and the need to provide 'good value for money'.

In responding to the survey data collected by the Operational Policing Review, ACPO recognised the public's preference for community policing and crime prevention over traditional crime fighting as salient police activities. ACPO's response also demonstrated its recognition that much police activity was service orientated rather than crime driven. The government was entirely correct when it argued that on a typical day only eighteen per cent of calls to the police were about crime and only forty per cent of police time was spent dealing directly with crime (Home Office 1993, para. 2.3). This analysis was to be entirely consistent with earlier evaluations of police activity conducted both at home and abroad (Kinsey 1985, Wilson 1968). The government's plans to remove ancillary duties and direct police to primarily crime fighting demonstrated both naivety and a serious misunderstanding of what the police could be expected to achieve in a crime fighting role. Despite recent and well publicised zero tolerance policing, effective crime fighting by the police depends almost entirely on the public (as victims or witnesses) to report offences and identify offenders. As has long been recognised, the discretion which is often claimed to be exercised by police over what offences are recorded, in fact only hides a deeper reality which is the discretion exercised by the public in deciding whether to report offences to the police in the first place. As successive British Crime Surveys demonstrate, the dark figure of unreported crime reminds us that the police can only 'fight' those crimes which are reported to them by the public. It has been the recognition of this simple truth by ACPO which has in part encouraged the re-orientation of policing away from simplistic crime fighting towards crime prevention and public reassurance functions.

The Audit Commission and the police

The police associations, particularly ACPO and the Police Federation, proved highly influential in defeating policy objectives set by the Major government. However they been less successful in resisting a process of creeping reform driven by the Audit Commission whose Police Papers have become a significant influence on the organisation of the police. The Commission has criticised internal bureaucratic police structures, the role of CID and the status accorded foot patrol. It has also made a series of recommendations for senior police managers, concerning the measurement of police activity, particularly in relation to determining policing outcomes (*Helping with Enquiries* 1992, *Checks and Balances* 1994, *Streetwise* 1996). The Audit Commission was careful to involve police representatives in working on these reports. Close collaboration with the police was to be a feature of the Commission's works, particularly early on when it considered the role of administrative support units, vehicle fleet management, income generation and performance review in police forces.

Rather like Home Office circulars, the Audit Commission's reviews are viewed as more than mere guidance or advisory statements. Following the Audit Commission's 1991 review of police internal structures, most police forces began to move from a two tiered division and sub-divisional structure towards single policing units, either basic command units or local command units. Again the Audit Commission in its important evaluation of police effectiveness and crime control, *Helping with Enquiries*, argued that, if properly organised and resourced, the police could have a significant impact on crime. Proper and effective policing organisation should include the targeting of 'known criminals' as an alternative to responding to incidents, and the development of crime intelligence units and new technology to evaluate local crime patterns. As for internal reorganisations, most police forces have adopted many of the recommendations outlined in this Report. This suggests that the organisational reform of the police has owed more to external recommendations than any internal debate within the police service.

Most recently in *Streetwise*, a report on foot patrol, the Audit Commission has discovered that at any one time of only around five per cent of the police strength can be expected to be patrolling the streets (Audit Commission 1996). The same report postulated that for an average size police force of 2,500 officers, this meant that at any one time around 125 officers could be expected to be serving a local population of about 1,000,000 (Audit Commission 1996, para. 8-10). Nevertheless the Audit Commission argued that foot patrol could not be seen as a panacea for all policing problems and that putting all officers on foot patrol would undermine 'strategies to tackle crime which required a higher degree of specialisation in non-uniform work' (Audit Commission 1996). It is as yet uncertain what influence *Streetwise* will have on police patrol. Yet the Commission's support for continued specialisation and its apparently rather limited support for patrol work has already been met with support by those who continue to espouse the traditional police model (Shattock 1996).

Elsewhere the Audit Commission has recommended the introduction of a social market approach to the provision of a police service. In a highly critical monograph, published by the Social Market Foundation, Howard Davies, the former Director of the Commission argued for the introduction of a purchaser-provider relationship to policing and for the creation of a strong lay management (Davies 1990). Similarly the Deputy Director of the Commission took the opportunity of a 1992 ACPO conference to recommend the adoption of a core functions approach with the disposal or contracting-out of those functions which impeded the delivery of primary police service. The Audit Commission appears, then, to have shared the Major government agenda of seeking to challenge professional dominance while hiving off activities to private companies. This agenda was well illustrated the following year when the then Home Secretary Michael Howard, addressing the British Security Association, stated that private companies could expect to benefit from the proposed police reforms initiated by the government, particularly following its review of core and ancillary duties.

Local police authorities

The Police and Magistrates Court Act has profoundly changed the local administration of police forces. The reformed police authorities, besides being in terms of membership much smaller than their predecessor bodies are also free standing, precepting authorities. In metropolitan areas this status followed the 1985 abolition of the metropolitan counties. Under the act the local police authority (LPA) has responsibility for the local policing plan, within which national objectives and local objectives and targets are identified, using this information police performance is monitored over the year. The drafting of the Local Police Plan (LPP) has been made the responsibility initially of the chief officer, although responsibility for the plan itself lies with the police authority. The police authority is also responsible for issuing an annual report designed to publicise the extent to which police performance has matched the targets and objectives set for it by the authority. As envisaged police authorities now have a more clearly directed function which is more managerial in function and performance driven, than their predecessor bodies. The new authorities are also supposed to be more interested in outputs and outcomes than inputs. To assist this movement towards a more managerial role, police authorities have been stripped of their former responsibilities for civilian personnel, buildings, motor vehicles and the budget. A residual responsibility for complaints against the police, established under the Police Act 1964, remains although it is unclear what oversight of police practice this responsibility generates in practice.

A government commitment to the delegation of budgets has meant that the new police authorities do not have financial responsibility for the police force. Budgets are delegated directly to the chief constable as the budget holder. Under the Police and Magistrates Court Act police bloc grants are subject to capping. However the bloc grant does give a new freedom to the budget holder to determine how the money is spent. The chief constable now can determine local spending priorities and also has responsibility for police establishments, delegated from the Home Office. Thus the chief constable as budget holder decides whether increased spending should go to police establishment, civilian staffing, or technology. Interestingly many chief constables have intimated that they do not intend to spend additional money on increasing force establishments.

Nonetheless financial delegation has had a significant impact. If the chief constable is the fundholder then the purchaser-provider split, encouraged by the Conservative government in other public services, is difficult to operate. The police are now effectively both purchaser and providers of service. The full implications of financial delegation has yet to be assessed. However it is clear that the new police authorities, unlike the old, do not even enjoy the symbolism of being ostensible budget holders. When asked recently what control they were able to exercise over the police budget, two elected members of a local police authority replied that 'they didn't control anything round here' (Loveday 1996). In some police forces the police authority is even dependant on the chief officer to fund its operations. Where local police authorities have set aside sums of money to support their function this dependence is necessarily less significant. Evidence suggests that a number of former county police authorities are now heavily reliant on the good will of the chief constable to provide money to support any additional activities which go beyond those specified in the Police Act. Nor in this situation are they likely to be able to employ a secretariat to assist the police authority in monitoring police performance. Generally police authorities remain entirely dependant on data generated by the police force for purposes of evaluation, although comparative performance data will be provided annually by the Audit Commission.

Independent members

As intended the selection process for independent members, which allows the Home Secretary a vetting power, resulted in the selection overwhelmingly of independents drawn from the self- employed, or from professional backgrounds. Those who survived the weeding processes of nomination lists were usually white, middle class males. A clear bias was demonstrated against both women and members of ethnic minorities. A stronger bias was to be demonstrated against known trade unionists, or those drawn from a partisan (Labour) background. Inevitably the criteria identified for initial selection meant that those selected exhibited similar characteristics. Those with a business background or business experience were preferred. The Conservative government's business managers were moreover to check nominations in an attempt to ensure consistency in selection. One result has been the arrival on police authorities of many business executives and the return of retired members of the military. Management consultancy is well represented on the new police authorities as is accountancy, while at least three police authorities have now retired brigadiers as independents (Loveday 1996). Contrary to the claims made in 1993 in defence of the nomination process, by then Home Secretary Michael Howard, shopkeepers and farmers were not to be better represented on police authorities following the reforms under the 1994 Act.

The continued operation of what has proved to be an arcane and elongated selection process for independents, clearly needs to be reviewed. Moreover as one senior police officer has recently observed, the secretive nature of the final selection process for independents gives too much power to the Home Secretary. Open and transparent accountability, which is so important for both the police and police authority, is unlikely to be achieved while government business managers have the power to pick over nomination lists in an attempt to ensure that their natural supporters are represented on the police authority. Independent membership of police authorities, along with many other patronage places on the numerous quangos created by the Thatcher and Major governments will of course now be a source of new patronage for the Labour government. This development was probably never envisaged by the Conservatives, who at the time, appeared to act as if their control of the executive could be expected to be permanent (Young 1990).

Police authority performance

An initial assessment of the new authorities suggests that the impact of independent members has not been very significant (Loveday 1996). While some independents have provided expertise on specific areas, their role has been limited by the police authorities' lack of executive and budgetary responsibilities. Monitoring performance is neither an onerous or overly significant function, particularly when authority members have no powers to affect changes to police performance. It is a matter of debate as to whether the identification of fresh targets for local objectives will of itself significantly alter policing practices. Moreover when police forces fail to achieve targets, the police authority can do little other than publicise the fact. Contrary to the Conservative government's expectations any failures to achieve the targets set for public services do not always appear to engage or stimulate the public's imagination. Nor is it always certain that police authorities are prepared to challenge publicly police performance, even when that performance falls significantly below the standards expected by HMIC. While under performing schools are subject to 'public shaming', police forces are unlikely to suffer the same fate.

Nevertheless police forces did achieve a number of key performance targets set nationally by the Home Secretary. Key indicators in 1995/6 and 1996/7 were linked to crime fighting and encouraged police forces to increase the arrest rate for violent crime and for domestic burglary. Between 1995 and 1997 many police forces were able to record increases in arrests in both categories of crime. Police success may have been linked to a wider change in the crime pattern which saw recorded crime rates fall for the fourth successive year in 1997. Yet serious doubts exist over how much reliance can be placed on official crime statistics and so on any government claims concerning the fall in crime. The 1996 British Crime Survey highlighted increases in the incidence of violent crime but noted that the threat of higher insurance premiums appeared to act as a significant disincentive for victims to report crime (British Crime Survey 1996). Nor was it entirely clear that changes in police recording practices might not have affected the overall crime profile for a police force area, for instance in 1995 HMIC had criticised service in the Metropolitan Police area for reclassifying reported offences to indicate a fall in the domestic burglary rate (Loveday 1995). Recording practices are not likely to be susceptible to police authority direction which means that the achievement of national or local crime objectives depends almost entirely on the integrity of police officers and their supervisors in determining what offences should be recorded and also how they are recorded. As with police crime clearance rates, recorded crime hides as much as it reveals and so statistical data relating to the objectives set by the Home Secretary and police performance needs to be treated with some caution (Coleman and Moynihan 1996, pp.120-21).

It may be too early to judge the overall performance of police authorities in determining local policing objectives and target setting for police. However it already noticeable that some police authorities appear happy to leave the Local Policing Plan to the chief constable and merely endorse whatever that officer decides is appropriate. This may in many respects be entirely appropriate as the chief officer will enjoy a monopoly of the information on which the local plan is based. No similar source of information or data independent of the police force is available to the police authority. Indeed these authorities will continue for the forseeable future to be entirely dependent on performance information provided by police officers. Anyway there is already some doubt over the exact status and value of the local policing plan. While some commentators see the plan as a vital fulcrum of accountability, others view it as merely encouraging collusion in a culture of performance measures, targets and league tables which, while emphasising quantitative outputs, fails to reflect qualitative issues or outcomes. There is also doubt as to who generates local performance indicators and objectives. Are these set by the chief officer after consultation with the police authority? Have the police authorities even in their smaller, more focused form the operational capability to do more than merely respond to and endorse the proposed objectives set by the chief officer? As the new authorities have only been in existence for a relatively short period, it may well be premature to question their effectiveness in this area. Yet early indications suggest that professional dominance is likely to remain a feature within the police service and this dominance is unlikely to be seriously challenged by the new police authorities.

Professional dominance

The impact of financial delegation of budgets to chief officers has already been considered. It is, of course, a matter of record that in public bodies budget holders are usually better able to determine priorities than non budget holders. The decision not to implement a purchaser-provider split between police authority and chief officer has prevented the introduction of social market disciplines which the Conservative government had espoused for other public services. If the purchaser-provider split has not been introduced, neither has strong lay management. Yet two other further important features of the social market, both identified by Howard Davies as being essential to a social market approach for public services, have not been introduced. These were individual contracts and the creation of a 'strong and realistic customer voice' (Davies 1991).

After the Police and Magistrates Courts Act 1994, all officers of ACPO rank were to be encouraged to enter into a new contract arrangements. Those appointed prior to the act would do so only voluntarily. Those promoted to ACPO rank after the act will be required to enter into a new contract arrangement with the police authority.

The contract was ostensibly designed to enable the police authority, or the Home Secretary, to terminate or not to renew a contract in cases of poor individual performance. Contract arrangements would also mean that the retirement age of senior police officers would generate some consistency and could be reflected in terms of individual contract arrangements. Any expectation that the contracts would be a means of penalising poor performance have, however, been entirely undermined by the arrangements entered into by police authorities.

As has been argued recently, by a senior police officer (Baker 1996), the whole basis for the Fixed Term Appointments (FTA) for ACPO rank officers has been questioned by the insistence that contracts are awarded, guaranteeing those officers a job until retirement, no matter how badly they perform (Baker 1996). Baker was to discover that of the contracts disclosed by police authorities, the appointment for chief officers averaged 4.8 years, for designated deputy chief constables the average was 5 years and for assistant chief constables the average was 8.25 years. This suggested that 'almost every FTA was aligned to the officers expected retirement date, rather than being linked to a time when performance would be reviewed and en extension of the FTA considered' (Baker 1996). How, it might be asked, could consistently excellent performance be encouraged by a ten year contract? Indeed in terms of contracts chief officers may now be better protected in post than they have been before. Thus the FTAs negotiated by police authorities, presumably with the support of the Home Office, effectively negated the conditions of managerial or contractual accountability which contracts ostensibly sought to create. Police performance has also been linked to external measures such as crime rates and responses to emergency calls. Police performance might, however, be equally linked to internal measures of management effectiveness and performance which could also be subject to equal by the authority. In particular improved performance in the whole area of equal opportunities and the reduction of the continuing problems of sexual and other harassment, which appear to characterise many police forces, could be included in chief officers' performance targets (Loveday 1996).

If contract arrangements leave much to be desired, police reform arguably has at least established the need for a strong consumer voice. The Police and Magistrates Courts Act was predicated upon the enhancement of existing police-public consultative mechanisms established under section 106 of the Police and Criminal Evidence Act 1984. Indeed it is worth noting that the government was to justify, at least in part, the sharp reduction in the number of elected members on police authorities by reference to the need to get 'policing closer to the community' by way of the existing police community consultative groups (PCCG's). While some commentators early on expressed reservations as to the efficacy of these groups, within official Home Office circles they were seen as having been a 'conspicuous success'. Evidence provided by officials to justify this interesting claim appeared to relate to the absence, despite the severe recession of the 1990s, of any of the major urban disturbances which had occurred in the early 1980s. Elsewhere some commentators have argued that with the Local Policing Plan, police authorities must now consider any views obtained from the police community consultative groups. Some commentators have concluded that the new responsibilities 'contrary to the cynical expectations of critics' may serve to stimulate 'greater commitment on the part of police authorities to the process of facilitating local policing policies' (Morgan and Newburn 1997, p.148). Nevertheless, at the risk of appearing overly cynical, consultative arrangements have not unfortunately provided an effective basis for formulating anything at all (Stratta 1990).

Evidence for the failure of consultative arrangements has been provided by successive HMIC reports, which together clearly raise questions about this method of identifying community interests. As those reports demonstrate, the failure of consultation processes suggest the existence of a large black hole in what was the centre of the Conservative government's strategy on policing. To date there has been very little community involvement or interest in setting objectives for the local plan. In the absence of the public at police consultative meetings (PCCGs), police representatives themselves often decide what the local priorities should be. HMIC reports from a range of police forces indicate that community involvement in developing local objectives remains highly problematic. Moreover alternatives to formal consultation have also proved to be disappointing. In Devon and Cornwall a series of open meetings, outside the consultative processes, held to identify police priorities drew a 'poor attendance' (HMIC 1995, para. 2.9). In Kent HMIC recommended that 'police forces should try new methods of consultation' in order to encourage public involvement (HMIC 1995, para. 2.55). In Humberside HMIC noted that requirement of the Police and Magistrates Courts Act for community consultation 'implies a requirement for better attendance and representation at PCCG's from a wider cross section of the community' (HMIC 1995, para. 7.33).

David Maclean as Minister of State, was surely right to argue in 1996 that there was no prescription on how best to achieve local consultation. Most recently the Home Office Police Research Group have sought to identify methods to improve consultation and extend it by way of social research and networking (Elliott and Nicholas 1996). There is clearly a need for an effective customer voice, but the PCCG's used by the Conservative government to justify the massive reduction in elected representatives are never likely to provide such a voice.

Alternatives to PCCG's will need to be evaluated, but the continuing obscurity of section 106 Committees, suggests that their abolition would not generate much public protest or even interest. The imbalance between police and public representation at existing PCCG's may mean that local objectives can be compromised if they are little more than what the police think the public might identify as appropriate local objectives. If this has become a common practice then the overall value of the Local Policing plan becomes itself a matter of concern.

197

Conclusion

Although the Police and Magistrates Courts Act was designed to improve police efficiency and highlight the police 'crime fighting' function, it would appear that post bureaucratic change has been one of adaptation, rather than of acceptance. Ironically the overall impact of change has tended to enhance and strengthen the position of professionals in the police service vis-à-vis central and local government. Recent comments from HMIC suggest that police authorities, once themselves a source of anxiety, to some chief officers have ceased to be a matter of either concern or salience. A new grant mechanism along with financial delegation has significantly augmented the position of chief officers who now have an immediate responsibility for spending decisions which may or may not meet with the approval of the police authority. Police authorities are responsible for monitoring performance. It would appear that local policing may be enhanced by reform, but it will be professionally driven and largely autonomous of lay management. Indeed the future role of the police authority remains uncertain (irrespective of independents constituting just under a third of its membership). Devolved budgets have ended any attempt to create a purchaser function for the authorities. Chief officers are budget holders, and when this interesting feature of the 1994 Act, is added to that of soft contracts the ability of the authority to influence police performance becomes increasingly questionable. If recent reforms have effected any changes, it appears that police autonomy has been enhanced rather than in any way challenged. For the police service this has been a reassuring conclusion to a process which only recently appeared to represent a major threat to both their professional standing and espoused operational independence.

This newly enhanced police autonomy could lead chief officers to pursue divergent pathways. Traditionalists may be expected to espouse the value of specialisation and status hierarchies. Alternatively more progressive officers may seek to challenge the espoused benefits of increasing specialisation, and encourage a more generalist approach possibly reducing police hierarchy and introducing smaller units of policing with the benefits of devolved budgets. How much change can be made to street level policing remains problematic. Staffing shortages, now a generalised feature of most police activity, mean that individual officers respond to public demands for service in a reactive mode. It would appear, however, that the lack of effective police provision that such staffing shortages generate may only reflect a deeper malaise within police organisations where the professional determination of policing objectives irrespective of public demand, has created and continues to sustain a staffing crisis. Reducing the bureaucratic hierarchy may provide only a partial solution to this crisis, although the two supervisory ranks of chief superintendent and deputy chief constable) have now been abolished. Of greater significance would be the introduction of a cultural shift to place greater emphasis on police-public contact by uniform personnel than on narrow specialist practices which remove the police from regular public contact.

Change in the police service has been driven very largely by external review rather than from within. The Audit Commission's increased demands for greater value for money made it the 'change driver' for the service. Research into the bureaucratic nature of police organisations provides a more meaningful insight into police activity than may be usually identified in the media. Moreover a more educated and questioning public is increasingly critical of the level and quality of service provided by the police. A more critical assessment of the role of the police as the publics' defender became, moreover, inevitable following the Thatcher government's systematic use of police forces to achieve largely political objectives during the 1980s, particularly during the miners dispute of 1984-5. While public opinion surveys consistently suggest that the police are held in greater esteem than estate agents or solicitors, it is clear that, as successive British Crime Surveys have shown, those who have been and are most likely to be victimised, remain the most critical of the quality of police service provided. The quality of service and the nature of police public contact remain crucial to effective policing and the extent to which the public will call for police service. For police managers, the bottom line might rightly be defined as the degree to which the public exercises its discretion to either call or *not call* for police service. A decision by members of the public not to call for police service, which is often a characteristic of high crime areas, may be viewed as a significant public indictment of the police services' commitment to 'fighting crime'.

References

Audit Commission (1991), *Reviewing the Organisation of Provincial Police Forces*, HMSO: London.

Audit Commission (1993), *Helping with Enquiries*, HMSO: London.

Audit Commission (1996), *Streetwise - Effective Police Patrol*, HMSO: London.

ACPO (1990), *Collected Conference Proceedings*, ACPO Summer Conference: Birmingham.

Baker, K. (1992), *Turbulent years - My Life in Politics*, Faber: London.

Baker, M. (1996), 'On What Authority?' *Policing Today*, September, Vol. 2, No. 3.

Coleman, C. and Moynihan, J. (1996), *Understanding Crime Data: Haunted by the Dark Figure*, Open University Press: Buckingham.

Cope, S., Charman, S. and Savage, S. (1997), 'Police Professionalisation: The Role of ACPO', Paper given to the Public Services Research Unit Conference, Cardiff Business School.

Davies, H. (1990), *Fighting Leviathan*, Social Market Foundation: London.

Elliot and Nichol (1996), *It's Good to Talk*, Police Research Unit Paper 22, Home Office: London.

Greensward et al. (1997), *The Criminal Investigation Process*, Rand Corporation: Lexington, Mass.

Home Office (1993), *Police Reform*, Cmnd. 2281, HMSO: London.

Home Office (1996), *Protecting the Public*, Cmnd. 3190, HMSO: London.

HMIC (1995), *Reports: Devon, Cornwall* and *Humberside*.

HMIC (1997), Interview with Sir Jeffery Dear, HMIC Worcester.

Loveday, B. (1990), 'The Road to Regionalisation', *Policing*, Vol. 6, Winter, pp. 639-60.

Loveday, B. (1996) 'Business as Usual', *Local Government Studies*, Vol. 22, No. 2, pp. 22-39.

Loveday, B. (1996), 'Auditing the New Police Authorities', *County News*, December.

Loveday, B. (1995), 'Criminal Justice' in Jackson, P. and Lavender, M. (eds.), *The Public Services Year Book 1995/6*, Chapman and Hall: London.

Marshall, G. and Loveday, B. (1984), 'The Police: Independence and Accountability' in Jowell and Oliver (eds.), *The Changing Constitution*, Oxford University Press: Oxford.

Martin, J. and Wilson, G. (1969), *The Police: a Study in Manpower*, Heinneman: London.

Merseyside County Council (1985), 'A Survey of Police Officers', MCC: Liverpool.

Jones, M. (1980), *Organisational Aspects of Police Behaviour*, Avebury Press: Aldershot.

Monkennen, E. (1981), *Police in Urban America 1860-1920*, Cambridge University Press: New York.

Morgan, R. and Newburn, T. (eds.), *The Future of Policing*, Clarendon: Oxford.

Nalla, M. (1992),'Perspectives on the Growth of Police Bureaucracies 1948-1984', *Policing Society*, Vol. 3, pp. 51-61.

Police Federation (1996), 'Patrolling: A Report by the Police Federation', February, Police Federation: Surbiton, Surrey.

Police Joint Consultative Committee (1990), 'Operational Policing Review'.

Reiner, R. (1991), *Chief Constables*, Oxford University Press: Oxford.

Reiss, A. (1971), *The Police and The Public*, Yale University Press: Yale.

Shattock, D. (1996), 'Demand for More Beat Bobbies "Misplaced",' *Police Guardian*, September, p. 5.

Scott, H. (1957), *Scotland Yard*, Penquin: Harmondsworth.

Stratta, E. (1990), 'A Lack of Consultation', *Policing*, Vol. 6, pp. 523-49.

Wilson, J. (1968), *Varieties of Police Behaviour*, Harvard University Press, Cambridge, Mass.

Young, H. (1990), *One of Us*, Pan: London.

12 Justice in the lower courts

John W. Raine

In this chapter the focus is upon the decline of traditional bureaucratic structures and changing power relationships in a part of the public sector characterised by the exercise of coercion and state authority. The chapter provides a case study of the impact of public sector managerialism within the administration of justice, and particularly of the professional role and status of the practitioners who work within the magistrates' courts of England and Wales. These courts are of interest both because of their significance within the overall context of judicial administration (they deal with over ninety-five per cent of criminal cases and with much civil case work as well) and because they amply illustrate the complexity of outcomes that has been one hallmark of change in the wider UK public sector. Specifically they illustrate the duality and conflict of trends, of professionalisation and deprofessionalisation taking place simultaneously. On the one hand we see here the role and status of professional officers having been subordinated by the imposition of a new manager cadre operating the regimes and doctrines of public sector managerialism, while on the other, we see the continuing development of professionalism in the staffing and running of the courts which is challenging traditional power bases and mores.

Managerialism and deprofessionalisation

The Thatcher reforms of public services have been extensively described and evaluated elsewhere in and beyond this volume (see for example Pollitt 1990, Raine and Willson 1993, Newman and Clarke 1996). Accordingly this chapter is confined to the particular reforms within the administration of justice and in magistrates' courts and their consequences. As elsewhere in the public sector, these reforms were ideologically driven and centred around the pragmatics of cost efficiency and demonstrable service effectiveness. Cost efficiency, captured in the euphemism of 'value for money', challenged traditional assumptions and approaches in budget making and service administration. Previously budgets were mostly calculated on the basis of past provision rather than on identified need, and services were provided mainly on the basis of professional discretion rather than according to costs or demand.

Recent reforms sought demonstrable service effectiveness through revised and more transparent accountability processes which overtook conventional professional accountabilities for practice and trumped the traditional public service ethic. Performance management techniques were increasingly employed to measure achievement at individual, unit and institutional levels against pre-determined targets and priorities, an approach that was very different from that associated with previous bureaucratic processing.

The impacts of these reforms on the magistrates' courts of England and Wales were on four distinct areas: the revision of the organisational framework, the development of strategic management, the pressure for greater efficiency and productivity, and the reshaping of the staffing organisation.

Revising the organisational framework

The magistrates' courts, as indeed the higher courts, were not subjected to the large-scale structural and market-oriented reforms associated, for example, with the health service. This reflected a number of circumstances, including the fragmented local organisational framework, practitioner resistance at local level - by magistrates and their clerks - the relatively low commitment to marketisation ideas within the Home Office and particularly on the part of Home Office ministers. Another factor was the political and constitutional difficulties that arose from the doctrine of the separation of powers which respected the independence of the judiciary from the executive arm of the state (Raine and Willson 1993) (James and Raine 1998).

Nevertheless somewhat behind the other public services, the magistrates' courts of England and Wales were placed under many of the same managerialist pressures as experienced elsewhere. Initially through exhortation and eventually by financial controls and performance monitoring, the government pressed them to become more efficient and effective. Indeed it is possible that a fuller managerialist agenda of market-style reforms would have eventually been introduced in this arena under the Conservatives. After all the history of bureaucratic processing in the administration of justice in the lower courts began in the contracting out by each local bench of responsibility for administration (as well as for the provision of legal advice in the court room) to a local practising solicitor.

However the Home Office reform agenda took a rather different path with the arrival of the last in the line of Conservative Home Secretaries, Michael Howard, and focused mainly on a policy agenda of getting tough of crime. As a result the main emphasis of managerialism for the magistrates' courts largely remained at the level of trying to meet the performance targets that were demanded of them by government while also coping with increasingly tight budgets.

Perhaps because of the neglect of the alternative of market mechanisms, the government felt it necessary to intervene artificially to restructure in pursuit of greater efficiency and effectiveness. Thus, following a Home Office Scrutiny of magistrates' courts (Home Office 1989), a set of reorganisation proposals were presented in a White Paper accompanied by a transfer of governmental responsibility from the Home Office to the Lord Chancellor's Department, from where the Crown Court and County Court were already organised. These proposals promised several significant changes in the organisational framework, the key ones of which were implemented under the Police and Magistrates' Courts Act 1994.

A key aspect of the new framework for local justice was the planned rationalisation in the number of local units for managing the lower courts. Prior to 1994 each shire county, metropolitan district and London borough area had its own magistrates' courts committee, a committee of magistrates from the area, the members of whom were elected by their colleagues on the local benches to undertake the governance and resource management role, particularly in relation to finance, staffing, buildings and equipment. The competence and effectiveness of such committees had been brought into question in the 1989 Home Office scrutiny study. The plan as outlined in 1992 was to halve their number by amalgamations and also to limit the number of magistrates on each committee to twelve, down from more than 30 members in some cases (Lord Chancellor's Department 1992).

Predictably the plan generated much opposition among magistrates and staff about the dilution of local identity. Perhaps not surprisingly, therefore, the initial approach of seeking voluntary amalgamations resulted in little rationalisation. Probably the Lord Chancellor and his department would have moved ahead to enforce more amalgamations in pursuit of further rationalisation. In any case this quickly became the policy of the new government, elected in May 1997, and a timetable for amalgamations was accordingly prepared for implementation.

A second and key aspect of the reform package was implemented in full prior to the election. This involved the establishment of a new top tier of managers - one for each magistrates' courts committee area - to act as chief officer for the courts' committee and to head the staff and administrative organisation within the area. This new tier of justices' chief executives, as they were called, was superimposed on the justices' clerks who had previously been the autonomous heads of profession in their own local court organisations. The argument for the change was based on the promotion of a more managerial culture which in turn would generate efficiency improvements. The thinking was that the new justices' chief executives, with responsibility for all the court administrative units within their areas, would be able to attack wasteful duplication and introduce more flexibility into the allocation of resources. Much was made of the argument that it would now be easier to transfer cases, staff and other resources between courts according to demand and supply pressures and so allow greater efficiency in the use of resources overall.

However the loss of status and authority by the justices' clerks was deeply felt. As a concession to them, the Lord Chancellor agreed that those appointed to the new posts of justices' chief executive would have to have legal qualifications like the justices' clerks, thereby making all justices' clerks eligible candidates. In practice management rather than professional skills and aptitudes have counted greatly in decisions over appointments. To the dismay of the Justices' Clerks Society, a few appointments were made of lawyers without any experience of magistrates' courts. The consequent low morale of the profession, pre-empted some tactical non-cooperation on the part of justices' clerks who questioned the authority of the justices' chief executives to decide administrative policy and practices within the local courts for which they themselves felt responsible (as they had always been). Here, the provisions of the Police and Magistrates Courts Act 1994, unfortunately offered insufficient clarity. A number of justices' clerks were so disillusioned that they sought early retirement which meant a loss of much experience for the courts. Many others were pressed to accept redundancy terms as victims of local reorganisation plans designed to help pay for the new (statutory) top tier of management.

Behind the plan for the new manager cadre of justices' chief executives lay the failure of the justices' clerks, as a body, to impress government that they were taking the new managerial agenda seriously. Certainly many members of the Justices' Clerks Society worked very hard in pursuit of greater efficiency and effectiveness in the running of their courts. Yet many others preferred to continue to project themselves primarily as lawyers first and foremost. They chose the courtroom rather than the office as their main work venue, devoting time to magistrates rather than to staff (the Scrutiny study, somewhat uncharitably, had described the role of justices' clerks in relation to magistrates as a cross between the family solicitor and butler) and preferring to focus on legal developments and legal training than on management initiatives and management training. For them professional status and responsibility was their main interest. Indeed some pursued parallel interests as authors and editors of legal texts or served on a part-time basis as stipendiary magistrates in other areas.

Characteristic of all professional groups in the preceding era of administrative bureaucracy, justices' clerks had long enjoyed considerable discretion in the pattern of activities undertaken and in the way they spent their time (Raine and Willson 1996). But of course the resulting diversity did not sit easily with the standardising and measurement-driven assumptions of the new managerialism. Happily the new culture did not meet with universal disapproval, and its ethos was embraced without difficulty in many areas. Indeed many justices' clerks, whose Society's logo was a pair of quill pens, had themselves felt that the traditional ways of working were not going to suit the future. For them bureaucracy was not only out of favour, it was also out of date. Others realised the seriousness of the government's 'commitment to greater efficiency and applied for the new justices' chief executive posts or mobilised their own internal reforms rather than waiting for change to be imposed. Others again, watching the reforms elsewhere, saw some useful approaches and techniques worth copying in their own organisations.

Whether by imposed or self-generated change, the organisational structures of the magistrates' courts changed in three main ways: they became less hierarchical, sometimes with whole tiers removed; they became leaner and tighter as jobs widened and staff numbers reduced; and they became driven by managerial rather than professional processes. This last characteristic is, of course, particularly significant within the context of this book. Professional structures begin from an assumption that 'the professional knows best', that the organisation exists to service that expertise and that the work needs to be individualised and dealt with case by case through the exercise of discretion. In contrast management structures assume that the best decisions are made at the top and that is why managers are paid the most. Most public service organisations had run both structures in tandem. Finance and support services had operated mainly through management structures while operational services had mainly worked through professional structures. The magistrates' courts were somewhat different. They had traditionally run almost exclusively on professional lines. The cadres of administrative and clerical staff employed by the courts never enjoyed the status, pay or prospects of their professional counterparts, the clerks. One effect of the reforms, however, was to give status and career opportunities to senior administrative staff and, in so doing, introduced a new tension - a tension between managerial and professional systems. The new status ascribed to management, most particularly through the appointment of justices' chief executives, meant that the most senior professionals - the justices' clerks - felt devalued with their autonomy increasingly challenged by seemingly unnecessary regulations and procedures.

Developing a strategic management perspective

A key characteristic of traditional bureaucratic services was that they were procedurally driven. The procedures may not always have been written down, but what the organisation did, and how it did it, was generally bounded, consistent and clear to all staff. Indeed the purpose of staff induction programmes was to introduce new appointees into the administrative constraints and regulations within which the particular organisation operated. In some contrast a key characteristic of the new managerialism was that the organisations were purpose-driven. Although that purpose was usually expressed in lofty mission statements and strategic planning objectives, the full implications were rarely discussed or understood below top manager level.

In its early and rational stages of development, managerialism was driven by an 'ideal' process model of visioning, planning, strategy, implementation, monitoring and review. Government departments required the organisations to prepare strategic business plans consistent with their own, to identify priorities and targets and to monitor, review and report on achievement. Again the magistrates' courts amply illustrate the point, in this case through the introduction of a new statutory duty required of the local courts committees to prepare and update strategic plans on a regular basis, the quality of which were to become subject to scrutiny by a newly-established inspectorate. While all this may have galvanised the attentions of the magistrates' courts committees and their justices' chief executives, there was often little awareness of the contents of the strategic plans, let alone of their consequences for the organisation of work within the court offices. Mostly it was a case of high level lip service to the vocabulary and principles of strategic planning but only very limited follow-through in terms of implementation, monitoring and feedback.

The possible inappropriateness of such rational planning mechanisms to complex, multi-stakeholder organisations such as the courts was largely unappreciated by the civil servants who dictated the reform process, as indeed, it was by some of the more managerially-minded justices' clerks themselves, well-read on the science of management, but insufficiently experienced in the art. The failure of the courts, as of other criminal justice agencies, to convey to government the distinctiveness within the field of public service of their particular role and functions, led to disillusionment and dissatisfaction with the reforms. Others simply worked harder and faster, mistakenly believing that this would in itself resolve what were in fact competing pressures. In this they became preoccupied with a series of new managerial methods and techniques, each of which seemed to promise enhanced performance. They included local organisational restructuring, changes of personnel at the top, the preparation of business plans, introduction of customer service, excellence and total quality initiatives, process 're-engineering' and many more. As in other organisational contexts such methods were always likely to be successful as levers to mobilise change, provided that adequate support was forthcoming to facilitate the change process. Often, however, they failed or were less than successful because they were used not as levers but as solutions in their own right, and without the necessary support for change being provided. In some instances over-enthusiasm for the fads of the pop-management literature generated initiative fatigue, organisational stress and machismo management. This, in turn, reinforced the image carried by the 'caring professionals' of the 'heartless managers' and generated much shroud-waving among those predisposed to cynicism.

Efficiency and productivity

Runaway public expenditure provided its own rationale for public service reform though again, the magistrates' courts were not initially exposed to cost savings to the same degree as other public services. Nevertheless, by the early 1990s, the parsimonious values of the management accountant had clearly become embedded in the courts and in the way policy in this domain was being developed and implemented.

Inevitably there were particular sensitivities about cost savings in relation to the pursuit of justice and debate about the relative cost efficiency of different sentencing decisions had always been frowned upon. But the managerial agenda of the mid 1980s onwards was inspired, of course, by commitment to cost-control and to making efficiency gains. The methods used to this end in magistrates' courts followed a well-trodden and unimaginative path already rehearsed in other public services. In 1992 cash limits were imposed to put a ceiling on the grant paid to support the spending of the local courts. Some funding was ring-fenced to require the courts to follow government-set priorities, notably for new accommodation and for training. A formula, based principally on workloads and performance, was developed to distribute the cash limited grant among the local areas. The resulting distribution differed markedly from the past pattern and it was necessary to introduce transitional arrangements to cushion the impact of change. Even then the formula had to be amended after a few years to introduce greater stability in the allocations, this time taking more account of past expenditure. By then, however, the annual index-linking of the cash limits had been abandoned and the overall budget reductions meant enforced cuts for many local courts.

The effects of pursuing greater efficiency and productivity in the magistrates' courts were twofold. Firstly most courts simply learned to do more with less. In the absence of a clear strategy from the government about the standards of provision expected, for example, how local should local justice be in rural areas, the spirit tended to become parsimonious and negative. In this respect the attentions of professionals became focused on cost-saving, service cuts and on low level processing activities. This was illustrated in the orientation of the Magistrates' Courts Information System (MIS) developed by government from the mid 1980s onwards, and which used a set of Key Indicators (KIs) to monitor and compare the performance of individual courts. Of the four such KIs, one concerned the quality of service, while the other three focused explicitly on efficiency and productivity, average cost per case, delays in case completions, and the level of outstanding fine arrears.

Secondly where financial pressures could not be brought to bear on services, productivity improvements were sought to address problems of delay and hence indirect costs. Throughout the 1990s the subject of delay-reduction remained high on the Home Office/Lord Chancellor's Department agenda and a series of initiatives were taken to tackle the lengthening time-scales involved in completing cases in magistrates' courts. In 1989 the Home Office established a 'Pre-Trial Issues' Working Group to develop national standards for the courts and other local criminal justice agencies to work to. Later a Home Office study of the delay problem recommended a series of procedural changes to expedite the progress of cases, which included the extension of powers traditionally those of the judiciary alone, to their legal advisers, the magistrates' clerks (Home Office 1997). At face value the argument seemed logical enough - that a case should only be put before magistrates when it was ready to proceed. But the recommendation was controversial in so far as it sought to categorise pre-trial decision-making as 'administrative' and therefore not the business of magistrates in the courtroom. Many on the bench saw the matter differently and regarded such decision-making as properly judicial. The same report also recommended that magistrates, not defendants, should in future decide if an 'either way' case should be transferred to the Crown Court to be heard before a judge and jury, and that prosecutors should be accommodated in local police stations (from whence they had been removed in 1985 when an independent Crown Prosecution Service was established) to improve co-ordination with the police and speed up file preparation and review. It was thus a report that, in offering managerialist solutions, challenged a number of professionally-defined and traditional standards within a justicial setting.

Staffing

The process of revising the organisational framework, of developing strategic management and of enhancing efficiency and productivity all had major implications for staffing in the courts. The advent of the new top tier of justices' chief executives, combined with the need to make cost savings because of tight cash limits, meant that many existing staff posts came under threat. As indicated, the number of justices' clerks declined sharply following the implementation of the Police and Magistrates' Courts Act 1994 as early retirement terms were settled on many with long-service records as a way of reducing costs. At the same time the case for retaining the rank of deputy justices' clerks was brought sharply into focus. In some areas the rank was summarily abolished and existing post-holders made redundant or down-graded. This inevitably unsettled those of similar status in other areas.

Staff in the magistrates courts, as a whole, paid a high price for the reluctance of a number in their midst to foresee the changes ahead, to move with the times and to implement their own reforms. Inconsistent and piecemeal policy-making and implementation meant that the implications of the reforms for staff were inadequately confronted. Elsewhere in the public services concerns over staffing were more comprehensively addressed by deliberate programmes of staff development designed to build understanding and motivation around the changes being made, particularly around customer service and quality. This was problematic in the courts, however, where the consumerist ideas had questionable relevance and where at the centre of proceedings was a reluctant 'user', namely the defendant or offender rather than a willing 'customer'. Quality initiatives remained therefore at the margins, focused for example on the provision of improved facilities, signposting, information provision and customer service training (Raine and Willson 1996).

The result was that, whereas in other services there were attempts to support staff in making difficult personal transitions in their practice, in magistrates' courts such support was very limited. Consistent with their own ethos, the stick, rather than the carrot, was used. An example of this was the way in which work patterns were increasingly standardised. In the interests of efficiency, transparency, performance and its measurement, clear specifications were required of the conditions for intervention, methods to be used and the standards of outputs to be achieved. In part this was required by legislation, as for example, in the tighter sentencing regimes imposed in the 1991 Criminal Justice Act and in the 1997 Crime (Sentences) Act. It was reinforced by policy documentation including guidance, circulars and advice notes and by the publication of recommendations initially from a 'good practice' group in the Home Office and subsequently from the newly established Inspectorate for Magistrates' Courts.

The increasingly rigorous application of standards meant that a price was also paid by professional practitioners, particularly the justices' clerks, in respect of initiative and responsibility for action, many of whom, in the interests of personal survival, chose to follow guidelines to the letter rather than pioneer or take risks with new projects.

Professionalisation in magistrates' courts

As elsewhere in the public service, the managerialist agenda of the 1980s and 1990s challenged and changed the status and role of senior professional practitioners within the lower courts. In establishing a new power base and a new dynamic to the administration of justice, it contributed in no small way to a process of deprofessionalisation. That said the period was also marked by a contrary trend, a trend which bore all the hallmarks of professionalisation, notably the growing pre-eminence of expertise within the particular occupational area (Freidson 1970).

This pre-eminence was evident in the significant growth in the employment of magistrates' clerks with legal qualifications, as solicitors or barristers, rather than the Diploma in Magisterial Law that had been specially developed in earlier times to protect standards of legal advice to lay magistrates in the courtroom. Although very few areas operated an official recruitment policy restricting appointments of court clerks to those with professional legal qualifications (Nottinghamshire led the way in this respect in the late 1970s), increasingly magistrates' courts' committees preferred to appoint barristers and solicitors or encouraged and supported existing Diploma qualified staff to return to college to obtain professional status. There was pressure in this direction from the heads of profession, the justices' clerks, who by law were required to hold professional qualifications. Eventually, in 1997, the new government submitted to the pressure and announced its intention to professionalise the court clerking function.

At the local level the question of qualifications had proved a divisive issue. The majority of long-serving court clerks, including most deputy clerks, lacked professional qualifications and were disinclined to return to study. But increasingly they perceived their status to be threatened by the many newly-appointed barristers and solicitors who were able to command extra pay increments on account of their qualifications. Many magistrates lent support to their long-serving diploma qualified clerks asserting that their long experience was to be more valued than paper qualifications. But with the advent in 1985 of a fully professionalised Crown Prosecution Service, replacing police officers as the presenters of the prosecution case in the courtroom, most justices' clerks came to the view that magistrates needed court clerks with equivalent professional status in order to maintain authority and protect the reputation of the court..

Another facet of the counter trend of professionalisation that took place alongside the managerialisation of the courts concerned the magistrates themselves. Criticisms of the lay magistracy had been long-standing, with concerns about the recruitment process, the social composition of the bench and inconsistency and leniency in sentencing. The Magistrates' Association had worked hard to address these concerns throughout the 1980s and 1990s by publishing more information about the magistracy, supporting more openness and encouraging more applications from local people to join the lay bench, issuing national sentencing guidelines to local courts and promoting more training. These developments met with a mixed response from magistrates themselves, some of whom were concerned that their discretion was being narrowed by the sentencing guidelines and that their lay status was being undermined by the amount of legal training and knowledge now expected of them.

In practice the issue was broader. The role of lay magistrates was being squeezed by professionals from three directions: from stipendiary magistrates, from justices' clerks and from the police. Outside London, where a stipendiary system had long existed, appointments of full-time stipendiary magistrates had been few and far between before the late 1980s. So it was not surprising that lay magistrates saw the succession of such appointments made thereafter as threatening their continued existence. Repeated statements of commitment to lay justice from the Lord Chancellor failed to provide reassurance. At a more mundane level a recurrent complaint of lay magistrates was that the newly-appointed stipendiaries were 'creaming off' the more complex, often more interesting, cases including remand hearings and the longer trials.

Others felt that their justices' clerks, their legal advisers and chief administrators, had become predisposed towards stipendiary magistrates. In many instances this was indeed the case. As professional lawyers themselves, and with considerable experience of the disadvantages of a lay system, many justices' clerks had long privately favoured a stipendiary system for its greater consistency, toughness on persistent offenders and speedier pace of work. Indeed many had seen the benefits of stipendiaries first-hand when they had 'borrowed' them from other areas to hear particular extended and complex cases, perceived to be problematical for a lay bench. This experience had led them to think that a permanent appointment in their patch would be an effective way to reduce delays, to achieve more consistency and to challenge the idiosyncrasies of the lay bench. A number of justices' clerks themselves sat occasionally as deputy stipendiaries, and many relished the opportunity to join the judiciary in this way on a full-time basis.

Alongside all this the justices' clerks themselves provided an additional pressure on the lay magistracy through their pursuit of delegated powers to act in place of appointed justices. The Justices' Clerks' Society continually argued for such powers, although often their efforts were thwarted by the influence at national level of the Magistrates' Association, usually strongly opposed to the idea. Even so steps in this direction were made. For example accompanying the establishment of a new Family Court system in 1990 were new procedural requirements that involved the delegation of substantial new powers to justices clerks. Moreover with concerns growing over the tardiness of court processing, there were further pressures from justices' clerks to be given powers to act as single justices in hearings. An initiative taken at Bexley magistrates' court in the early 1990s amply illustrates this. Here all defendants were required shortly after charge by the police to appear before a clerk, not a bench of magistrates, for a pre-hearing at which matters such as legal aid, representation and hearing dates would be decided. Despite the fact that the scheme was deemed to have a questionable basis in law, it was quickly adopted by several justices' clerks at other courts and even attracted support from the Home Office because it appeared an effective way of increasing case completion rates (Raine 1994). The Magistrates' Association registered strong opposition to the scheme because they felt it infringed their authority and down-graded what they regarded as 'judicial' decisions to the status of 'administrative processing'.

The further instance of the squeezing of the lay magistracy by professionals came from the police whose powers were increasingly extended in ways that eroded the traditional framework of accountability towards the bench. An important instance of this concerned the extension to police officers of powers to attach conditions to bail previously reserved for the judiciary. This was made possible under the Criminal Justice & Public Order Act 1994 following a recommendation in the report of the Royal Commission on Criminal Justice (Runciman 1993). Prior to this the police had had two options after charging suspects. They could release them on police bail, which was unconditional, to attend court at a later date. Alternatively they could hold them overnight in police cells to appear before magistrates on the following morning. There the prosecution would typically argue either that the defendant should be remanded in custody until the date of trial or, if the court was inclined to grant bail, that certain conditions should be attached, such as a curfew or weekly reporting at a local police station.

The key arguments cited in favour of extending the power to the police to attach conditions to bail mainly concerned the more efficient processing of defendants, mainly through reducing the number of people kept overnight in police cells, reducing the number of 'overnight remand' cases with which magistrates' courts had to deal and reducing the court based work of the Crown Prosecution Service (CPS) and defence solicitors. But the extension of the power to police officers meant that the responsibility for constraining a person's liberty, through the imposition of bail conditions such as curfew or weekly/daily reporting, was passed from an independent judiciary to the executive. It also meant that this would often be done without the benefit of representations by the defence. It was a case of professionalising bail with conditions, by extending the responsibility for imposition from a part-time volunteer magistracy to full-time trained custody officers within the police. However if that professionalisation process was intended to produce better decision-making, research findings suggested it failed to do so. A study based on six local areas highlighted inconsistencies and idiosyncrasies in how the police applied bail conditions and found little evidence of custody officers having received special training to equip them for this new role (Raine and Willson 1996).

Managerialism, deprofessionalisation and professionalisation: making sense of the trends

The trends described in this chapter - of managerialisation and of simultaneous deprofessionalisation and professionalisation - describe some intriguing inconsistencies in the direction and nature of change in the magistrates' courts in the 1980s and 1990s. The argument, as in other chapters of this volume, is that managerialisation, being the antithesis of professionalisation, was a significant factor underpinning the diminishing status and influence of the key professionals, in this case the justices' clerks. But what the analysis of experience in this particular institutional setting also reveals is a simultaneous counter tendency. Paradoxically this counter tendency towards professionalisation might also be understood as a consequence of managerialism although, as elsewhere in the public service, it was a continuing process the origins of which predated the advent of the new managerialist doctrines of the 1980s. For example it was the managerial imperatives of reducing delay and increasing productivity in the court room that underlay the justices' clerks' pursuit of more delegated powers from magistrates and their support for the appointment of more stipendiaries. Similar considerations also underlay the extension of powers to the police in relation to bail conditions.

So what were the main outcomes of these conflicting tendencies for the magistrates' courts and for those who worked within them? Three such outcomes can be identified. The first outcome was how the principles and practices of management became rooted in the thinking of personnel at all levels within the courts and increasingly shaped their perspectives and priorities at work. Justice and judicial administration was seen as a function to be managed in much the same way as any other public or privately provided service. The old adage 'what price justice?', initially the rallying cry of the critics of managerialism in the courts, no longer seemed a respectable position to adopt. For sure there continued to be rumblings of concern about the extent to which efficiency considerations were now driving criminal justice policy and practice, for example over the proposal to remove the right to elect jury trial in 'either-way' cases. But more significantly the new conventional wisdom was that the courts, like all public bodies, had a responsibility to use their publicly-provided resources wisely and would have to justify their requirements against other public policy priorities.

This was illustrated both in the acceptance, albeit with some reluctance, of the imposition of cash limited funding and in the widespread acknowledgement that summary justice needed an overhaul to become more productive and to reduce delays. In the same way there was fairly widespread endorsement of the government's arguments for enhanced accountability, greater transparency and more information about performance in judicial administration as part of a revised approach to public accountability in the public services generally.

In this respect the lower courts had come to view themselves less as a branch of the state and more as another public service, along with health, street cleansing, education and so on, which the taxpayer was being asked to support. The approaches and philosophy of the new public sector consumerism were generally embraced by the courts, with little regard for the possible consequences in terms of potential loss of their constitutional separateness, judicial authority and dignity that might flow from such submission to market and consumerist principles (Raine and Willson 1996). At the same time the centralising, indeed, nationalising, of 'local justice' - increasingly under the control of the Lord Chancellor - though regretted by many, was never seriously challenged. The extent of acquiescence to such nationalisation was symbolised in the suffixing of the word 'service' to 'the magistrates' court' and the widespread adoption by local courts of the 'MCS' logo (Magistrates' Courts' Service) which had been coined by the Lord Chancellor's Department.

By the mid 1990s, then, there was widespread adherence to the doctrines of managerialism, particularly the need to increase efficiency, among court professionals and magistrates alike. Somewhat ironically, however, there were few obvious indications of cost efficiency or productivity gains being made. Time intervals for completing cases remained stubbornly long, mainly as a consequence of new legislative pressures, conformance with new administrative procedures, over-committed defence lawyer practitioners and shortages of prosecutors or of courtrooms. Cost savings resulting from closed courts, computerisation or staff restructuring, were generally more than outweighed by initiatives to improve 'customer service' through new accommodation, better training and the like. The costs of the new management tier of justices' chief executives, together with all the associated overheads, also bore heavily on budgets. And, as local courts were closed and the workload transferred to larger regional centres, so much of the goodwill of lay magistrates was eroded with the result that justices' travel and subsistence costs escalated, as many more now claimed their entitlements. As elsewhere the budgetary realities resulting from public sector managerialism were rarely quite as the rhetoric had suggested or the optimists had anticipated.

The second outcome of the conflicting trends illustrated by this analysis was the demoralisation of personnel and the generation of uncertainty and confusion about role and responsibility boundaries. Of course, as in any restructuring, there were those who benefited directly by the opportunities of change and whose position and capacity to influence were greatly enhanced. But overall the reforms had a deleterious effect upon morale among magistrates and staff alike and created as many problems about the division of responsibilities as they solved. Most serious in this context was the effect of the establishment of the new top manager cadre of justices' chief executives over the justices' clerks. The superimposition of such managers with authority emanating not merely from the magistrates' courts committees which they served, but also from legislation and from the emphasis now being given to management by the Lord Chancellor's Department, was a recipe for strife. In many areas the justices' chief executives sought to assert themselves over their professional colleagues by also acquiring for themselves the powers that the law had traditionally bestowed on justices' clerks. Such actions were opposed by justices' clerks, but there was little that they could do if the Lord Chancellor was minded to endorse applications for 'joint appointments'. In such situations some justices clerks resorted to guerrilla tactics designed to thwart the designs of their new bosses (in fact the new Lord Chancellor in 1998 quickly indicated his dislike of joint appointments, and this helped clear the air to some degree).

Nevertheless role conflict and confusion did not abate and continued to focus on the definition of respective areas of responsibility of justices' clerks and justices' chief executives. Justices' clerks generally resisted attempts by the justices' chief executives to influence the ways in which the courts were administered and justices' chief executives reciprocated by claiming statutory authority for the deployment of administrative staff. Here, as indicated, the legislation unfortunately provided insufficient clarity of interpretation and the position was hardly helped by the Lord Chancellor's reluctance to regulate in favour of one particular model for practice. As a result the arguments were protracted and rarely satisfactorily resolved. Allies to the justices' clerks' position were usually to be found among the local benches, the chairs of which were mostly predisposed towards decentralised authority. Allies to the justices' chief executives, on the other hand, were mainly on the magistrates' courts committees - increasingly comprised of the more business-wise and commercially-minded members of the bench, who were inclined to support centralisation in pursuit of more efficiency and control.

Restlessness and dissatisfaction was not confined to the top tiers but permeated throughout the court organisations. As indicated the position of deputy clerks looked increasingly vulnerable once the reforms were made. Moreover the position of many more staff was brought into question in 1997, when the Lord Chancellor's Department announced its intention to pursue a Private Finance Initiative for a national computerisation initiative for the courts. This followed the failure of a similar project within government (the MASS project) and seemed likely to lead to the transfer of many, perhaps most, of the court administrative staff from employment by the courts themselves to the winning private bidder. More than that, it seemed likely to result in further and major restructuring of the pattern of magistrates' court provision across the country into a format more suited to the requirements of the successful private contractor.

The third outcome of the conflicting trends explored in this chapter flowed directly from such anxieties and disaffection among the personnel resulting from the reforms. This was the prospect of a serious recruitment problem with potential implications for the nature of local justice and its administration. There were several aspects to this problem. The professionalisation trend in favour of court clerks with barrister or solicitor qualifications was problematical in so far as, with the decline in the number of justices' clerkships, there were fewer opportunities for staff to achieve the top grade. Thus many new entrants did not stay long, realising the prospects to be limited, and sought careers in private practice, where the pay and prospects were mostly better in any case.

In parallel a recruitment problem loomed in relation to the lay magistracy. Indeed the problem was already apparent in many areas in the 1980s when Local Advisory Committees, the panels of mainly magistrates in each local area responsible for finding, interviewing and recommending appointment to the Lord Chancellor, were encountering difficulties in filling places on the bench. Particularly difficult was the achievement of a 'balanced' bench in terms of a cross-section of occupational backgrounds, which as a result of previous criticism of the narrow class-base of the magistracy, had been given additional emphasis as a recruitment criterion. While it was usually not difficult to find white, middle-aged, spouses of successful professional practitioners willing to join the bench, the task of finding representatives from other social groups, notably those of younger age and from ethnic minority backgrounds, was altogether more difficult (King and May 1985). The mounting pressures of job insecurity and threat of unemployment during the 1980s had a deleterious effect on the recruitment process. Fewer people were prepared or able to meet the expectation of a fortnightly or weekly bench commitment. At the same time employers had become less tolerant of absence for public service responsibilities. The privatisation of the public utilities, traditionally fertile recruitment grounds for the magistracy, did not help in this respect. The closure of many of the smaller local courthouses and amalgamation of neighbouring smaller benches was also a factor since it diluted the 'localness' and closely knit social community of the bench - always an attractive aspect for would-be-recruits. Then there was the impact of the professionalising tendencies within the magistracy, the ever increasing expectations for more training, the time involved and legalistic nature of which, served to rule out many potential candidates.

Conclusion

The magistrates' courts of England and Wales provide an intriguing case study of the effects of contrasting trends - of managerialisation, deprofessionalisation and professionalisation - upon a public institution and upon the practicalities whose working domain it represents. In many respects the outcomes of the changes seem negative - unfulfilled expectations of management-inspired reforms, demoralisation of staff, recruitment difficulties and the like. On the other hand here was an institution that throughout its history had been the subject of criticism for its elitism, inconsistency and its remoteness from the public whose interests it purported to secure.

Were these outcomes so different from those from other parts of the public service described in other chapters of this volume? Did the fact that the nature of the managerialism that befell the courts, largely without the kind of market or quasi-market conditions that were imposed in health, for example, result in a different pattern of outcomes for professionals? And were the contradictions between managerialism and professionalism and the resistance to change any more or less fierce in the courts than in other quarters?

In pondering these questions it is necessary to consider the potential distinctiveness of the courts that might derive from their particular role and position within the context of state responsibility and from their special constitutional circumstances arising through the separation of powers. Here, in particular, it is important to reflect upon the institutional significance of the courts and what this might imply for the nature of the change process and of reactions to it. The distinction drawn by Selznick (1957) between organisations and institutions may be of some significance in this context. He defined an 'organisation' as a system of consciously co-ordinated activities, as a rational instrument, engineered to do a particular job and an 'institution' as more a natural product of social needs and pressures; a responsive, adaptive organism:

> Organisations are technical instruments, designed as means to definite goals. They are judged on engineering premises; they are expendable…Institutions may be partly engineered, but they also have a 'natural' dimension. They are products of interaction and adaptation; they become the receptacles of group idealism; they are less readily expendable… .

> Organisations are characterised by 'designed' behaviour; institutions by 'responsive' behaviour. In an organisation, efficiency and function are the most important things; the organisation embraces change if it offers prospects for greater achievement. In an institution any threat of change is fiercely resisted; feelings of personal loss are strong and there is an instinctive fight for the status quo.' (Selznick 1957, p.68)

Might it be that many of the problems arising from the imposition on the lower courts of public sector managerialism in recent years are attributable to the tendency to treat this particular institution as though it were an organisation and to subject it to pressures that could ultimately be undermining of its institutional status and stability?

References

Friedson, E. (1970), *The Profession of Medicine*, Dodd, Mead: New York.

Home Office (1989), *Report of a Scrutiny Study of Magistrates' Courts*, HMSO: London.

Home Office (1997), *Review of Delay in the Criminal Justice System* (Narey Report), Home Office: London.

James, A. and Raine, J. (1998), *The New Politics of Criminal Justice*, Adison, Wesley, Longman: Harlow.

King, M. And May, C. (1985), *Black Magistrates*, Cobden Trust: London.

Lord Chancellor's Department (1992), *A New Framework for Local Justice*, London: LCD.

Newman, J. and Clarke, J. (1997), *The Managerial State:Power, Politics and Ideology in the Remaking of Social Welfare*, Sage: London.

Pollitt, *Managerialism and the Public Services*, Blackwells: Oxford.

Raine, J. and Willson, M. (1993), *Managing Criminal Justice*, Hemel Hempstead: Harvester Wheatsheaf.

Raine, J. and Willson, M. (1996), 'Managerialism and Beyond: the Case of Criminal Justice', *International Journal of Public Sector Management*, Vol. 9, No. 4, pp. 20-33.

Selznick, P. (1957), *Leadership in Administration*, Harper and Row: New York.

13 Conclusion

Martin Laffin

The aim of this book has been to examine how the professions have adapted to major changes in the structure and context of the contemporary public sector in Britain. As was pointed out in the introductory chapter, the idea and ideal of professionalism and individual professions have profoundly shaped the welfare state. The various chapters in this book demonstrate how that idea and ideal has been and is subject to serious challenges in the cases of the eleven professions. Elected and appointed policy makers now dispute professional claims to special knowledge and to altruistic service. Policy makers are increasingly discriminating over sources of advice and willing to impose their own views on professional practice, especially as they struggle within an uncertain financial environment. How have the professions responded and adapted to these changes? This concluding chapter answers that question by summing up the findings under the three headings identified in chapter 1: the national or macro level, the institutional or meso level and the practice or micro level.

The national level

At the national level this book began with the observation that professional influence over policy has declined over recent years, in particular that the professions are losing their once pre-eminent role as the definers of social problems (Perkin 1989 and ch. 1). This book contains much evidence to support this loss. In the face of this loss of influence what have the leaders of the professional associations done to try to shore up their influence?

The starting point is the recognition that professional associations are broadly political bodies whose major purpose is to articulate, organise and promote the values and interests of their members - usually and inevitably the most vocal and influential of those members. The professional associations of the eleven professions studied display considerable diversity. At least three different types of association can be detected. Firstly the traditional professional association to which a substantial number of practitioners belong such as the British Medical

218

Association, Royal College of Nursing and Royal Town Planning Institute. Secondly coordinating associations which represent the management elite of the profession. Almost all the local government professions have coordinating associations which monitor and seek to form a coordinated response and input into national policy making. The most powerful example of such an association mentioned in this book is the Association of Chief Police Officers (ACPO). Thirdly some professions are represented collectively through trade union rather than professional associations - both school and university teaching illustrate this pattern. Significantly, of course, the majority of public sector professionals typically combine professional membership, or at least a sense of professional identity, with trade union membership, indeed they are more likely to belong to a trade union than a professional body.

The associations representing the more successful professions, and often it is the coordinating associations rather than the mass membership associations, did come over the immediate post-war period to act as 'autonomous sources of influence' on the formation of public policy (Laffin 1986, p. 221). As such they formed an integral part of the inter-organisational and inter-governmental relationships that constitute the public sector. Traditionally they have formed a vital part of the feedback loop between national and local levels, distilling what is 'national' from the particularities of the local. In so doing defining and redefining public problems, and spreading best practice and innovation. Of course this process did and does reflect the values and interests of the profession, though seldom quite in the crude way hypothesised by New Right public choice theorists.

To examine further the changing struggle of the professions to shore up their influence it is important to understand the strategic choices available to the leaders of the associations. Four possible strategies can be identified - conserver, prospector, advocate or passive. Those associations that adopt conserver strategies are typically found in the older professions which have few reasons to change and plenty of reasons to resist change. These associations insist on exclusivity and sharp boundaries between practitioners and the laity. The British Medical Association (BMA) is a prime example of a conserver association - though even the BMA has more recently recognised the need, in its core values initiative, for clinicians to think more widely about their roles and responsibilities (Hunter, ch. 2).

Similarly the Royal Town Planning Institute has stuck to a conserver strategy. The Institute has resisted recent pressures to widen the membership intake by loosening the requirements to embrace new activities undertaken by some planners, such as in tourism and economic development (this point emerged during the discussions at the June seminar). Meanwhile many professional planners at the practice level have themselves continued to prospect for new opportunities in economic development and tourism. Such shifts among the rank and file illustrate the central management problem for any profession's leaders. They have to balance the need to protect the 'core' identity of the profession and standards of entry against the need to retain relevance for members, and potential members, whose actual practice may be diverging from the professional mainstream. Particularly where the world of practice is changing rapidly, the leadership can experience difficulties in limiting the degree of divergence.

In contrast to conserver associations, prospector associations are more recent aspirants to professional status. As such their leaders are very actively seeking to make new professional claims and recruit new members. The Institution of Environmental Health Officers, for example, has adopted such a strategy to define and expand their niche in local government as Paul Thomas relates (ch. 8).

Like prospector associations, advocate associations are marked by a high degree of activism. Advocate associations seek to establish themselves as significant policy actors by becoming more like think tanks, producing research and commentaries on public policy matters, and in this way establishing their claims to policy expertise in the minds of policy makers and the public. The Chartered Institute of Public Finance and Accountancy (CIPFA) and the Chartered Institute of Housing (CIH) are good examples. CIPFA has sponsored the establishment of the Public Finance Foundation and the leaders of the profession have become active in commenting on current issues of financial management in the public sector. Similarly the CIH has drawn considerable media and policy maker attention to itself through several landmark reports and media comments. Both associations are not driven just by an abstract interest in public policy, both see their strategies as a means of attracting and maintaining membership, perhaps in the case of CIPFA to make it more attractive as an amalgamation partner. However whether this increase in public profile has also expanded their policy influence remains an open question requiring further research.

Finally passive associations are those caught in the bright headlights of change and are unable, or unwilling, to respond strategically to the new challenges. The national nursing bodies seem to match this strategy. As Ackroyd (ch. 3) points out the nursing leadership remains trapped within a dated model of professionalism which prevents them from responding effectively to new threats and opportunities.

Another significant development related to the strategies of professional associations has been the disappearance of some specifically public sector associations. As Keen and Murphy point out CIPFA has sought to amalgamate with a much larger institution with a largely private sector membership. This move reflects the ways in which public sector accounting practice are converging with private sector practice and so the boundary between the two are blurring. Similarly in recent years the Institution of Municipal Engineers has been subsumed by the Institution of Civil Engineers, reflecting similar convergence of practice as well as a strong preference among public sector engineers to join the larger institution and see their careers as potentially at least extending beyond the public sector. Again the implications of such a shift require further research.

As the chapters in this book make clear, then, the professional associations have had to struggle to shore up their influence as well as their membership over recent years. Their leaders have recognised the limitations of conserver strategies and increasingly favoured the active prospector and advocate strategies. Significantly even the medical profession has lost some of its old influence. The profession was marginalised during the implementation of the Griffiths Report. As Hunter (ch. 2) points out in contrast to 1948 when their sensibilities and freedoms were treated with great care, the last Conservative government ignored the profession when faced with the more urgent necessity of keeping the Treasury from interfering in the affairs of the NHS. Moreover the BMA has been willing to commit itself to losses of professional power at the practice or micro level in exchange for influence at the national level.

In fascinating contrast the police have been the only profession which has clearly gained policy influence over recent years. Loveday tells how the elite, coordinating association ACPO has become a powerful policy actor, most notably in removing the teeth from the performance management reforms recommended by the 1993 Sheehy Inquiry (ch. 11).

To refer back to the argument of chapter 1 this decline in professional influence, extending across the professions (except the police), must be understood as more than simply a consequence of an extended period of Conservative government. Professionals now find themselves in a very competitive marketplace for policy ideas and advice. What was formerly a fairly stable system characterised by the dominance of professionalised policy communities has been replaced, across most policy fields, by a diversity of competing policy voices. To underscore this point, under Labour all the signs are that the professionals' influence will not be restored.

The institutional level

As I argued in chapter 1 the growth of the welfare state was characterised by the professional colonisation of the bureaucracy, in particular the professional domination of the top jobs. Top and senior managers were appointed on the basis of professional reputations rather than their management competences or their attachment to the local or employing organisation. These managerial professionals justified their monopoly of the management roles associated with their profession in terms of their claims to specialist expertise and commitment to the particular service. Significantly medicine was the exception, only more recently have doctors in any numbers moved into senior jobs within the NHS though the doctors have always constituted the single, most important source of influence within the NHS.

Notably some professions have been more successful than others in holding onto the reins of managerial power. Nurses have lost their place around the senior management table and have not enjoyed great success in winning general manager posts. Housing management has lost out to the trend in local government towards multi-disciplinary departments. In contrast, for example, the great majority of directors of social services and of education are still drawn from social work and teaching backgrounds.

This position of dominance has come under serious challenge. Of course the idea of professional achievement as a good preparation for management has long been questioned, not least by the corporate management movement of the 1970s in the public sector (see ch. 1). The present challenges go beyond such a critique of professional credentials and education. Circumstances have moved on significantly over the last twenty years. Professional training, especially in the service professions, looks less and less appropriate to managing in finance driven organisations which depend on networks and contracts to get things done.

Central government policy makers have sought to impose their own views on what constitutes sound management practice on local government, the health service and other decentralised agencies. They have done this in a variety of ways - through introducing market competition, inspectorial bodies, placing new reporting requirements on agencies and encouraging the emergence of new managerial cadres to implement value-for-money approaches, most notably in the health service and the magistrates' courts. Generalist managers or administrators have a long history in the health service but recent years have seen a considerable enhancement of their role, following the creation of chief executive posts at hospital and health authority levels.

Meanwhile those leading local, employing organisations, at least partly as a result of the structural changes engineered by central government mentioned above, have come to emphasise the particular needs of their organisation rather than professional reputations in selecting senior staff. They prize, usually potential, commitment or loyalty to the local organisation as highly or more highly than professional commitments. In other words a form of localism is re-emerging and beginning to reverse the historical victory of professional cosmopolitanism. The reasons for this reversal are clear - increased competition among public organisations shifts loyalties towards the local organisation, the devaluation of professional status stressed in chapter 1 weakens professional claims to the top jobs, policy makers are increasingly identifying public policy problems that cut across professional boundaries, and they are looking to recruit managers capable of controlling rather than reflecting professional demands against a background of uncertain public finances.

Of course the nature of management as well as of professionalism is changing. The weakening of direct, bureaucratic controls in many public sector organisations is transforming management roles. Top managers are having to see their roles in more strategic and policy-focussed ways, certainly less as leaders of their professional colleagues. For example in local government, as Keen and Murphy (ch. 4) point out, chief financial officers have had to meet new expectations that they should be resource planners and adopt a client or customer focussed relationship with their service department colleagues. Moreover the development of a core-periphery distinction within local government in which a policy core makes policy which is then implemented, at least in principle, by service delivery organisations, not necessarily within the public sector, opens up some new and serious challenges to local government. Who should belong to the policy core and who to the service delivery periphery? The evidence suggests that this question will be answered primarily on other grounds to those of purely professional reputations and affiliations. However as Rao observes, 'The question of the location and form of the strategic role in the competitive local authority has yet to be fully thought through, and councils are likely to grapple with these second-order effects of competition to the end of the century' (1996, p. 123).

The practice level

The central theme that emerges at the level of practice are the considerable pressures on professionals at the front-line service level. The response of policy makers to social problems has long ceased to be one of shoring up professional self-regulation and autonomy. Instead the contemporary policy response is to impose new expectations and requirements on professional practice, circumscribing traditional professional claims to cognitive superiority and service in the public interest. Professionals at this level, in all eleven professions, face intensified demands for accountability which increase the difficulties of reconciling their professional ideals with the pressing realities of everyday practice. Furthermore these professionals have experienced work intensification following expectations that they should achieve more with fewer resources.

Many commentators, as noted in chapter 1, have argued in a neo-bureaucratic vein that these pressures constitute 'Neo-Taylorist' pressures involving the intensification of control over their work by management (for example Pollitt 1990). Ackroyd (ch. 3) takes issue with this argument, pointing out that Taylor set out to specify in great detail the work required of factory workers in terms such as specifying the time required to complete individual tasks. Ackroyd points out that nurses, and I would add other professional workers within the public sector, have not been subject to comparable controls. Indeed the managers, of hospitals and most other public sector organisations, would face insuperable problems given their own limited knowledge of professional practice and of monitoring if they were to pursue such a control strategy. Managers still have to rely on the self-organisation of the professional, which is precisely the condition that Taylor sought to eliminate. Hoyle and John, in their chapter, make a similar point in rejecting the concept of 'proletarianisation' as unhelpful. I would add, too, another reason that managers avoid over specifying practice level work, which is that they delegate, often tacitly, significant service rationing decisions to frontline workers. It is also important to recognise that these demands for tighter control over professional work emanate from elected policy makers. At least in part such demands reflect very real concerns among the electorate over questions of service quality and accountability. They cannot be explained simply in terms of a drive for greater savings or efficiency.

Central government controls now extend right into areas once assumed to fall well within the domain of professional judgement and decision making. Teaching provides a good example: a national curriculum has been imposed on schools, and ministers have even sought to specify how much time should be spent on reading and mathematical activities in primary schools. But the problems of policing and enforcing such requirements are obviously enormous. Policy makers still have to reckon with the existence of irreducible areas of discretion enjoyed at the practice level by professionals. This discretion forms the basis for the micro-power of the professions (Hunter ch. 2). Even the former Conservative government had to make significant concessions to teachers' micro-power to introduce the national curriculum. The Department of Education and Science itself admitted that it required the commitment of the teachers themselves to make things happen within the national curriculum: 'Teachers cannot but must be trusted' (Bowe, Ball and Gold 1992, p. 17). In addition several contributors note the severe problems of trying to measure performance in the case of professional work.

At the same time the nature of the work has changed. The classic or traditional view of the professional practitioner, even within public sector organisations, was of someone whose work was conducted with considerable independence from the employing organisation, was technical and client-focussed, and relied on the efforts of the individual practitioner. The new view of professional practice places less emphasis on the technical specialist and client-focussed aspects of the work and instead stresses the management of resources, inter-dependency rather than independence, generic competences and redefines 'clients' as 'customers'. Accordingly service professionals are acquiring new competences particularly in the management of budgets, contracts and inter-organisational relations. Arguably these new competences enhance rather than detract from discretion at work, service professionals are now less dependent on the finance experts, for example, as Keen and Murphy (ch. 4) show. Furthermore, again as Keen and Murphy make clear, areas of expertise are blurring as the accountants encroach on the service professionals' turf and the latter become able to challenge the accountants on their own turf.

It is not only professional competences that have changed. Professional commitments are also shifting away from the traditional cosmopolitan professionalism towards a localist attachment to the employing organisation. Like their colleagues in senior management, practice level professionals experience expectations that stress loyalty to the employing organisation or even department rather than to professional standards of practice and conduct or to the 'client'. Clough (ch. 6) describes how social workers are facing new pressures to see their prime loyalty to the organisation rather than to the client or a set of professional ethics: the issue pressed on practitioners is how to save costs and practice defensively to protect the employer. Similarly Murphy and Keen relate how accountants in devolved units are expected to meet the 'internal customer' needs of their service departments or business units. In universities, too, Henkel (ch. 10) shows how localist loyalties are modifying the values of what was a strongly cosmopolitan profession.

These pressures are having a significant impact on professional careers. Professional careers, like professional roles, have become more uncertain especially as work performance is assessed against criteria that are no longer narrowly professional. Hoyle and John (ch. 9) raise the possibility that some teachers are adopting a role as 'new entrepreneurs' within schools, seeing fresh career opportunities in the new requirements for management roles in a market-driven environment. Similarly Huw Thomas (ch. 8) points to how individual planners are acting entrepreneurially in moving into new areas of activity, particularly tourism and economic development.

Nonetheless 'professionalism' remains an important touchstone for many, perhaps most who work in the public sector. In local government, for instance, a recent survey of local government officers in four authorities found that over ninety per cent placed 'professionalism' as among the most important characteristics of an officer whereas less than 30 per cent valued 'enterprise' (1994, p. 23). Similarly Lowndes (forthcoming) emphasises how organisational changes are likely to be more effective if they mesh in with rather than conflict with professional values. These findings suggests that officers are still attached to an ideal of public service and that the cognitive assumptions of their profession strongly shape their views of how business should be conducted within their organisations.

The future of professionalism

This book began by posing the question of whether the old categories of bureaucracy and professionalism were adequate to the challenges of understanding the changes presently sweeping through the public sector. The contributors to this book mostly agree over the limitations of these old categories but are less agreed over what new conceptual categories should be introduced to aid that understanding. They reflect the uncertainty and continuing debate over the prevalent direction of change in the public sector - is it moving beyond bureaucracy to new forms of organisation or is bureaucracy simply being reinvented? This debate between the post-bureaucratic and neo-bureaucratic schools of thought runs through the book. In the neo-bureaucratic vein Hoyle and John, in their chapter, are concerned with the internal changes that have taken place within schools that they argue are introducing 'bureaucratic' ways of doing things into schools. Meanwhile others, such as Rhodes (1997), Kooiman (1993) and Laffin (ch.1) stress the growing importance of inter-organisational, networked relationships over the traditional, intra-organisational bureaucratic relationships in how the public sector works. However these different views may not be as quite as far apart as they first appear. Ironically it is at least partly the need to cope with this more uncertain, post-bureaucratic environment that is leading schools, and similar public service organisations, to replace their former 'structural looseness' with a neo-bureaucracy of defined roles and structures.

Public sector professions are all facing broadly similar pressures of work intensification, threats to established bureaucratic careers, and demands for greater accountability and outside control. Thus the contemporary notion of professionalism that is emerging is more limited than the traditional notion. It provides a context and a basis for negotiation with others rather than a final statement of who should be accepted as knowledgeable and trustworthy. The collective standing won by their profession is not as powerful a resource for professionals as it once was and often now fails even to ensure them a place at the policy-making table; traditional concepts of professionalism no longer guarantee them access to the top jobs at the institutional level; or to autonomy at the practice level. Professional membership is no longer accepted automatically as a guarantee of competence and neutrality, a loss of status which is very unlikely ever to be retrieved. Even so the members of many professions will continue to have a considerable influence over services though significantly more at the micro or practice level than in national policy making arenas. For as long as service delivery methods involve the exercise of significant discretion, professionalism will be significant in ensuring that such discretion is exercised predictably. Professionalism, then, is likely to persist because it offers a structure and language for coping with the problems of accountability and control created by discretionary work.

References

Bowe, R., Gold, A. and Ball, S. (1992), *Reforming Education and Changing Schools*, Routledge: London.

Kooiman, J. (1993), 'Governance and Governability: Using Complexity, Dynamics and Diversity' in Kooiman, J. (ed.), *Modern Governance*, Sage: London.

Laffin, M. (1986), *The Professions and Policy: The Role of the Professions in the Central-Local Government Relationship*, Gower: Aldershot.

Lowndes, V. (forthcoming), 'Management Change in Local Government' in G. Stokes, (ed.), *The New Management of Local Government: Markets, Hierarchies and Networks*, Macmillan: Basingstoke.

Perkin, H. (1989), *The Rise of Professional Society England Since 1880*, Routledge: London.

Pratchett, L. and Wingfield, M. (1994), *The Public Service Ethos in Local Government*, CLD and ICSA: London.

Rao, N. (1996), *Towards Welfare Pluralism: Public Services in a Time of Change*, Dartmouth: Aldershot.

Rhodes, R. (1996), *Understanding Governance: Policy Networks, Governance, Reflexivity and Accountability*, Open University Press: Buckingham.

Index

accountability 99, 136, 137-8, 148, 154, 165, 166, 168, 179, 202, 223
accountancy 42, 46, ch. 4 *passim*, 206
Adam Smith Institute 80
architects 77, 110
Association of Chief Police Officers (ACPO) 188, 195, 196, 219, 221
Association of University Teachers (AUT) 165
audit 29, 61
    performance 61
    external 175
auditor 57, 68
Audit Commission 5, 59, 61, 63, 64, 65, 66, 69, 81, 115, 132, 183, 190-1, 193, 199

Baker, K. 187
Bains Report (1972) 129
Bevan, A. 24
'Best Value' 6, 142
British Association of Medical Managers (BAMM) 28
British Association of Social Workers (BASW) 103
British Medical Association (BMA) 23, 27-9, 31-3, 218-9, 221
British Medical Journal 28
British Property Federation 81

bureaucracy, ch. 1 *passim*, 50-2, 66, 70, 76, 78, 87, 108-10, 113, 125, 136, 142, 146, 156, 162, 198, 202, 222, 225
Bromley 65
building control 131
Burnham Agreement 147

Callaghan, J. 151
Central Council for Education and Training in Social Work (CCETSW) 94
Central Council for Nursing, Midwifery and Health 39
Central Housing Advisory Committee (CHAC) 111
centralisation 8, 24, 34, 61-2. 67-8, 76, 118, 121, 152, 158, 176
Chartered Institute of Environmental Health (CIEH) 141
Chartered Institute of Housing (CIH) 108, 109, 113, 114, 117, 124, 220
Chartered Institute of Management Accountants 57
Chartered Institute of Public Finance and Accountancy (CIPFA) 56, 58-9, 60, 65, 220
chief constables 185, 192
chief executive 21, 106, 203-5, 208, 213, 214

chief financial officer 66, 67, 70 (see also Treasurer)

Citizens' Charter 135

City Challenge 83, 84

Clarke, K. 24, 184, 187

classical management theory 2

Committee of Vice-Chancellors and Principals (CVCP), 165, 169

community care 96, 100, 102, 104-6, 108, 118-9.

see also social care

community health services 26, 34

community pharmacy

community work 95

Competing for Quality 130

Compulsory Competitive Tendering (CCT) 6, 63, 67, 71, 79, 81, 83, 85, 96, 114, 119, 130, 132, 138

consensus management 21-2, 42

Conservative government (1979-97) 5, 7, 18, 61, 79, 82, 83, 96, 100, 103, 106, 112, 114, 118, 121, 124, 146, 153, 159,162, 171, 186, 189, 193, 197, 221, 223

consultants
hospital 21
private sector to public sector 58-9

Consultative Committee of Accounting Bodies (CCAB) 58

consumer 69, 96
complaints 104
see also customer *and* service user

consumerism 49, 113, 208, 212

contracts 6, 10, 11, 13, 25, 26, 65,, 92, 104, 118, 119, 124, 130, 132, 195, 222
contract culture 25
employment 41, 118, 143,156-7, 163, 168, 174,176-7, 179, 187-9, 195-6

contracting out 64, 76, 78, 82, 85, 137, 140, 142-3, 191, 202, 222, 224
see also outsourcing

contractor-client relationship 6,12, 14, 57, 66, 85, 130-1
see also purchaser-provider split

Cornwall 197

corporate management movement 10

corporatist bargain 164

Coventry 80

courts, ch. 12 *passim*

Criminal Investigation Departments (CID) 185-6

Criminal Justice Act 1991 211

Criminal Justice and Public Order Act 1994 211

Crosland, T. 148, 164

Crown Prosecution Service 207, 209, 211

Crowther Report 148

Cullingworth Report (1969) 112, 126

curriculum 149, 156-7
national 153, 157, 223
higher education 166, 178

customers 49, 163, 178, 208, 213, 222, 224
see also consumers *and* service users

customer service departments 61, 65, 68, 96

Dearing, R. 154

decentralisation 8,68, 76, 118, 121, 124, 152, 173, 198, 214
see also devolution

deprofessionalisation 14, 29, 78, 141, 215
see also proletarianisation

developers 82

development plans 77

Devon 197

devolution 68-70
see also decentralisation

direct labour organisations 63, 130

doctors ch. 2 *passim*, 41, 46, 139
see also medicine

domesticated v. wild organisations 147

economic development 83-4, 87, 224
education
schools ch. 9 *passim*
higher 153, ch. 10 *passim*
certificate of secondary education 148, 152, 153
vouchers 153
Education Act (1944) 151, 153, 154
Education Act (1976) 151
education
directors of 12
local education authorities 103, 148
efficiency 23, 30, 31, 33, 40, 42, 45, 52, 63, 66, 114, 117, 121, 204
and effectiveness 61, 62, 115, 183, 201
versus quality 166
elected members 66, 67, 70, 132-3, 135, 143, 192, 223
Employment, Department of 171
enabling role
in local government 10, 119, 130
engineers 40, 77, 85, 110, 112, 166, 220
enterprise zones 81, 82
environment 83
sustainable development 87, 141
Environment, Department of 80, 86, 116
Environment Agency 140, 143
environmental health officers 85, 108, 119, ch. 8 *passim*, 220
environmentalism 7
equity 92
Europe 108, 136, 153
expertise ch. 1 *passim*, 58, 94, 209

family court system 210
feminism 7
finance, departments of ch. 4 *passim*

general practitioners (GPs) ch. 2 *passim*
General Social Services Council 103
Griffiths Report (1983) 22-3, 39, 40, 220.

Hall, P. 80
health ch. 2 *passim*, ch. 3 *passim*
health authorities 103
health and safety at work ch. 8 *passim*
Health and Safety Executive 135, 143
Her Majesty's Inspectorate of Constabulary (HMIC) 189, 194, 197
Her Majesty's Inspectors of Schools 148-9
see also OFSTED
Heseltine, M. 81
hierarchical v. collegial relationships 4, 172
hierarchy 1-2, 4, 8-10, 12, 14-5, 23-4, 34-5, 40, 45, 48, 50-1, 76, 78, 119, 132, 142, 163, 204
higher education 78, ch. 10 *passim*
elite, mass and universal systems 163-4
Higher Education Funding Council 168, 169
Hill, O. 110
Hollow government 11
Home Office 184, 187, 190, 192, 196, 197, 202, 203, 207, 208
Home Secretary 187, 184, 189, 193-5, 196, 202, 203, 207, 208, 211
hospitals ch. 2 *passim*, ch. 4 *passim*
housing ch. 7 *passim*, 136, 140, 143, right to manage 123
and social services 104
Housing Act (1996) 122
Housing Act (1988) 118, 120
Housing Act (1980) 113
Housing Action Trusts 120, 122-3
Housing Corporation 122

Housing Investment Plans 112
Housing and Local Government Act
(1989) 118
housing management 14, 221
see also social housing
Housing and Town Planning Act
(1947)
Howard, M. 187, 191, 193, 202
Hurd, D. 189

information technology 8, 166
Inner Urban Areas Act (1978) 78
Inspectorate for Magistrates' Courts
208
Institute of Chartered Accountants in
England and Wales (ICAEW) 59
Institution of Civil Engineers 220
Institution of Municipal Engineers
110, 111, 220
Investors in People (IIP) 132
Jones, R. 80
justice 92
  criminal 183, 206
justices' clerks ch. 12 *passim*
Justices' Clerks' Society 204, 210

Kensington and Chelsea 65, 123
Kent County Council 67, 197
knowledge 1-3, 7-9, 13, 57, 95, 112,
  116, 164, 166, 167, 176,179, 218,
  223, 225
  knowledge workers 57, 71
  modes 1 and 2 167
  and post-modernism 167
  knowledge society 171
Labour government 5, 7, 28, 34, 64,
  79, 96, 103, 112, 114, 126, 142,
  159,171, 221
Labour in opposition 136, 147
Lambeth 67
lawyers 204, 210, 213
league tables 86
Lee-Potter, J. 28, 29, 31
learning organisation 97
'Local Agenda 21' 83, 141

Local Government Act (1992) 130
Local Government Act (1972) 61
Local Government and Finance Act
  (1988) 63, 130
Local Government Planning and
  Land Act (1980) 63, 130
Local Government Act (1933) 129
local housing companies 124
localism 222, 224
  see also local orientation
local orientation v. cosmopolitan
  orientation 57, 68, 70, 221
  see also localism
Lock, D. 80
London Docklands 81
Lord Chancellor's Department 203,
  207, 210, 213, 214

magistrates 94, ch. 12 *passim*
Magistrates' Association 210-1
magistrates'   courts   information
  system 207
magistrates'   local   advisory
  committees 214
Major, J. 82
Major government 183, 187
  see also Conservative government
managed care 33
management ch. 1 *passim*, 18, 23,
  29, 30, 31, 39, 64, 119, 126,
  147,163, 173, 179, 183, 209, 212,
  215, 221, 222
  management buy-outs 65
  management revolution 42
  management by walking around 46
  myths and models 31-4
  new management 40, 46, 53
  performance management 25, 29,
  33, 134, 196
  private sector 25
  styles 96, 98
managers 11, 18, 20, 22, 23, 26, 27,
  29, 30, 32, 42, 43, 48-9, 51, 93,
  97, 99, 101, 131, 138, 203, 205-6,
  213 221, 223

middle managers 69, 76, 98
management consultants 176, 193
managerialism 19, 21, 26, 29, 32, 34, 50, 52, 66, 201-2, 204-5, 208, 213, 216
markets 2, 6 , 8-11, 24, 26, 109, 118, 125, 163, 202, 213, 215
  internal markets 6, 23
  managed markets 24
  market testing 6, 64
  markets and networks 117
  see also quasi-markets
marketisation 6, 25
Meat Hygiene Service, 133, 143
medicine 13, ch. 2 passim, 38, 94, 95
  see also doctors
micro-power, medical 28, 223
mental health 100-1
Miners' Strike 199

National Audit Office 59
National Health Service 6, ch. 2 passim, ch. 3 passim, 129, 221, 222
  see also health
neo-bureaucracy 155-6, 223, 225
Neo-Taylorism 9, 44, 223
  see also Taylorism
networks 5, 9, 11, 32, 35, 109, 117, 119, 123, 126, 132, 167, 222
Newcastle-upon-Tyne 80
new public management 8, 25, 41, 43, 51, 126, 163, 173
  see also managerialism
New Right 5, 7, 149, 219
new towns 77, 79, 120
Newson Report 148
non-profit sector 10
  see also voluntary sector
nurses 12, 21, 22, 32, ch. 3 passim, 139, 223
normative model 33
Northern Ireland 94

occupational closure 38

Office of Science and Technology 171
Ombudsman 84
outsourcing 64-5, 121
  see also contracting-out
Office for Standards in Education (OFSTED) 5, 155, 158
owner-occupier sector 108
parents 148, 150, 153-4, 158-9
partnerships 12, 133
patients 20, 28, 42, 45, 48-52 passim
Pattern, J. 154
Pennington Report (1997) 136
planning, town ch. 5 passim, 108, 142
planning, departments of ch. 5 passim
police 94, 95, 108, 136, 139, ch. 11 passim, 209
  civilian staff 186, 192
  Metropolitan 185
  traffic 185
  uniform patrol 184-5, 191
police authorities ch. 11 passim
  local policing plans 195-6
Police Act (1964) 184, 192
Police Community Consultative Groups 196-7
Police Federation 188
Police and Magistrates' Court Act 187, 188, 192, 195-6, 198, 203, 208
Police Operational Review 185, 190
policy communities 5
polytechnics 162, 164, 168, 172, 179
poor relief 92
Posen Review (1992) 187-8
post-bureaucracy ch, 1 passim, 76, 78, 87, 109, 117, 118, 132, 134, 137, 143, 158, 225
post-fordism 158, 163
priority estates project 117
private finance initiative 214
private sector 10, 11, 12, 19, 25, 32, 53, 57, 58, 61, 65, 71, 76, 77, 82,

98, 100, 104, 108, 113, 119, 121, 142, 143, 163, 170

privatisation 5, 152

probation officers 100, 102

professionalism ch. 1 *passim*, 38, 50, 77, 95, 106, 112, 140, 141, 155, 156, 157, 163, 76, 205, 224

collegiate and patronage models of professional control 57, 66

cosmopolitan orientation 57, 68, 69, 70, 177, 224

'default' 148

definition of 3

discretion 3, 4, 13, 26, 34, 35, 52, 57, 76, 78, 82, 134, 135, 139, 140, 163, 190, 199, 202, 204, 205, 210, 223, 224, 226

'new entrepreneurial' 157, 224

'new mode' 113

professionality 157

professional associations 218-221

proletarisanisation 14, 223

see also deprofessionalisation

Protecting the Public 186

public choice theory 3

public health inspectors 129, 134

purchaser-provider split 10, 20, 23, 25, 40, 67, 71, 100, 104, 163, 191, 192, 195

see also client-contractor

quasi-markets 10, 39, 62, 97

see also markets

refuse collection 130, 131

regulation 3, 105-6, 117

Research Assessment Exercise (RAE) 169, 170, 174, 177

residential homes 93-4, 99, 100-3, 105

residualisation 111, 118, 124

right to buy 108, 113-4, 124

Robbins Report (1963) 164

Royal Commission on Criminal Justice 211

Royal Commission on the NHS (1974) 22

Royal Town Planning Institute (RTPI) 77, 78, 81, 82, 83, 85-7, 219

schools ch. 9 *passim*,

comprehensive 148, 151, 159

grammar 148, 153

grant maintained 154-5, 158

local management of schools 154, 158

Schools Council for Curriculum and Examination 147

scientific management p. 43

see also Neo-Taylorism

Scotland 120

Scottish Office 116

service level agreements 64, 132

service users 97, 98, 104, 105

see also consumers and customers

Sheehy Enquiry (1993) 187-8

social care 92, ch. 6 *passim*

and older people 92, 100

direct social care 93-4

see also community care

social housing ch. 7 *passim*, 83

see also housing and housing management

Social Market Foundation 191

social movements 7

social problems 3-4, 7, 11, 106, 218, 222-3

social services ch. 6 *passim*

social work 14, ch. 6 *passim*, 136, 139, 221, 224

street-level bureaucrats 139

structure plans 83

Surrey County Council 60

Surveyors 77, 85

Taylorism

the myth of, p. 43-45

see also Neo-Taylorism

teachers 12, 94, 95, 136, 139, 219, 221, 223
  headteachers 147, 151
  school ch. 9 *passim*
  higher education ch. 10 *passim*
Teacher Training Agency 154, 156, 158
technological change 8, 117, 121, 122
Tenants' Charter 113, 122
Thatcher, M. 24, 148, 153, 201
  government 40, 79, 199
  see also Conservative government
think-tanks 7
tourism 83, 224
town clerk 111
Trade and Industry, Department of 171
trading standards officers 131
training and enterprise councils 134, 137
Treasury 22, 124
treasurers 60, 63, 111
trust 25-26

United States 33, 184
universities 13, ch. 10 *passim*, 224
University Grants Commission 164-5, 168, 170
Urban Development Areas (UDA) 82
Urban Development Corporations (UDC) 84, 137

value-for-money 5, 61-2, 65, 130, 132, 189, 201, 222
vice-chancellors 178
voluntary sector 12, 14, 95, 96, 98, 100, 103, 108, 120, 142, 170

Wales 120, 123, 124, 168, 185, 202
water supplies 129
Weber, M. 2, 12, 19, 50-1, 147
welfare state 1-5, 7, 8, 10, 12, 15, 43, 218, 221
Working for Patients (1989) 24
Welsh Office 116
Westminster L.B. 65
William Tyndale School 151

For Product Safety Concerns and Information please contact our EU
representative GPSR@taylorandfrancis.com Taylor & Francis Verlag GmbH,
Kaufingerstraße 24, 80331 München, Germany

Printed and bound by CPI Group (UK) Ltd, Croydon, CR0 4YY

08/05/2025

01864360-0002